JESUS CHRIST

THE WARRIOR
"A CALL TO ARMS!"

Gloria A. Perales

Gotham Books

30 N Gould St.
Ste. 20820, Sheridan, WY 82801
https://gothambooksinc.com/

Phone: 1 (307) 464-7800

© 2024 *Gloria A. Perales*. All rights reserved.

No part of this book may be reproduced, stored in a retrieval system, or transmitted by any means without the written permission of the author.

Published by Gotham Books (March 26, 2024)

ISBN: 979-8-88775-124-5 (H)
ISBN: 979-8-88775-122-1 (P)
ISBN: 979-8-88775-123-8 (E)

Because of the dynamic nature of the Internet, any web addresses or links contained in this book may have changed since publication and may no longer be valid.

The views expressed in this work are solely those of the author and do not necessarily reflect the views of the publisher, and the publisher hereby disclaims any responsibility for them.

ACKNOWLEDGEMENT

Much gratitude and appreciation for reviewers and editors of this book! A great and special thank you to my brother, Dr. Daniel Arredondo, DDS who painted the picture of Jesus on the cover and others in this book. May the Lord be glorified in all that we do and say through Jesus Christ. I give to each of you, my beloved, my love in Jesus, Mary, Our Heavenly Father and all the Holy ones who have reached perfection.

TABLE OF CONTENTS

Ignite The Blazing Fire!	1
Introduction	3
Need Your Approval	5

PART I

Hope In The Glory of God	6
The Message of Christ On Earth	8
Jesus Christ The Warrior	10
The Armor of God	18
Obedient Mind To Christ	19
Be Perfect As My Father Is Perfect / Help Me Notify Every Christ Believer	20
The Word of God Is Alive!	28
Stop A Grieving World	30
Deliverance	34
A Changed Life Bearing Fruit	43
New Era Of Unconditional Love	44

PART II

What About The Roman Catholic Church?	46
What Part of The Bible Do You Not Believe?	55
Who Is The Devil?	60
Prayer of Renunciation	65
Prayer of Resistance And Rebuke	66
Who Are The False Prophets?	68
Who Are The False Christs?	71
Who Is The Antichrist?	76
What Power Does Satan Have Over Me?	77

How Can I Begin To Obey? I Am Helpless!	81
What Is Repentance & Fear of The Lord?	83
Why Is The Virtue of Charity A Great Virtue?	86
Why Is The Virtue of Humility A Great Virtue?	87
What Exactly Does "I Am The Way" Mean?	88
What Does "I Am The Truth" Mean?	89
Who Are The Righteous?	96
What Is Grace?	100
What Is Your Blessing?	104
Who Is The King?	106
Who Is The Servant of Money?	116
Who Is Like Our Fathers Of Great Faith?	122
In What Timeline Is Faith Executed?	129
Who Is The Thief?	130
Who Is The Murderer?	131
Who Are The Living, Who Deny The Dead Life?	135
Who Is The Worker Of Inequity?	142
Am I Born Again?	143
Who Is Your Father?	148
Who Is Your Mother?	152
The Word of God Transforms!	155
What Is The Significance Of The Rosary?	158
Why The "Hail Mary"?	159
Why Was Mary Chosen To Be The Mother of Our Lord?	166
Will The Divorced, Adulterers, And Homosexuals Be Chaste At The Coming of The Lord?	168
How Do We Become Blameless?	176
Why Do I Suffer?	177
When In Time Did They Change "Our Lord's Prayer"?	180

Do Earthly Possessions Possess You?	183
What About Statues And Graven Images?	193
What Are False Gods?	200
What About the queen of heaven in Scripture & Mary Mother of God?	204
Why Was Jesus Silent In Front of The Courts?	209
How Great Is The Mercy of Our Lord?	211
Who Should We Trust?	214
Why Is The Divine Mercy Chaplet So Important?	216
How Can We Stop War?	218
Who Will Listen To The Life Saving Commands of The Lord?	224
What Is The Sign of Jonah?	231
What Is And How To Use Sackcloth And Ashes?	234
Why Is The Scapular A Sign Of Salvation?	240
Should We All Wear Sackcloth?	241
Am I Without Sin?	244
Does Hell Exist?	246
Where Is The Kingdom of Satan?	249
Do I Do As Our Shepherd Has Taught?	251
What Is Religion?	254
How Can We Make His Joy Complete?	259
Who Are The True Apostles of Today?	261
Who Do You Think Is The Person Most Prayed For?	264
Who Is God?	266
What About The Sabbath?	269
Why Must I Give My Free Will To The Lord?	273
Who Will Follow Jesus?	275
What Should My Greatest Passionate Desire Be?	277
Who Are The 144,000 In The Book Of Revelation? Can We Be Part of That Number?	279

Are The Keys To The Kingdom of Heaven Used As The Lord Intended?	282
Will You Be Part of Today's Finale?	286

PART III

The Eucharistic Host Like My Baby	292
The Greatest Anguish Vs Love	294
St. Michael The Archangel	294
The Chaplet of St Michael	294
A New Chaplet of Mercy	296
Obedient Mind To Christ	296
The Armor of God	297
Worldwide Agreement of Hope-Pray Without Ceasing	297
Steps To The Narrow Road	300
Steps To The Rebellion of Love	303
Imitating The Bible Events	306
The New Testament The Greatest Commandment	308
The Old Testament The Ten Commandments	309
Renewal of The Ten Commandments	311
The End	314
References	315

IGNITE THE BLAZING FIRE!

I Pray hoping ...

> *^{17} That the God of our Lord Jesus Christ, the Father of Glory, may **give to you a spirit of wisdom and revelation in the knowledge of him;** ^{18} And that having the eyes of your heart full of light, you may have knowledge of what is the hope of his purpose, what is the wealth of the glory of his heritage in the saints, ^{19} And **how unlimited is his power to us who have faith**,* Eph 1:17-19 BBE

> *^{24} **For our salvation is by hope:** ... ^{25} **But if we have hope for that which we see not, then we will be able to go on waiting for it**. ^{26} And in the same way the Spirit is a help to our feeble hearts: for we are not able to make prayer to God in the right way; but the Spirit puts our desires into words which are not in our power to say; ^{27} **And he who is the searcher of hearts has knowledge of the mind of the Spirit, because he is making prayers for the saints in agreement with the mind of God**.*
> Ro 8:24-27 BBE

Our Lord desires for us to unite to Him and to make His joy complete.

> *by being of the same mind, maintaining the same love, united in spirit, intent on one purpose.* Php 2:2 NASB

The Lord has great plans for us. He loves us! Yet, we see in this world that discord is everywhere. The Lord said that angels of light are devils in disguise, also, ministers of righteousness are devils in disguise. Mat 24:24 says that even the elect might be deceived. Are we ignorant vessels of clay being held captive? Are we blind to the spiritual life that surrounds us. So truly, who are we? Truth must be sought; the Lord reveals. We must remember that only the Lord can cast out Satan. We must trust Jesus and follow Him!

The Lord said He came to divide. We must follow Him and help Him divide. He said that this world is in the power of the evil one. That statement is easy to believe because our world is in turmoil and in much chaos. Many suffer. It is time for ALL BELIEVERS in CHRIST to gather as the Lord requests in *1Cor 1:10*! We must Love Unconditionally, Pray, Fast, Repent and Unite.

> *"Whoever is not with me is against me, and whoever does not gather with me scatters.* Mat 12:30 NIV

The Lord desires to unite Himself to us with the baptism He is anxious to undergo. He will fill us with grace upon grace and no evil thing will be able to touch us and we will sin no more. We will be true children of God and in Him we will truly live, move, and have our being.

> *"I have come to cast fire upon the earth; and how I wish it were already kindled!* **"But I have a baptism to undergo, and how distressed I am until it is accomplished!** *"Do you suppose that I came to grant peace on earth? I tell you, no, but rather division;* Luke 12:49-51 NASB 1995

Years ago, the Lord led me to believe that He is coming in my lifetime. Of course, only He knows when he is coming, nevertheless, **perhaps this book contains the spark that ignites or kindles the blazing fire**. I hope it will inspire and motivate us to take the first step in faith. The Lord made a covenant saying that He would teach each one of us. We must desire it and reciprocate all that He came to exemplify. If you do not believe, repent in Sackcloth and ashes, and let the Lord teach you too. I am no different than you. Trust In Jesus!

INTRODUCTION

So much has happened in my life. We know the story of doubting Thomas. The Lord said in John 20:29 NKJV *Blessed are those who have not seen and yet believe.* I am sure, I am not the only one who has experienced unbelievable spiritual occurrences. In any case, I have been given a great aspiration to proclaim the message in this book. Although it may seem like many messages, really there is not many at all. Our God is a God of simplicity. In the section of Who is Who? and What is What? I hope to bring awareness in the hearts of men of the written Word of God as not normally disclosed. You might be shocked but please read, this is not to condemn but rather to make aware. All questions and answers are supported by scripture usually followed by prayer for the salvation of those who might be lost, or to give us strength to do Gods will, according to that question.

I first repented using sackcloth and ashes in 2004. Afterwards, I was drawn to sleep in sackcloth based on scripture in Joel 1:13. During that time, I believe I was being enlightened as documented in this book. God promises to teach us, in the covenant He made in Hebrews 8:10-12 and Jeremiah 31:33. I have learned that we have been misdirected by leaning on human understanding. In any case, I stopped sleeping in it in 2011 after my mother passed away.

In June 2022, after receiving a phone call by two different publishers regarding the same book in the same week (I wrote in 2010 which was dormant), I felt an urge to sleep in it again. I am amazed, that the Lord began to enlighten me again.

Today in 2023, I believe that sleeping in it gives some sort of clearance for the Lord to teach us. It is sacrificial for us to sleep in it for Our Lord, certainly it is not lush, soft, and comfy. I have grown accustom to it. I believe it is necessary to first repent in it with ashes and then sleep in it. Learning does not always come while under the cloth, the Lord is very creative.

We must desire and want to love and please God more than anything in the World. His desperate desire for us is shown in the passionate love of Christ and His loving death for us. And so, we also must desperately desire to be as Our Father desires: Perfect as Our Father is Perfect, willing to imitate Jesus.

Through Ignorance, we are held captive in a prison that deceives us, by making us feel, say, and do ungodly things. We believe what we feel instead of the truth. We must live by faith and not by sight. The wicked warden is weak, but makes us think otherwise. He is a liar. The only Stronghold we need is Our Great God and by His Holy Spirit we are more than conquerors. We are set free.

Lack of knowledge causes us to perish! Ignorance is the wardens' strength.

I pray that we will all run the race to attain the grace beyond grace that the Lord desires to give us. I give to you my love in Jesus and Mary! Thank you and may the Lord be your reward.

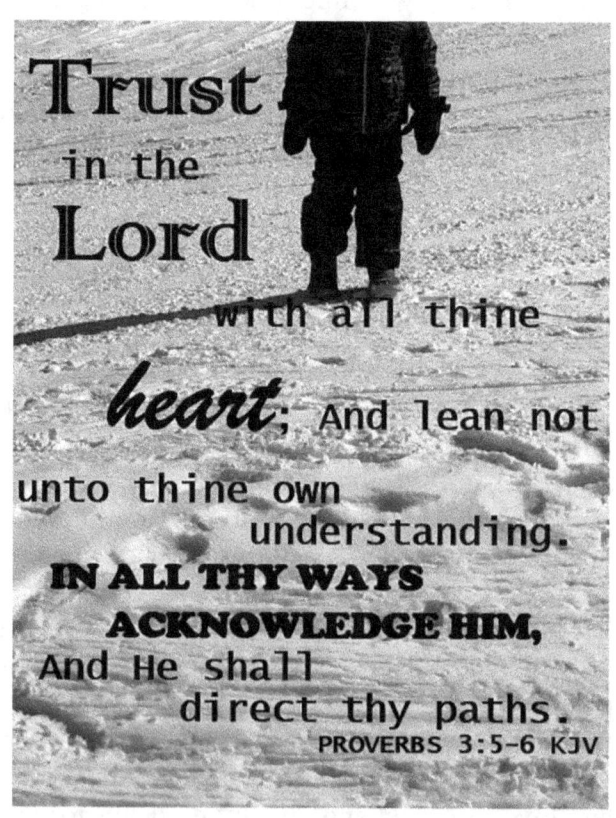

The following prayer is about me and if you want, then include yourself in this prayer. I need your permission - Please say yes, I beg you! Ask your friends for me to also read and say yes. Thank you!

NEED YOUR APPROVAL

on the following prayer so the Lord will answer my prayer, PLEASE SAY "YES!!!" I ASK MY FAMILY AND THE WHOLE WORLD… Please give the Lord permission on my behalf. Please pray the following for and with me:

Beloved Father, I offer to you GLORIA, as a living sacrifice, as she has requested. I give you permission Lord, to do with her as you will, whether the sacrifice be in charity, in thanksgiving, in praise, in worship, or in atonement. Let thy will be done in Gloria's life. I detach myself from Gloria in respect to all that is of the world and unite myself to her in all that is in unity with you Oh Lord. Teach me Lord, to love as you LOVE.

Gracious, loving, and fulfilling Lord, satisfy our hunger and thirst to know you and to be in your presence. I trust in your great goodness beyond understanding. All Glory, Blessings, Honor, Might, and Power are Yours Dearest and Most Beloved Father through Jesus Christ and the Holy Spirit. Blessed Mother Pray for us that we may be made worthy of the promises of Christ. Thank you to my beloved on earth, who said Yes! Highly exalted is Our Great God, our King of Everlasting Love! Hosanna in the Highest! Blessed is He who comes in the Name of the Lord. Thank you, Father, for hearing our prayer. SAY "YES" right now!!! "YES" Tell the Lord if you want this prayer to also apply to you, and I say "YES"

We must REPENT as if trying to SAVE OUR OWN LIFE!!! Also pleading for the dead!!!

PART I

HOPE IN THE GLORY OF GOD

In our lifetime, have we given the great virtue of Hope the recognition it requires? In Who is Who and What is What? section of this book, we see the great value of hope and I am hoping, you hope with me as one.

For our salvation is by hope. Romans 8:24 BBE

*Now **faith is** the substance of things hoped for, and **the sign that the things not seen are true**.* Heb 11:1 BBE

But stay alert at all times, praying that you will have strength to escape all these things that are going to take place, and to stand before the Son of Man." Luke 21:36 NASB

Rejoicing in hope; patient in tribulation; continuing instant in prayer; Ro 12:12 KJV

*[17]**Pray without ceasing.** [18]**In everything give thanks:** for this is the will of God in Christ Jesus concerning you.* Thessalonians 5:17-18 KJV

*For in hope we have been saved, but hope that is seen is not hope; for who hopes for what he already sees? **But if we hope for what we do not see, with perseverance we wait eagerly for it.*** Ro 8:24-25 NASB

For whatever was written in earlier times was written for our instruction, so that through perseverance and the encouragement of the Scriptures we might have hope. Ro 15:4 NASB

Now may the God of hope make you full of joy and peace through faith, so that all hope may be yours in the power of the Holy Spirit. Ro 15:13 BBE

But I will hope continually, and will yet praise thee more and more. Ps 71:14 KJV

Sustain me according to Your word, that I may live; And do not let me be ashamed of my hope. Ps 119:116 NASB 1995

but sanctify Christ as Lord in your hearts, always being ready to make a defense to everyone who asks you to give an account for the hope that is in you, yet with gentleness and reverence; 1Pe 3:15 NASB 1995

And everyone who has this hope fixed on Him purifies himself, just as He is pure. 1John 3:3 NASB

Therefore, prepare your minds for action, keep sober in spirit, fix your hope completely on the grace to be brought to you at the revelation of Jesus Christ. 1Pe 1:13 NASB 1995

AND IT SHALL BE IN THE LAST DAYS; GOD SAYS, "THAT I WILL POUR MY SPIRIT ON ALL MANKIND" Acts 2:17 NASB

THE MESSAGE OF CHRIST ON EARTH

In few words, what can be said to make a difference in our lives? We must remember the life of Christ which we are to live to become like Him. In all He spoke, I would say there are three words of great significance that could give summation of the message of Christ, Our Lord. These words portray the life we are to live to become like Him. They are **Each Unconditional: "Love," "mercy" and "repentance."** We must reciprocate, what He came to demonstrate: His Life. We must do what He has requested of us!

We are certain that we are of God, but
all the world is in the power of the Evil One.   1John5:19 BBE

For our preaching is not about ourselves,
but about Christ Jesus as Lord,
 and ourselves as your servants through Jesus.   2Cor 4:5 BBE

For this reason am I loved by the Father,
because I give up my life so that I may take it again.
 John 10:17 BBE

Greater love hath no man than this,
that a man lay down his life for his friends.   John 15:13 KJV

We know the love of God in this way:
because he laid down his life for us.
And so, we must lay down our lives for our brothers
1 John 3:15 CPDVTSB

We know that no one who has been born of God sins;
but He who was born of God keeps him,
and the evil one does not touch him.   1John 5:18 NASB

⁴ *"Or how can you say to your brother,*
'Let me take the speck out of your eye,'
and behold, the log is in your own eye?
⁵ *"You hypocrite, **first take the log out of your own eye,***
and then you will see clearly

to take the speck out of your brother's eye. <u>Mat 7:4-5 NASB 1995</u>

*But Jesus, turning to them, said,
Daughters of Jerusalem,
let not your weeping be for me,
but for yourselves and for your children.* <u>Luke 23:28 BBE</u>

Repent as if to save your life! Use sackcloth and ashes. Forgive everyone both living and dead! Be Merciful! Pray that the Lord will forgive them too!

*No one can by any means redeem another
or give God a ransom for him* <u>Ps 49:7 NASB</u>

The men of Nineveh **will stand up with this generation at the judgment, and will condemn** *it because they repented at the preaching of Jonah;* <u>Mat 12:41 NASB</u>

JESUS CHRIST THE WARRIOR

He was born in a stable, laid in a manger filled with straw. His Mother's veil was his blanket. He rode on a donkey. He walked the earth with nowhere to lay his head. He was meek and humble. He came to equip His Army: His Armor includes the Helmet of Salvation, the Belt of truth, the breastplate of Righteousness, our feet Shod with the Gospel of Peace, and He gave us the Sword of the Spirit which is the Word of God.

Who would think, that He came as a warrior?
Yet, He implies it in His Word.
Jesus did not come to bring peace on earth,
He came to divide the kingdom of Satan on earth!
He came to gift to us incorruption and immortality!
He tells us He wants to baptize us. It is a second Pentecost, we will be filled with the Holy Spirit and grace upon grace.

"I have come to cast fire upon the earth; and how I wish it were already kindled! "But I have a baptism to undergo, and how distressed I am until it is accomplished! "Do you suppose that I came to grant peace on earth? I tell you, no, but rather division; Luke 12:49-51 NASB 1995

He said you are either for me or against me, **those who are with me gather**, those who are against me scatter. We are like the people ready to stone the prostitute, judging each other, and judging the churches. The body of Christ is scattered filled with pride, selfishness, and self-glory. Their master is money, they need it because it is the master of this world. This world is filled with suffering and so much deception, chaos, and confusion. Who would prefer to live in a world like this, when they can live healthy, worry free, in peace, harmony and love? The Lord said that *"no eye has seen, no ear has heard, no heart has imagined, what God has prepared for those who love Him"* 1Cor 2:9. No man can understand the glory that will behold them. Jesus draws the line on the ground and says let the one without sin cast the first stone.

Let us look at scripture Mark 3:26. It says that if Satan is divided, he will come to an end. Well turn that around, in Satan's kingdom, Christians are divided and they are coming to an end. Many Christians are persecuted, suffer, and die for their belief in Jesus. Why do they suffer so much, if God is so powerful? The truth is that Satan is victorious because our sinfulness and disobedience is the cause of our own misery. Christians are weak, lacking in faith with contradicting doctrines or beliefs. Christians are in discord complying with Satan's game. They are like mobsters in clicks or gangs competing against each other, attempting to profit for their own benefit. Christians think in the flesh, not in the spirit. They think their victory is their own. We must repent in sackcloth with use of ashes and allow the Lord to teach us and to be our Victor. He is Our Victor!

Although believers love Jesus, they continue to disobey and have not gathered. We have been stubborn and have taken our own stand believing our ways are the best way, the right way. Truly, there is only ONE way. Jesus said He is the WAY. As believers in Christ, we walk blindfolded, not knowing who we are and as Jesus said on the cross "they know not what they do." Many believers do not realize that they are rebels in the kingdom of Satan. They are rebels for Jesus Christ the Warrior. So what does that mean? Ok, let us turn that around, Satan (Lucifer) a good angel at the time gathered with his followers more good angels, together, they rebelled against God and were cast out and down to earth. They became labeled as devils, and Satan became the father of sinners. They lost their beauty and the peace of God left them.

The earth is the kingdom of Satan. This is discussed in Part II of this book. Believers of Jesus Christ are against Satan, they are FOR Christ. Believers are sinners in Satan's kingdom and because there are so many different doctrines and beliefs, they are in discord. They are scattered and weak. They have not gathered as the Lord has pointed out. Now, it is our turn to form a rebellion. We must gather and rebel against Satan and end his kingdom, so that Our Lord's Kingdom will come. The Lord tells us how, when, and where, we must desire to obey.

Today, the question is, whose side are you on? Will you be part of the peaceful and loving rebellion? Jesus came to wage WAR

WITH THE KINGDOM OF SATAN. Will you join His Army?
> *And if Satan is at war with himself,*
> *and there is division in him,*
> *he will not keep his place but will come to an end.*
> Mark 3:26 BBE

> *⁵³ The father shall be divided against the son, and the son against the father; the mother against the daughter, and the daughter against the mother; the mother-in-law against her daughter in law, and the daughter in law against her mother-in-law.* Luke 12:53 KJV

He speaks about division in families because some will choose to sin and continue in the ways of the devil because "they do not know what they do." Other sinners that have been converted to believe in Christ, will be faithful to Christ, until transformation, when they are truly born again, when no evil can touch, harm, or make them to sin.

We must draw the line and stand with Jesus Christ, Our Warrior! He came to convert us and make believers out of us. He taught us love, truth and the way. We must live by faith and not by sight. No matter what the obstacle, stand firm! We must be merciful as He is merciful! He said He desires that all will be saved, perhaps that includes His angels and Satan. Perhaps, we stand in the gap with mercy for them as well. He wants to fill us with grace upon grace with the baptism he is anxious to undergo. We must take the first step!

He says all are guilty! The devil is the father of those who sin. The world is in the power of the evil one. We are all sinners and united to the kingdom of Satan. Sin is the chain that binds us to Satan. If anyone thinks they do not sin, they must read this book to find out who they are. It is important that we help the Lord divide! We must be rebels for Jesus Christ the Warrior. God against Satan!

> *And so all Israel shall be saved: as it is written,*
> *... they are enemies for your sakes: but*
> *..., they are beloved for the fathers' sakes.*
> *... Even so have these also now not believed,*
> *that THROUGH **YOUR MERCY***
> THEY ALSO MAY OBTAIN MERCY.

> *For God hath concluded them all in unbelief,*
> *that he might have mercy upon all.* _{Ro11:26-32 KJV}

Our Lord Jesus Christ is our advocate and stands before Our Father in Heaven pleading for our salvation. In following Jesus, we also become the advocate. We plead before Jesus for the salvation of the remaining unbelievers and the dead who may have seemed lost. Standing for them, we hope that they still have a second chance for their salvation; truly hoping that ALL will be saved as Our Lord desires. Imitating Jesus, we surrender ourselves as an advocate for them, pleading to the Lord to be merciful to the lost, the worst of sinners. And we, forgive them too, because "they know not what they do" or have done, no matter how much they have hurt us or anyone else.

> *¹⁰ Now* **I BESEECH YOU, BRETHREN**, *by the name of our Lord Jesus Christ, that ye all speak the same thing, and* ***THAT THERE BE NO DIVISIONS AMONG YOU****; but that ye be perfectly joined together in the same mind and in the same judgment. ¹¹ For it hath been declared unto me of you, my brethren, by them which are of the house of Chloe, that there are contentions among you. ¹² Now this I say, that every one of you saith, I am of Paul; and I of Apollos; and I of Cephas; and I of Christ. ¹³ Is Christ divided? was Paul crucified for you? or were ye baptized in the name of Paul?*
> _{1 Corinthians 1:10-13 NKJV}

The hope of our salvation comes through perfection and there is only one way to be perfect. The Lord left instructions, **He is our living instruction sheet**; and before He comes, we must follow Jesus:

> *And* ***whoever does not bear his cross*** *and come after Me* ***cannot be*** *My disciple.* _{Luke 14:27 NKJV}

> *Then Jesus said to His disciples,* **"*If anyone wants to come after Me, he must deny himself, take up his cross, and follow Me.*** _{Mat 16:24 NASB}

I always thought that bearing our cross was basically bearing our sufferings. However, it is more than that. To follow Jesus, we truly must be willing to bear the cross for the salvation of others even unto death as Jesus has done. We must do as He has done. He tells us how, when, and where, we must obey.

For the word of the cross seems foolish to those who are on the way to destruction; but to us who are on the way to salvation it is the power of God. 1Cor 1:18 BBE

For it is a sign of grace if a man, desiring to do right in the eyes of God, undergoes pain as punishment for something which he has not done. 1Pe 2:19 BBE

*For this reason I make request to you, brothers, by the mercies of God, that you will **give your bodies as a living offering**, holy, pleasing to God, which is the worship it is right for you to give him.* Ro 12:1 BBE

We know the love of God in this way: because he laid down his life for us. And so, we must lay down our lives for our brothers 1 John 3:15 CPDVTSB

So, who is willing to join the Army of Jesus Christ the Warrior? **WHERE?** in the Roman Catholic Church, where the lion's den will form and our love will be tested. The Roman Catholic Church where Jesus promises victory! Peter is the key! **WHEN?** We must take the first step in faith! **HOW?** Gather! Love, Repent, Fast, and Pray, Call to Heaven! Unite! Desire to be born of God with the new Pentecost!

He left us instructions; He clearly states that He came to divide the kingdom of Satan and tells us where to unite and how to make His joy complete.

[18]*And I say also unto thee, that **thou art Peter, and upon this rock I will build my church; and the gates of hell shall not prevail against it.** * [19]*And I will give unto thee the keys of the kingdom of heaven: and whatsoever thou shalt bind on*

earth shall be bound in heaven: and whatsoever thou shalt loose on earth shall be loosed in heaven. <u>Mat 16:18-19 KJV</u>

make my joy complete by being of the same mind, maintaining the same love, united in spirit, intent on one purpose. <u>Php 2:2 NASB 1995</u>

So, how is it that we can make His joy complete?

- **be of the same mind**: simply by desiring to demonstrate love as Jesus did, even unto death;
  So that as Jesus was put to death in the flesh, do you yourselves be of the same mind; for the death of the flesh puts an end to sin; <u>1Pe 4:1 BBE</u>
- **maintaining the same love:** simply unconditional love, unconditional mercy, unconditional forgiveness;
  For to this end also did I write, that I might know
  THE PROOF OF YOU,
  Whether ye be obedient in all things.
  To whom ye forgive any thing, I forgive also:
  For if I forgave anything, to whom I forgave it,
  For your sakes forgave I it, in the person of Christ;
  Lest Satan should get an advantage of us:
  for we are not ignorant of his devices. <u>2Cor 2:9-11 KJV</u>
- **united in spirit:** by uniting and allowing the Lord to baptize us in Spirit so that we can truly be born again, the Pentecost
  *But Jesus answered, "You do not know what you are asking. Are you able to drink the cup that I am about to drink **and be baptized with the baptism that I am baptized with**?" They said to Him, "We are able."* <u>Mat 20:22 NKJV</u>
- **intent on one purpose:** to be an advocate as Jesus was, for the salvation of the living and the dead, even the worst of sinners. We must plead for their mercy.
  For you have been called for this purpose, since Christ also suffered for you, leaving you an example for you to follow in His steps, <u>1 Peter 2:21 NASB</u>

> *¹⁵ And I said, 'Who are You, Lord?' And the Lord said, 'I am Jesus whom you are persecuting. ¹⁶ But get up and stand on your feet; for this purpose I have appeared to you, to appoint you a minister and a witness not only to the things which you have seen, but also to the things in which I will appear to you; ¹⁷ rescuing you from the Jewish people and from the Gentiles, to whom I am sending you, ¹⁸ to open their eyes so that they may turn from darkness to light and from the dominion of Satan to God, that they may receive forgiveness of sins and an inheritance among those who have been sanctified by faith in Me.'* <u>Acts 26:15-18 NASB</u>

Today, we need to realize that Jesus came to divide the kingdom of Satan, so that Satan's kingdom will come to an end. He came to wage war. We have not understood the parables, codes, and hints Jesus spoke while on earth. Most preachers have misled us. They have been blind guides, not knowing they are leading souls to destruction, including their own. Much has been hidden from us. We must pray that the Lord will help us to Not Lean on Human understanding, and help us to accept all truth, especially if against things we have been accustomed. Pray that the Lord will lead all of us to the truth. Let us pray and hope that He will be our stronghold helping us to take the first step of faith, unafraid. Believe!

> *³²and you will know the truth, and the truth will make you free."* <u>John 8:32 NASB 1995</u>

This earth is Satan's kingdom, the Lord even said it while on earth. He wants to claim us and the earth as His own! We must gather!

> *And the great dragon was cast out, that old serpent, called the Devil, and Satan, which deceiveth the whole world:* **he was cast out into the earth, and his angels were cast out with him.** <u>Rev 12:9 KJV</u>

> *Jesus answered, "My kingdom is not of this world. If my kingdom were of this world, my servants would have been*

fighting, that I might not be delivered over to the Jews. But my kingdom is not from the world. <u>John 18:36 ESV</u>

We have been blinded by lies. We have believed that we are free indeed, but we are not yet free! By faith, we are free! We live in a world of suffering, turmoil, abuse, deception and lies.

We have been standing in the sidelines. The Lord does not want us to fight with swords, guns, knives, or any carnal weapon. He does not want us to protest any harm inflicted upon us. He tells us to let them slap us on both cheeks. We do not have to stay and tolerate such behavior; we can do as Jesus did. We can leave simply to avoid, as Jesus did and pray for them.

Does the severity of the sin matter, we are all sinners? According to the word of God, the devil is the father of sinners. Jesus loves us no matter how sinful we are. Did the severity of sin matter to Jesus? Probably not, He came to save everyone. Salvation is of utmost importance and Jesus demonstrated that. He loves us just the way we are, yet tells us to sin no more. This can be done only with His grace, but we must desire it and try. We must be willing to give ourselves as Jesus did, forgiving, loving unconditionally, and demonstrating true mercy in every circumstance.

The point here, is that the Lord desires everyone to be saved. We must partake in unconditional love and mercy and advocate as Jesus did. He is calling everyone to repentance. He is making everyone aware of their sins.

We will truly be set free when the Army of God gathers, at which time our love will be tested and Our Protector and Our Victor, Jesus, will heal us and do all He has promised.

He wants to claim the earth as His own. Let us crown Him King and Lord of all. Let us bring forth the Royal Diadem and Exalt His majesty and omnipotence. Let us submit to His desire to save all, and do as He has asked. The weapons of our warfare are mighty through God to the pulling down of strongholds. We are strengthened with unity, prayer without ceasing, unconditional love, forgiveness, and unconditional mercy. We must desire to fight the battle with Him, by standing still and knowing that He is with us!

He will fight the battle, not us, we are only vessels of clay submitting to the power of an Almighty and Glorious God who loves us. **Pray and Exalt Him!**

Allow your vessels of clay, to be set free by Jesus Christ the Warrior. Be free indeed! We are held captive in these prisons of clay. Awake all you sleepers! In the Name of Jesus!
Rebels against the kingdom of Satan… Rebels for Jesus Christ the Warrior, Army Rise up! Let the rebellion begin! Repent in sackcloth using ashes and Gather!
THIS IS A CALL TO ARMS! Love, pray, fast, repent, and unite!

PRAYERS:
THE ARMOR OF GOD
Finally, I am strong in the Lord, and in the power of his might. I put on the whole armour of God, that I may be able to stand against the wiles of the devil. I wrestle not against flesh and blood, but against principalities, against powers, against the rulers of the darkness of this world, against spiritual wickedness in high places. Wherefore I put on the whole armour of God, that I may be able to withstand in the evil day, and having done all, to stand. I Stand therefore, having my loins girt about with truth, and having on the breastplate of righteousness; And my feet shod with the preparation of the gospel of peace; Above all, taking the shield of faith, wherewith I shall be able to quench all the fiery darts of the wicked. And I take the helmet of salvation, and the sword of the Spirit, which is the word of God: Praying always with all prayer and supplication in the Spirit, and watching thereunto with all perseverance and supplication for all saints; Ephesians 6:10-18 KJV personalized as a prayer

I believe I wear the Armor of God for all eternity, and I also ask Your protection Dear Lord, upon all beloved on earth. In the Name of Jesus. Amen.

OBEDIENT MIND TO CHRIST

For though we walk in the flesh, we do not war after the flesh: (For the weapons of our warfare are not carnal, But mighty through God to the pulling down of strong holds;) Casting down imaginations, and every high thing that exalts itself against the knowledge of God, and bringing into captivity every thought to the obedience of Christ; And having in a readiness to revenge all disobedience, when my obedience is fulfilled. 2Cor 10:3-6 KJV

Lord make me, and my mind obedient to You; bless me, protect me and keep me from all harm. Remain with me and in me always. I also ask Your protection upon the minds and bodies of all beloved on earth. In the Name of Jesus. I pray.

One last note on this topic:

We must repent using sackcloth and ashes, the sign of Jonah, which the Lord said is the only sign we would see. In Mat 12:41 it says that because the men of Nineveh repented at the preaching of Jonah, they will be at OUR judgement, and will condemn us because we have not repented. Please the Lord, repent using sackcloth and ashes!

He answered, "A wicked and adulterous generation asks for a sign! But none will be given it except the sign of the prophet Jonah. Matthew 12:39 NASB

The men of Nineveh **will stand up with this generation at the judgment, and will condemn it** *because they repented at the preaching of Jonah* Mat 12:41 NASB

The sign of Jonah is deep and bitter repentance using sackcloth and ashes for people and animals.
More detail on that topic is in this book.

BE PERFECT AS MY FATHER IS PERFECT
HELP ME NOTIFY EVERY CHRIST BELIEVER

All Orthodox Catholics and Every Church of Every Denomination

To the first of seven Churches in the Book of Revelation: the Church of Ephesus, you appear to be almost perfect, but not… for you are nothing without love….

> *[4] But I have this against you, that **you are turned away from your first love**. [5] So keep in mind where you were at first, and be changed in heart and do the first works; or I will come to you, and will take away your light from its place, if your hearts are not changed.* Rev 2:4-5 BBE

The second Church Smyrna: the Lord warns Smyrna that they will face persecution. The Lord encourages them to be faithful unto death and the crown of life will be theirs. They too must keep in repentance and unconditional love allowing the Lord to be their strength.

Pergamum, the third Church, has lost its way. It is a place of conflicting beliefs and compromises. They have let false teachings and worldly influences corrupt their faith. They have fallen prey to cults; heretics are their leaders. Sexual immorality and eating food sacrificed to idols is their stumbling block. Their faith is corrupt. Jesus asks them to repent, they are fallen.

Thyatira, the fourth Church, has allowed wickedness to flourish in the name of inclusivity. The false prophetess leads people astray enjoying their wicked behavior. These are not willing to repent, sickness, death to their children, and great tribulation are their punishment, unless they repent. To those who have held fast to the things of the Lord, He will place no further burden and encourages them to overcome and continue in His work until the end.

Sardis, the fifth Church, appears to be alive but is the dead church. This church is spiritually dead. They have neglected their spiritual vitality. Their fervor is lacking and their deeds incomplete.

The Lord tells them to awake; there is hope with a change of heart and repentance.

Philadelphia, the sixth Church, is a church sustaining its faith. They have kept His Word and not denied His name. They must hold fast and overcome. The Lord has placed them before an open door, which no one can shut.

Laodicea, the seventh Church, is neither hot nor cold. They are lukewarm and the Lord wants to vomit them out of His mouth. Although they are wealthy, He says they are poor, pitiful, wretched, blind, and naked. He wants them to change their ways and repent earnestly. He says that he rebukes and disciplines those whom He loves.

The above churches simply symbolize the challenges and triumphs of faith we face today. We are made aware of the importance of changing our ways, loving unconditionally, repenting, and keeping our eyes on the Lord. Every church today has flaws, all are constantly challenged by the temptations of this world. Resisting, Rebuking and Renouncing Satan becomes difficult for those who do not acknowledge God in every instance of their life.

Resolving every one of the issues addressed to the seven churches seems very simple in the eyes of Our Lord. The solution every time is Repent and Love Unconditionally. Keep the faith and follow Jesus. Who is willing?

We must find our true first love. Knowing that we believe we love God first, perhaps it is time to demonstrate our greatest love. We must desire to be low and humble like Jesus. He wants us to be as He is: Perfect as Our Father is Perfect.

We in the flesh think we can never be perfect. However, He came to show us the way. He asks us to make His joy complete and He tells us how. He beseeches the churches that there be no division among them by uniting. He tells each of us to offer our bodies as a living sacrifice, willing to die for another. That is how we know love, true love, by loving unconditionally putting every obstacle aside. Satan will make the transition difficult, but Our Lord is the victor! OUR VICTOR!

There is only one way to be perfect as Our Father is Perfect and that is to return to God, and follow Jesus. But what does that mean? It means exactly that, imitate Him. We must do as He has taught. We must be willing to enter the Lion's den with the intent and purpose for the salvation of all, the living, and the dead. Being merciful to even the worst of sinners hoping for their salvation. We are the advocate for the remaining unbelievers and **for the dead waiting to rise by asking mercy for them as well, because**

> *THROUGH YOUR MERCY*
> *THEY ALSO MAY OBTAIN MERCY* Ro11:26-32 KJV.

The question arises as to when should this occur. The answer is "now." As exemplified throughout the Bible, we are shown, that first faith is executed and then the Lord's responds. By taking the first step in faith the Lord will respond. What are we to do to take that first step is noted throughout this book. How do we take that first step is easily defined. We must pray without ceasing, exalt the Lord, love unconditionally, and gather in the Roman Catholic Church, at any location in the world. In addition, we must be merciful to the worst of sinners both living and dead, and plead for their mercy. Keep your eyes on the Lord, not on the sinner, pray for them. Yes, the Church is in error, but the Lord will rectify.

We must forgive and pray for the dead who have hurt us and perhaps, lived a life without love; they themselves tormented, not knowing anything else.

We must lay down our crown at the feet of Jesus willing to enter the lion's den, the Roman Catholic Church. The Lord has promised victory there. This is not to say that the Roman Catholic Church is the Lion's den, but only to say that as believers in Christ gather, a lion's den might form. Stand firm! Be still and know that He is Our Victor!

The Lord says to make His joy complete by uniting in the same spirit. This is the true baptism, spirit to spirit which the Lord is anxious to bestow upon us. This baptism will give us grace upon grace where no evil can harm or touch. We will truly be born again. This will be the result of our taking the first step in faith. We must decide to love as He loves and unite in unconditional love joining the army of God in the Roman Catholic Church.

Surely if the Lord said to Peter that he is the rock and the gates of hell will not prevail against it, then certainly all churches, all believers in Christ, need to demonstrate the greatest Love and unite! Doctrine, the law of this world, made things imperfect!

Do the churches realize that in *1 Cor 1:11-13* the Lord is talking about all Churches of today? All are not united! There are many contentions among them... nothing has changed, pride and selfishness infiltrate the leaders of the churches that refuse to love unconditionally, ignoring the woes of Saint Matthew. The kingdom of God on earth is scattered, it is living in the power of the evil one. We must clearly divide forming the Army of God with Jesus Christ the Warrior. We are rebels in the kingdom of Satan. Trust in Jesus!

According to scripture *1 John 3:8* sinners are of the devil. We are all sinners. All are guilty.

He who sins is of the devil, for the devil has sinned from the beginning. For this purpose the Son of God was manifested, that He might destroy the works of the devil. 1John 3:8 NKJV

One who is born of God does not sin, cannot sin and the evil one does not touch him. Jesus came to divide the kingdom of Satan by converting us. We who believe in Jesus Christ, as Our Savior and God, are converted in the faith of Jesus. Our transformation is not complete, we must be born again, born of God with the Baptism of the Holy Spirit as noted in *Luke 12:50*.

Now realizing that Christians must gather, it is time for us to take the first step of faith like our fathers of great faith. *Mat 11:20-30* tells us that we should have repented long ago in sackcloth and ashes. We should question what our Christ believing church has taught us, and ask the Lord to teach us all truth, and help us not to lean on human understanding.

The Lord made a Covenant, a promise, to teach us. First repent using sackcloth and ashes, and then ask the Lord to teach you while using sackcloth. Most importantly of all teachings, be like Jesus and demonstrate unconditional love, unconditional mercy even to the merciless, and unconditional repentance for surely, we have contributed to all chaos. Forgive, your preachers, teachers, priests, scribes, pharisees (those who think themselves of highest sanctity), blind guides and hypocrites, be merciful as Our Lord is merciful and Love unconditionally.

> *[10] " For this is the Covenant that I will make with the house of Israel after those days, says the Lord:*
> ***I Will** Put My Laws into Their Minds, And*
> ***I Will** Write Them on Their Hearts, and*
> ***I Will** Be Their God, And They Shall Be My People.[11] " And **They SHALL NOT TEACH EVERYONE** his fellow citizen, and everyone his brother, saying, 'Know the Lord,'*
> ***FOR ALL WILL KNOW ME**, from the least to the greatest of them. [12] " For I Will Be Merciful to their iniquities, AND I WILL REMEMBER THEIR SINS NO MORE."*
> <u>Heb 8:10-12 NASB 1995</u>

THE KINGDOM OF GOD IS SCATTERED! It is time to gather! **Unite to the Army of Jesus! A divided kingdom cannot stand!** It is time to **Love your brother!**

> *[10] Now I beseech you, brethren, by the name of Our Lord Jesus Christ, ...THAT THERE BE NO DIVISIONS AMONG YOU;* <u>1 Corinthians 1:10 KJV</u>

We must unite in unconditional love! **We must divide the kingdom of Satan!** Come back to the Roman Catholic Church! Why? Because the Lord has promised victory in the church of the APOSTLE PETER.

> *And I say also unto thee, that thou art Peter, and upon this rock I will build my church;* **and the gates of hell shall not prevail against it.** <u>Mat 16:18 KJV</u>

The Lord has told us to have no division among us. The truth is there is too much division and confusion. If you are a church leader, question yourself as to who you truly are? Desire to take the speck out of your own eye! I am of non-denominations; I am Catholic; I am Orthodox; I am Protestant; I am Pentecostal; I am Methodist; I am of another denomination; I am your preachers name; I am of what or who? Yes, beautiful speakers, but disguised as angels of light and ministers of righteousness. Do not misunderstand, although the Bible says angels of light and ministers of righteousness are devils in disguise, they have been beacons of light to the lost-on earth. As sinners, they might be devils in disguise, but they are good devils. Repent so that you might believe. I am no one to tell you who you are, do you know who you are? Pray and seek, the Lord reveals.

> *We know the love of God in this way: because he laid down his life for us. And so,* ***we must lay down our lives for our brothers*** *1 John 3:15 CPDVTSB*

In the following verse, the Lord is telling the Churches to repent, and if you do, he will wage war with the demons in the Churches with the Word of God, the Sword of the Spirit, "and **the gates of hell will not prevail**" as mentioned in *Mat 16:18*. Do not wait for Judgement Day! Repent in sackcloth and ashes!

> *¹⁶* ***Repent;*** *or else* ***I will come unto thee quickly****, and will* ***fight against them with the sword of my mouth****. ¹⁷ He that hath an ear, let him hear what the Spirit saith unto the churches; Rev 2:16-17 KJV*

> *To him who overcomes I will give of the fruit of the tree of life, which is in the Paradise of God. Rev 2:7 BBE*

> *Be faithful until death, and I will give you the crown of life. Rev 2:10 NASB 1995*

> *He who overcomes will not come under the power of the second death. Rev 2:11 BBE*

To him who overcomes I will give of the secret manna, and I will give him a white stone, and on the stone a new name, of which no one has knowledge but he to whom it is given. Rev 2:17 BBE

²⁶ He who overcomes, and keeps my works to the end, to him I will give rule over the nations, ²⁷ And he will be ruling them with a rod of iron; as the vessels of the potter they will be broken, even as I have power from my Father: ²⁸ And I will give him the morning star. Rev 2:26-28 BBE

He who overcomes will be dressed in white, and I will not take his name from the book of life, and I will give witness to his name before my Father, and before his angels. Rev 3:5 BBE

Him who overcomes I will make a pillar in the house of my God, and he will go out no more: and I will put on him the name of my God, and the name of the town of my God, the new Jerusalem, which comes down out of heaven from my God, and my new name. Rev 3:12 BBE

*¹⁹ 'Those whom I love, I reprove and discipline**; therefore be zealous and repent*** Rev 3:19 NASB 1995

²⁰ 'Behold, I stand at the door and knock; if anyone hears My voice and opens the door, I will come in to him and will dine with him, and he with Me. ²¹ 'He who overcomes, I will grant to him to sit down with Me on My throne, as I also overcame and sat down with My Father on His throne. ²² 'He who has an ear, let him hear what the Spirit says to the churches.'" Rev 3:20-22 NASB 1995

Be Merciful to Your Brothers as Our Lord Is Merciful to You! Live In Unconditional Love!

*Let the sinner give up his way,
and the evil-doer his purpose:
and let him come back to the Lord,*

*and he will have mercy on him; and to our God,
for there is full forgiveness with him.* <u>Isaiah 55:7 BBE</u>

*⁶ Make search for the Lord while he is there,
make prayer to him while he is near: ...
⁸ For my thoughts are not your thoughts,*
or your ways my ways, says *the Lord.* <u>Isaiah 55:6-8 BBE</u>

Were a soul like a decaying corpse so that from a human standpoint, there would be no (hope of) restoration and everything would already be lost, it is not so with God. The miracle of Divine Mercy restores that soul in full. Diary of St Faustina ¶1448

And being made perfect, he became the author of eternal salvation unto all them that obey him; <u>Heb 5:9 KJV</u>

THE WORD OF GOD IS ALIVE!
*"And blessed is she who believed
that there would be a fulfillment
of what had been spoken to her by the Lord."*
Luke 1:45 NASB 1995

BELIEVE!

THIS IS A CERTAINTY!
the words which I have said to you are spirit and they are life.
John 6:63 BBE

Because you have not repented you do not believe!
The WORD made you out of dust and gave you the breath of life!
The WORD became flesh in Mary's womb, Jesus. Jesus is God.
The WORD through Jesus becomes the Living Bread.
EAT of the Bread of Life, so that you may obtain life everlasting!
Our Lord Loves You! Please repent and offer your heart, mind, and soul to Jesus! He is waiting for you to invite Him into Your heart…
He wants to teach you all things!
Beloved Father, give to us, Jesus, the finisher of our faith!

Repent That You Might Know the Truth!

and ye, when ye had seen it, ***repented not afterward, that ye might believe him.*** _{Mat 21:32 KJV}

In other words, with a contrite Heart, Repent of the things you do not believe, That perhaps the Lord will reveal His Truth In His Unfathomable Mercy and Everlasting love.

Behold, the eye of the LORD is upon them that fear him, upon them that hope in his mercy; _{Ps 33:18 KJV}

Know this: Fear of the Lord is a beautiful gift from the Lord; a fear so profound of being separated from Him; a fear of offending Him, a fear and sorrow of being the reason for His many tears.

Enter ye in at the strait gate: for wide is the gate, and broad is the way, that leadeth to destruction, and many there be which go in thereat:
strait is the gate, and narrow is the way, which leadeth unto life, and few there be that find it. _{Mat 7:13-14 KJV}

[18] "I have seen his ways, but I will heal him; I will lead him and restore comfort to him and to his mourners,
_{Isaiah 57:18 NASB 1995}

Do you desire to enter in at the narrow gate? Few there be that find it! Therefore, Seek! Therefore, repent to please the Lord!

Do not be afraid!

STOP A GRIEVING WORLD

How many in this world are grieved? How many think they are helpless and that all hope is gone? How many think they are not grieved, not realizing that it is they that grieve others? The Lord says my people perish because of lack of knowledge.

St Francis De Sales in his book *An Introduction to a Devout Life* page 268 states the following:

"The sorrow that is according to God," saith Paul, "worketh penance steadfast unto salvation: but the sorrow of the world worketh death (2Cor. Vii.10)." Therefore, sorrow may be either good or bad, according to its results upon us. Undoubtedly there are more bad than good results from it; **for the good results are but two, namely, penitence and mercy;** *while there are six evil results – anguish, indolence, indignation, jealousy, envy, and impatience;*

What can we do? We can seek true love and ask the Lord to teach us to live in it. True love is found in loving God first with all our heart, mind, soul, and strength. In *Luke 6:42* the Lord says we can help our brothers if we first take the speck out of our own eye.

We must desire to help break the yoke that surrounds us. With a change of heart and a mind of Christ, we learn to embrace our sufferings in the love of the Cross. The Lord reveals a burden that is truly light when we bless our enemies and are willing to love unto death. Repent, be merciful and forgive! Pray and fast! Hope greatly for our deliverance!

^{24}" Come to Me, all who are weary and heavy-laden, and I will give you rest.
*^{29}***Take My yoke upon you and learn from Me, for I am gentle and humble in heart,** *and you will find rest for your souls. ^{30}" For My yoke is easy and My burden is light."* Mat11:28-30 NASB 1995

Put on the whole armour of God, that ye may be able to stand against the wiles of the devil. Eph 6:11 KJV

Submit yourselves therefore to God.
Resist the devil, and he will flee from you. Jas 4:7 KJV

Be sober, be vigilant; because your adversary the devil, as a roaring lion, walketh about, seeking whom he may devour: 1Pe 5:8 KJV

Prayer:
Lord, please teach me to bow down in an acceptable way and to be pleasing to You. Help me to trust you and to acknowledge you in all my ways. Give to me wisdom, knowledge and understanding. Teach me to be obedient. Lead me to those whom you want me to help. Make me and Mold me to be the repairer of the breach, the restorer of paths to dwell in, as you desire, that the yoke of many will be broken. Teach me to draw out my soul to the hungry, and to satisfy the afflicted soul. Guide me continually and like a spring of water, let not my waters fail. Please allow my health to spring forth speedily. Teach me to keep the Sabbath holy as a delightful day unto the Lord, that you may feed me with the heritage of Jacob our father. All Glory, Honor and Power are Yours Most Beloved Heavenly Father in the Name of Jesus. Amen.

    The mercy of Our Lord is there for everyone who desires it. It brings much peace and love. We also must be merciful towards those who have hurt us. Repent with a contrite heart and desire to love God first. Let Him be our stronghold. Let us pray that the Lord will give to everyone a sound and merciful loving heart. Let us pray that He will beckon everyone to the abode of His endless mercy and love that we may dwell in the House of the Lord together as one.

    As for me, I am running a race with great hope. I seek desperately and desire greatly to die to this world that I may have life in Jesus. I trust in Him and believe His Word and the messages he sent to me. Every day is a day closer to the fulfillment of it.

On December 19th, 2005 I heard a voice clearly but somewhat distant. It was of a woman I thought to be Our Blessed Mother. She did not identify herself. In my thoughts I repeated what she said. Her words were biblically spoken, like in King James language. When I woke up, I could not repeat them, word for word, because I do not talk that way. I do know the content of the message. It was this:

"Your prayers are blessed and the Lord has heard them and He will answer"

In the Book of *Daniel 10:12-14* it took twenty-one (21) days for the heavens to answer. They came as soon as they received his prayer. The prince of the Persian kingdom resisted the angel for 21 days. I attribute the same happening to me because of the clearance provided through prayers with true bitter repentance with the use of sackcloth and ashes. I have been sleeping in it for so long. The Lord also led me back to confession after so many years of not going. I believe this also to be necessary. I was wondering which prayers the Lord was going to answer, by this time I had already published One, One Love, One Hope, One God, so I assumed it was those prayers.

I also look for sins to confess with much sorrow claiming them as my own hoping to please my Lord. I desire to have a pure and immaculate heart, white as snow. Of course, only the Lord can grant that grace! I repent of sins I did not think were mine so that the Lord will show me His truth. I seek it and I want it desperately. I know I am of a wicked and evil generation and I desire desperately to be holy to please our beloved Lord. I desire to allow the Lord to teach me. I desire to not lean on human understanding. I pray that He will make me to accept all truth especially if it is against something I have been taught by man. I ask for the strength to change and to accept all that He desires. I also realize that the Lord teaches us in many ways. His creativity is immense, beyond our understanding. We must diligently seek the Lord with all our heart, mind, soul, and strength so that we may find Him.

> *"But from there you will seek the LORD your God,*
> *and you will find Him if you search for Him*
> *with all your heart and all your soul."* <u>De 4:29 NASB 1995</u>

Prayer:
LORD HEAR OUR PRAYER

Lord Hear our prayer, let the words of our mouth and the meditation of our hearts be acceptable to You every moment of our being in time and eternity. Give to us a sincere desire to pray so that we may have a fervent soul of the righteous, so that our prayers may be pleasing to You. Teach us to pray with our whole heart, mind, and soul. Make us to be heard by You – and as a Father to His children -- answer us.

Forgive us Lord for not denying ourselves as we should, teach us how Lord, so that we may be pleasing to you.

Forgive us our inequities and the inequities of our fathers and relatives, especially of those deceased that might still be suffering for their sins whom you have judged. Bring them Lord to your everlasting Light that they may enter into eternal rest in your loving light and dwelling place which you have prepared for us. Make us Lord to repent pleasing to you.

Lord, we beseech you to **grant to us the grace of increased power of our prayers** that as one day is as a thousand days, so then, is one of our prayers **multiplied in your unfathomable love for the benefit of our brethren and those most in need of prayer. As you granted to Elisha a double portion of Elijah's spirit, so then, we ask the same for the benefit of our brethren.** Lord, we also ask that you allow the whole church, all angels, and saints to intercede for us in union with Mary Most Holy. Please Lord, deliver us from evil. Thank you, Father, for hearing our prayers.

DELIVERANCE

I used to think deliverance occurrences were as shown in Hollywood movies. They are publicized as scary and something to be afraid of. I know now that, that is a false representation. There is no fear in the presence of God; it says in the Word of God, Satan was cast out like lightening from the heavens.

> *And He said to them, "I was watching Satan fall from heaven like lightning* Luke 10:18 NASB 1995

The very presence of God and His almighty power is very real. We must have no doubt. **There is no fear in the presence of God and His Love is ever present conquering our enemies.** Satan truly flees like lightening. The Lord is all powerful and He is creator of all things including Satan.

One day in June 2005 I went to a Catholic Church to see a guest speaker giving testimony of the Living presence of Christ in the Living Bread, the Eucharist, our Holy Communion. I would usually sit in the front section of any church when I would hear a guest speaker giving a teaching or testimony. This day however, after his speech there was a brief intermission before the laying on of hands. This is when the elders pray over you. I moved to the very back of the church. A friend came to me and started talking to me. While we were talking, we began to hear wailing. There was a woman at the altar being delivered from demons.

I had never seen a deliverance before and wanted to go to the front of the church. On this night, my friend insisted that we should not do that. She said you must be prepared for deliverance. She encouraged me to go outside with her during the deliverance. I was reluctant but she insisted so I went. We were outside talking and the church had a bullhorn and I could hear the wailing. It sounded ere. She began to tell me of an incident in which she was present at a deliverance. She was one of the persons praying over the person being delivered. The evil creature bit her. She said it hurt and that it left a bruise on her body. She said that they jump around. Well, I did not know what to think of that, I was just glad I was outside. That was Thursday.

(Today in 2024 I can truly say that the devil cannot cast out the devil. If the devil jumped around as she mentioned, then truly the Lord was not there. The Lord and His almighty power is greater than any evil thing. Again, Satan was cast out of heaven like lightening. We must have faith.)

The Lord is great and greatly to be praised!!! In Him we live move and have our being! We cannot do any kind of deliverance on our own accord; the battle is not ours; it is the Lord's. It is a spiritual battle.

On Saturday, little did I know that the Lord was preparing me for what was about to happen in my life. I do not exactly know what time it was. I do know, it was at least an hour and a half before church that the mother of my son's friend called me hysterical and crying. She told me my son was dying, he had consumed mushrooms or something and could not breath.

My son was in England and I did not have a phone number for him. I did not know how to contact him. I told her to start praying the rosary. I also called my other son and told him his brother was dying and that he needed to start praying the rosary right away. I was with my mother and told her to also pray the rosary. I also had a CD playing on the radio with prayers of the divine mercy with beautiful meditations of the passion of Christ. I know the Lord was leading me. I began to order protection over my son in the name of Jesus by the power of the Holy Spirit as commanded by Our Heavenly Father. I asked the Lord to send the angels to protect and guard him. I asked St Michael the Archangel to come to his defense. I asked for the intercession of Our Blessed Mother, the saints, and the WHOLE Church. A very short while (minutes) after all these things occurred, my son called me. I started praying silently in tongues, he could not hear me, but the devil could. He briefly said hi and I was waiting for him to tell me what was going on while I prayed in tongues. He asked me "what is that?" when he heard me praying in tongues, but I was praying quietly. Not too much was said. The deliverance began. I had never seen a deliverance. I did not know what needed to be done. I was innocent of any procedures or words that needed to be spoken. I did not do this deliverance; I was a shell of dust used by My Lord. Literally, the Lord arose in me.

We must remember that the devil cannot deliver the devil. It is the Lord Himself that will do it for us. We must submit to the Lord and His divine will. We must repent to be made clean. I cannot even say that I personally prepared myself for the deliverance that is in fasting or confession. I do not remember; however, I have kept in the fruit of repentance through confession on a frequent basis and as I mentioned, I have been sleeping in sackcloth for a very long time (years). I also had been giving up small things to the Lord as often as I can because I am weak in keeping from eating all day. This deliverance was totally the work of Our Lord and I in the flesh was surprised by such an event, but the Lord Our Deliver, Our Leader, Our teacher, Our God, Our Father was in lead. Our Lord knows all time and His time is always right. He prepared me!

I want to emphasize the need in a deliverance to ask for the **intercession of Our Blessed Mother**. the angels and saints and **THE WHOLE CHURCH, in heaven and on earth**. They must all be called to intercede for us.

During the deliverance I was exalting the Lord greatly! He loves it! There was a couple of other things said over the telephone. These words came out of my mouth and left a great impression in my heart:

**"THERE IS NO FEAR
IN THE PRESENCE OF MY LORD!"**

"THERE IS NO DISTANCE FOR MY GREAT GOD!"

I was in the United States and my son was in England. This deliverance occurred over the telephone. As we were speaking a friend knocked on my son's door in England. When he knocked on the door, I told my son to tell him that he was talking to me and he needed to be alone. (This is how the Lord prepared me on Thursday). His friend left and later told him he was foaming at the mouth and so he began to pray for him as well. The Lord is great, he sent another prayer warrior in my son's defense.

It took around forty minutes and the last outcry was a loud wailing and expelling of the demon. My son was left in confusion and the Lord led me to bind the spirit of confusion. By this time, it was time for me to go to church where I stayed in prayer.

I later asked my son if during the deliverance he was hurting in any way. He said no. He said he remembered laying on the floor with his legs crossed like on the crucifix and could not take them apart. I remember he told me that he could hear kicking and fighting, it was as though all of heaven was in his room. Glory and Praise to Our Lord, Our Deliverer. Our Lover, Our Redemption.

In more recent years 2022-2023 I asked my son about this occurrence and he does not remember it as I wrote it years ago (above), but it is all in the Lord's hands, I will not judge, only the Lord saves.

The devil who is full of pride and vain glory makes people to think he is something to be afraid of. The devil is a professional liar! Be proud of nothing! BE NOT PROUD! Pride was Satan's fall.

So how do we stop a grieving world? By taking the speck out of our own eye, **then we can help our brethren.** By repenting, being merciful, loving and forgiving, praying, and fasting!

*By **lovingkindness and truth** iniquity is atoned for, and by the fear of the LORD one keeps away from evil.*
Pr 16:6 NASB 1995

*You hypocrite, first **take the log out of your own eye**, and then you will see clearly to take the speck out of your brother's eye.* Mat 7:5 NASB 1995

Then you will call, and the LORD will answer; You will cry, and He will say, `Here I am.' If you remove the yoke from your midst, The pointing of the finger and speaking wickedness, Isa 58:9 NASB 1995
(Say NO to pointing the finger and cursing!)

We must know who we are. We must live in the spirit. We are earthen vessels. Acknowledge the Lord, allow Him to be your stronghold! So how do we stop a grieving world? Perhaps like you stop a war by fasting and praying. Putting down our weapons! The Lord says those who live by the sword die by the sword. We must pray and fast …emptying ourselves of our pride, anger, and wicked ways. We must desire to please the Lord and be merciful towards each other. We must keep to repentance, forgiveness, and love always and unconditionally, embracing every humiliation. Can we truly tell those who have hurt us:

"I am sorry, please forgive me, it is my fault!"

We must give Our Lord our crowns and give Him His throne as mentioned in "Who is the King?" We must follow Him! He is our living instruction sheet! We must reciprocate!

> *¹⁰The four and twenty rulers go down on their faces before him who is seated on the high seat, and give worship to him who is living forever and ever, and take off their crowns before the high seat, saying, ¹¹ It is right, our Lord and our God, for you to have glory and honour and power: because by you were all things made, and **by your desire they came into being**.* Re 4:10-11 BBE

Perhaps we must hope harder and have a greater desire that He may truly deliver us from evil today and now. Desire as He desires.

> *In hope against hope he believed, so that he might become a father of many nations according to that which had been spoken, "SO SHALL YOUR DESCENDANTS BE.*
> Ro 4:18 NASB 1995

> *And for this cause my heart was glad and my tongue full of joy, and my flesh will be resting in hope:* Ac 2:26 BBE

> **For our salvation is by hope** Romans 8:24 BBE

Perhaps the more we desire, the more He desires. We reap what we sow. Return to the Lord all that He has shown to us. He repeatedly requests for us to repent and to return to Him, and so, let us beg him repeatedly; let us repent completely, so that He will return to us, as He desires us to return to Him.

Loving unto death! We must do as He does.
Be as He is. Love as He Loves.

I believe that those who are faithful will die for the love of God for the love and salvation of mankind, the living, and the dead. I believe the great deliverance or the rapture will occur when we do surrender completely to the Lord. This would be when believers decide to love unconditionally and unite. The elect will lay down their crowns at the feet of Jesus and die for those most in need, most unruly, most unloved as Jesus did. Perhaps this is when the Priests, preachers, and such give to the Lord his place at the altar. Could this be the Apostasy? Can we give back the table of the Lord to Jesus, Our High Priest according to the order of Melchizedek?

> *¹ For this Melchizedek, the king of Salem, a priest of the Most High God, who gave Abraham his blessing, meeting him when he came back after putting the kings to death ² And to whom Abraham gave a tenth part of everything which he had, being first named King of righteousness, and then in addition, King of Salem, that is to say, King of peace; ³ Being without father or mother, or family, having no birth or end to his life, being made like the Son of God, is a priest forever.* Heb 7:1-3 BBE

> *¹¹ If therefore perfection were by the Levitical priesthood, (for under it the people received the law,) what further need was there that another priest should rise after the order of Melchisedec, and not be called after the order of Aaron? ¹² For the priesthood being changed, there is made of necessity a change also of the law.* Heb 7:11-12 KJV

According to scripture forming the priesthood changed the law and therefore made it imperfect. Is it then reasonable to believe that if we truly desire the Lord to perfect the Church it must be returned to Him?

> *For, on the one hand, there is a setting aside of a*
> *former commandment because of its weakness*
> *and uselessness (for **the Law made nothing perfect**),*
> *and on the other hand there is a **bringing in of a***
> ***better hope, through which we draw near to God.***
> Heb 7:18-19 NASB 1995

And so also if there is a setting aside of the former commandment because the Law made nothing perfect thus, we live in imperfection. And so, if through this imperfection a greater hope is found. A Hope for the return of Our Lord that we may return to Him, then let us indeed return to Him passionately with all of our hearts, mind, strength and soul.

Is this what the Lord refers to in *Matthew 26:29*, that He will not drink of this fruit of the vine until that day? Can we give Him back His throne on earth? Let us unite and keep in prayer that the Lord will guide us to all truth.

There is no greater love!

> *But I say to you that from now I will not take of this fruit*
> *of the vine, till that day when I take it new with you in*
> *my Father's kingdom.* Mat 26:29 BBE

> *No one can by any means redeem another or*
> *give God a ransom for him* Ps 49:7 NASB

> *And he supposed that his brethren understood that God*
> *was granting them deliverance through him, but they did*
> *not understand.* Acts 7:25 NASB 1995

*⁸ "But do not be called Rabbi; for One is your Teacher, and you are all brothers. ⁹ "Do not call anyone on earth your father; **for One is your Father, He who is in heaven**.*
*¹⁰ "Do not be called leaders**; for One is your Leader, that is,** **Christ.*** Mat 23:8-10 NASB 1995*

Therefore, holy brethren, partakers of a heavenly calling, consider Jesus, the Apostle and High Priest of our confession; Heb 3:1 NASB 1995

*Where Jesus has gone before us, as **a high priest forever** after the order of Melchizedek.* Heb 6:20 BBE

¹Now the main point in what has been said is this: we have such a high priest, who has taken His seat at the right hand of the throne of the Majesty in the heavens, ² a minister in the sanctuary and in the true tabernacle, which the Lord pitched, not man. Heb 8:1-2 NASB 1995

We must understand that redemption comes from the Lord and no one comes to the Father unless He beckons. We know that the battle is not ours. We are weak but He is strong. We know that He desires for all to be saved. **Let us then walk in faith knowing that we are all saved although it may not appear to be that way.** Let us then submit to Our Lord, resist, rebuke and renounce the devil and he will flee. Let us gather in One Church, with a thick cord of strands that cannot be broken, opening heaven's door! Let us give to the Lord His Kingdom on earth!

And if one prevail against him, two shall withstand him; and a threefold cord is not quickly broken. EC 4:12 KJV

And if Satan is at war with himself,
 and there is division in him, he will not keep his place but will come to an end. Mark 3:26 BBE

Today this world lies in the power of the evil one as noted in *1 John 5:19*. This means that everyone is bound by sin to this evil world. This earth is the kingdom of Satan, as noted in Part II supported by scripture. We must realize that it is the Kingdom of God that is scattered and shattered. Our Lord Jesus Christ came to divide this evil world, so that we who trust in Him, may come to the knowledge of these circumstances and the hope of our salvation. Our Heavenly Father sent His only Son to saves us, to teach us, and to initiate our gathering. We are all sinners, all are guilty. **Believers and lovers of Jesus Christ Our Lord and Savior, must unite.** Jesus came to divide and we must join the cause. **If Satan is at War with Himself, he will come to an end.** We must join the army of Jesus Christ the Warrior by gathering!

In the book of *Daniel*, the three children that were thrown into the burning furnace, praised, blessed, and exalted the Lord, and so shall we! Love unconditionally!

Scripture tells us to anoint our head with oil, also fast and pray. As a protective measure, we should do it.

> *"But you, **when you fast,** **anoint your head** and wash your face* Mat 6:17 NASB
>
> *Let your clothes be white all the time, and **let not oil be lacking on your head.*** Ec 9:8 NASB 1995

Matthew 17:21 has been removed from the bible, it says that some spirits cannot be cast out unless you pray and fast.

> *[19]Then the disciples came to Jesus privately and said, "Why could we not drive it out?" [20]And He said to them, "Because of the littleness of your faith; for truly I say to you, if you have faith the size of a mustard seed, you will say to this mountain, 'Move from here to there,' and it will move; and nothing will be impossible to you. [21]["But this kind does not go out except by prayer and fasting."]* Mat 17:19-21 NASB 1995

A CHANGED LIFE BEARING FRUIT

For this reason I say to you, The kingdom of God will be taken away from you, and will be given to a nation producing the fruits of it. Matthew 21:43 BBE

"Abide in Me, and I in you. As the branch cannot bear fruit of itself unless it abides in the vine, so neither can you unless you abide in Me John 15:4 NASB 1995

All discipline for the moment seems not to be joyful, but sorrowful; **yet to those who have been trained by it, afterwards it yields the peaceful fruit of righteousness.** Heb12:11 NASB 1995

[22]But the fruit of the Spirit is love, joy, peace, patience, kindness, goodness, faithfulness, [23]gentleness, self-control; against such things there is no law.
Gal 5:22-23 NASB 1995

THE FRUITS OF REPENTANCE

A changed life:

Doubt	.... Believe	/ FAITHFULNESS
Ignoring God	...... Acknowledging God	/ PROCLAIM
Anguish	...... Blessedness	/ JOY
Immorality	.... Right-minded	/ GOODNESS
Indolence/lazy	.... Serve others thru God	
Indignation	...... Complacency	/ LOVE
Jealousy	.... Trust	/ SELF-CONTROL
Envy	.... Benevolence	/ KINDNESS
Impatience	...... Serene	/ PATIENCE
Pride	.... Meek	/ GENTLENESS
Hatred	...... Unconditional Love	/ PEACE

every tree that does not bear good fruit is being cut down and thrown into the fire. Mat 3:10 NASB

NEW ERA OF UNCONDITIONAL LOVE

PART II

WHO is WHO?
And
WHAT is WHAT?

WARNING!!!

Jesus Came to SAVE – Not to Condemn!!!
These writings are not meant to condemn …
They are meant to alert and make aware…
I too am a sinner running the race

These are strong words and thoughts…
Discern for yourselves
ask for the Help of the Holy Spirit

All things are imperfect until perfection comes!
My Hope is that you may act, contemplate, and consider what is written in this section. And keep the following in mind:

> *You hypocrite,* **first take the log out of your own eye***, and then you will see clearly to take the speck out of your brother's eye.* <u>Mat 7:5 NASB 1995</u>

This is a Call to Arms! Love, pray, fast, repent, and unite!

REPENT AND BE READY!
Above all things written in this book

Contemplate and DESIRE

THE UNCONDITIONAL: LOVE OF GOD MERCY and REPENTANCE

Desire
TO LOVE HIM and OTHERS AS HE LOVES YOU

RECIPROCATE EVERYTHING TO THE LORD (RETURN TO GOD)

DESIRE TO PLEASE HIM
AND LOVE HIM FIRST

ABOVE EVERYONE AND EVERYTHING

WHEN HE SAYS "REMEMBER ME" YOU SAY TO HIM
LORD REMEMBER ME,
RECEIVE ME AS YOUR OWN
SAY "YES LORD!
MAKE ME PERFECT AS MY FATHER IS PERFECT

FULLFILL YOUR DESIRE IN ME AND WITH ME!"

TRUST IN JESUS NO MATTER WHAT!
MAY YOU BE BLESSED!

What about THE ROMAN CATHOLIC CHURCH?

"Whoever is not with me is against me, and whoever does not gather with me scatters. _{Mat 12:30 NIV}

make my joy complete by being of the same mind, maintaining the same love, united in spirit, intent on one purpose. _{Php 2:2 NASB}

All believers in Christ have not gathered for the glory of God in unconditional love. They have not attempted to make the joy of the Lord complete. (The topic joy and discord are discussed throughout the book.) We have been disobedient. We have not followed Jesus.

Jesus walked a long treacherous road on His way to Calvary. Although a short distance, because of the crowds and the state of His injured body, the procession could have taken a few hours. Those few hours probably felt like an eternity to the Lord. He carried His cross after having been crowned with thorns, and whipped 40 times. Fragile as He was, Jesus carried His cross, walking to His crucifixion, soldiers whipped him and pushed him, and with others mocked Him, and did all sorts of wicked things to Him. The punishment seemed endless. As He hung on the cross, He prayed and said "Father forgive them for they know not what they do." Such a brutal demonstration of love, imprints the heart of a believer with so much love, compassion, and sorrow in His suffering, yet joy ignites. His sacrifice has given us the hope of our salvation and assumption into heaven, and the resurrection of the dead.

Jesus taught us how to separate ourselves from our sinfulness. He came to convert us and make believers out of us. He taught that the sinner must have a change of heart and repent. Although Jesus came as a kind, gentle, humble, and meek man, He spoke in codes, parables, and hints. We have not understood all that He spoke. He came as a Warrior of Love. He came to wage war in the name of love. In His teachings He tells us **who** the enemy is, and that He loves them and so should we. He tells us **where** the battleground is and that the gates of hell will not prevail at that battleground. He tells us **what** we must do to fight for the cause. We must repent, love, be merciful as He is, and gather. He tells us **when** this needs to occur as exemplified in the Bible. We must live by faith and not by sight. We must take the first step in faith and then the Lord will respond.

Our Lady of *Medjugorje* has repeatedly asked us to "Return to God." St. Faustina has told us to "reciprocate." The word of God says to "copy" or "imitate" or "follow Jesus." Contemplating the life of the Holy Family and the things that happen in our lives gives us a source and root of understanding, but only in a minute way. The absolute greatness and omnipotence of the Lord and the plans He has for our redemption is beyond our understanding. We must submit to Him! We must look at the examples left for us to imitate. We have found that history repeats itself, so we must analyze and respond accordingly.

He said that Peter is the Rock and the gates of hell will not prevail against it. The true church is the Roman Catholic Church, the rock, the church of the apostle Peter. This is where the Lord has promised that the gates of hell will not prevail. This is the battle ground. Jesus is our Victor; He is Our Warrior of Love.

> *And I say also unto thee, that thou art Peter, and upon this rock I will build my church; and* ***the gates of hell shall not prevail against it.*** Mat 16:18 KJV

In this world, any Army would defend its troops in trouble. They would respond to the needs of their troops without hesitation or devise a plan to succeed. We cannot see the spiritual realm. However, the Lord tells us in Eph 6:12 that *"we do not wrestle against flesh and blood, but against principalities, against powers, against rulers of the darkness of this age, against spiritual hosts of wickedness."*

The Roman Catholic Church is under attack, it is an obvious call to arms for the Army of God to gather. Now, imagine the Roman Catholic Church as a person of Jesus Christ, and all its angels of light and ministers of righteousness, as those whipping, mocking Jesus and doing all sorts of wicked things to the Church, trying to discredit it. Those are the devils in disguise, sinners, such as we, (we are all included in our evil ways, we are all guilty). We point fingers and are quick to judge. Yet, those persecuting the Church, believe in Jesus Christ, like us. They are believers causing division, keeping to the kingdom of Satan. Those devils in disguise or sinners, are not demonstrating unconditional love, they judge and contribute to Satan's kingdom. They do not know what they do, nor do they know who they are! They cling to the law which made things imperfect, the law which causes us to sin. We have been troops that have been imprisoned, blindfolded, and brainwashed to think different thoughts against each other and against the churches.

> *the god of this **world (Satan) has blinded the minds of the unbelieving** so that they might not see the light of the gospel of the glory of Christ, who is the image of God.*
> 2Cor 4:4 NASB

As mentioned, history repeats itself. And so, we must act upon the repetition of history. This time however, instead of rebellious angels rebelling in heaven, we are rebellious sinners rebelling against Satan in his kingdom on earth. Believers in Jesus Christ do not know that they are rebels in the kingdom of Satan! We who are the converted Love Jesus. We have faith in Jesus Christ. WE ARE BELIEVERS OF JESUS CHRIST, OUR WARRIOR OF LOVE, Our Victor. We must follow Jesus into battle and divide the kingdom of Satan.

We might not be literally crucified as He was, but as we grow in number with cords that cannot be broken, we will be stronger in the Lord. **The Lord will be stronger in us. He will be our stronghold!** And as we unite, the Lord will be pleased! And only He knows the right time to allow Pentecost to fall upon us, the baptism that will not allow Satan or his evil spirits to torment us anymore. Why? Because we will belong to God. He will claim us as His own. We will be His children and we can sin no more.

> ⁸*the one who practices sin is of the devil; for the devil has sinned from the beginning. The Son of God appeared for this purpose, to destroy the works of the devil.*
> ⁹***NO ONE WHO IS BORN OF GOD PRACTICES SIN,***

because His seed abides in him; and, he cannot sin,
because he is born of God. <u>1John 3:8 NASB 1995</u>

We know that Jesus Christ came to divide the kingdom of Satan. We also know that Satan will do anything to keep us from dividing his kingdom. Remember, we are vessels of clay and Satan knows it. Many of us do not understand that we are spirit beings! Can we unite? Can we unite, as sinners believing in Jesus Christ Our Warrior, loving Him, and standing firm in all that He came to demonstrate, following Him and uniting ourselves to Him and each other. Can we stop fighting each other and form the rebellion against Satan for the Glory of Jesus Christ? Can we join all our brothers who believe in Jesus Christ no matter the doctrine, differences, or dislikes?

We are born to love unconditionally. It does not matter if we have heard of homosexuality, adultery, murders, wars or any other sin, in the church or out of the church. We are all sinners. We must forgive and love unconditionally. Yes, there is compassion for the treacherous things that are occurring in the world. Yes, it is not right. But yes, Jesus says to forgive and to love. **And more importantly, we can put a stop to all that, by taking the first step in faith.** We must trust Jesus. He came to show us the way! When we do gather, the lion's den will form and our love will be tested! We must stand firm, be silent, love unconditionally, fast, pray, plead for mercy upon the living and the dead, and exalt the Lord.

God can do anything. He can make a camel go through the eye of a needle, if He wanted. The truth is, He wants to gift us incorruption and immortality. He wants to make us Perfect as He is, as His Father is, and as He made Mary. He can make us to qualify as an elect, or to be the same as the 144,000 in the book of Revelations. He can make us chaste, blameless, truthful, undefiled, virgins, immaculate, and anything He desires. Know that we love a God of impossibilities. He is merciful and loving; we must obey. Do we desire it, is the question? We are scattered! We must be one! Why the Roman Catholic Church? Because scripture tells us that the Lord has promised victory in the church of the apostle Peter. It is the battleground. Love your brother! A divided kingdom cannot stand!

We must fall like a choice vessel to be a choice vessel! **These are the elect, those who are willing to die innocently for the love of the guilty.** Be as He is, Sow as He sows, Love as He Loves!

Come Back To The Roman Catholic Church! GATHER!

The Lord points out to the Churches that there should not be any divisions among them. We are like a football team making touchdowns on the wrong side of the field. Therefore, because Christians are divided in the kingdom of Satan, the kingdom of God is shattered. Christians are scattered. Reflecting on what Jesus said on earth: The kingdom of God is not of this world and notably not here.

> *"My kingdom is not of this world. **If My kingdom were** of this world, **My servants would** fight, so that I should not be delivered to the Jews; but now My kingdom is not from here."* John 18:36 NKJV

He came to gather His Army and unite believers who have faith in Him. He is talking in code, "if it were, they would…" He said His servants would fight if His Kingdom was here. If we want to be His servants, we must form a rebellion of love. Our fight is to gather, to repent in sackcloth and ashes, love, fast, and pray. He says that there are many contentions causing confusion and disunity. We are in unity with the kingdom of Satan. We participate in Satan's kingdom because we are sinners and Satan is the father of sinners. Christians are persecuted and fight each other because they continue to think they are the ones in control and they think they need to save people.

> *None of them can by any means redeem his brother, Nor give to God a ransom for him—* Psalm 49:7

Believers are playing Satan's game. They think they must convert people. Conversion comes from the Lord, and only the Lord beckons. They fail to acknowledge the Lord in all they say and do. They think they are born again but we know they are not because they still sin. They believe the scary things in the book of Revelations because they think they are going to continue living in the kingdom of Satan. It is funny that people believe the dragons and such terror will occur, knowing Lucifer and his followers were cast out of heaven like lightening. Only if we remain a sinner, in Satan's cloister might we feel the threat, he threatens with. The Lord repeatedly offers a solution to our sinfulness: forgive, repent, and love.

We are rebels for Christ and we must gather. We must be willing to accept the fact of who we really are, and who we can be, if we obey Jesus!

We must desire to walk in the Spirit. Only the Lord can fight our battles. We are scattered living in pride or love of money. Preachers ignore the requisites that the Lord prescribed and they certainly do not inform their congregations that the Lord desires to teach us. They fail to inform their congregations that they, the congregation need to live in unconditional love, forgiveness, repentance, mercy, and unity. Instead, they mock other believers in Christ or misguide them, and some tell their congregation that they are born again, which is false. The Lord even asks if we were baptized in the name of Paul. That means that no person can baptize with the baptism the Lord desires to bestow upon us. Only the Lord can give us the baptism He is anxious to undergo, the baptism to be born again, born of God, Spirit to Spirit. It is the second Pentecost! We who gather and love unconditionally, will be the recipients. However, I am hopeful, that if we plead for the mercy of the worst of sinners, the Lord will also be merciful and they too will receive the Holy Spirit, so that ALL will be saved.

> *there are contentions among you. Now this I say, that every one of you saith,* **I am of Paul**; *and I of Apollos; and I of Cephas; and I of Christ. Is Christ divided?* **was Paul crucified for you? or were ye baptized in the name of Paul**
> <u>1 Cor 1:11-13 NKJV</u>

> *Now* **I beseech you**, *brethren, by the name of our Lord Jesus Christ,* **... that there be no divisions among you;**
> <u>1 Cor 1:10 KJV</u>

The Lord desires that all the Churches unite. He begs us to have no division among us. It is the Kingdom of God that must unite, so that Satan's kingdom can be divided and can be finished.!!! We who have faith in Jesus, are the rebels against Satan and must divide his kingdom! Satan and his devils are the perfect example in rebelling against heaven, now we must rebel against Satan by gathering and rebelling in his kingdom on earth. This is a heavenly rebellion. Normally you think a rebellion is violent, but this one, is a **rebellion of Love for the salvation of all**!

We do not need carnal weapons. The weapons of our warfare are mighty through God to the pulling down of strongholds as noted in Eph 6:10-18. We must also repent in sackcloth with use of ashes, unite, fast, pray without ceasing, live a life of unconditional love, forgiveness, and unconditional mercy. We must desire to fight the battle with Him, by **standing still and knowing that He is with us!** He will fight the battle, not us, we are only vessels of clay submitting to the power of an Almighty and Glorious God who loves us and has left us the code to victory where the gates of hell will not prevail. **Pray and Exalt Him!**

> *For, said he, they trust in their weapons, and in their boldness: but **we trust in the Almighty Lord, who at a beck can utterly destroy both them that come against us, and the whole world.*** 2Macc 8:18 DRB

Let us then revolt against ourselves, we of a wicked generation! **Let us unite and finish this!** Do we trust the Lord? Can we allow Him to lead us? We must!

Can we allow Him to Shepherd us? Are we afraid that the money supporting our churches/homes/selves will no longer be available to us? Are we afraid thinking we must support ourselves, not believing the Lord is our provider? The Lord told the apostles to go without a purse? Money is the god of this world. We must have faith; He will do the same for us. To put your heart at ease, meditating on Corinthians we contemplate how to handle this issue: we must live in this world as if not, spend money as if for the Lord. Acknowledge Him in your spending. We must not attach ourselves to money or anything or anyone. In other words, be of a mindset, preferring to first obey God, love God and be willing to submit to His every command, no matter what the consequences for the salvation of all living and dead.

We must be Christian brothers giving freely, forgiving unconditionally, and loving completely unto death for the salvation of the living and the dead. Who can say they know "love in the perfection of Our Father"? Could we or would we take the place of Jesus on the Cross? How deep is our love? May the Love of God fill us with His grace to receive from the Lord all that He desires. May He strengthen us and give us courage.

We are His sheep; He is our shepherd. The good shepherd leads his sheep. Sheep rely on their shepherd for survival. We have failed to follow Jesus, and keep our eyes on our Good Shepherd. Truly, we must follow Jesus, He came to show us the Way. We might not get crucified as He did, but the Lion's den will form as we gather and we will have to enter in faith, Trusting Jesus, without doubt!

And when he has sent out his sheep,
he goes before them, and the sheep follow him,
because they know his voice. John 10:4 CPDVTSB

Love one another! We must remove the walls that separate us. Christians stop rejecting believers of Our Lord Jesus Christ! The differences and quarrels are stumbling blocks! More clearly said, they are lying demons using you, tormenting you, keeping you from true love. The tongue is set on fire by hell. Satan makes us only believe what is convenient for our torment.

And the tongue is a fire, a world of iniquity. The tongue is so set among our members that it defiles the whole body, and sets on fire the course of nature; and it is set on fire by hell James 3:6 NKJV

The Lord even says in Rev 2:16 that if we repent, He will come to us quickly and fight with the sword of His mouth, the Word of God!

Repent; *or else **I will** come unto thee quickly, and will **fight against them with the sword of my mouth.*** Rev 2:16 KJV

The sign of Jonah is repentance in sack cloth and ashes!!!
With a true and sincere bitter appeal to the Lord for mercy and forgiveness towards all.

Do it for the Lord! Repent in sack cloth and ashes!!! Why sackcloth? This is what the Lord has prescribed. The Lord says confess and be reconciled one to another; we must attempt to reconcile with those whom we have conflict. Confessing to our preachers, priests, and religious leaders helps us to be reconciled one to another. If it seems irreconcilable, then we must pray for them and ask the Lord to be merciful to them and self. However, in sackcloth we confess to God directly and are attempting to reconcile to God according to the sign of Jonah, the only sign Jesus said we would see. In sackcloth we plead for the living and the dead, it seems to be a clearance to heaven, like a telephone line. We must plead for the dead who may have seemed lost, it is their second chance to salvation. This is just like us; we have a second chance, Jesus came the first time, now it is our turn to prove our love!
THIS IS A CALL TO ARMS! Repent, Fast, Pray and Unite!

Prayer: Jesus, we Trust in You! Your plans for our salvation are perfect. Help us Lord to submit ourselves to you and to take the first step in faith, courageously, with our eyes fixed on you. Help us to unite and show you the proof of our love, so that we may be like you. Forgive us for the times we have judged the Roman Catholic Church and all Churches, help us to love our brothers and to let go of the imperfect laws that separate us from your love. Help us to be merciful to those who have been the worst of sinners, to every preacher, leader, priest, and religious both living and dead. We plead for mercy upon all sinners. Help us to gather without hesitation in unconditional love, even unto death. Guide us and help us to gather in helping you divide the kingdom of Satan. Come Lord Jesus and deliver us from evil. Remove from our lives every attachment that keep us bound to Satan and his kingdom and bind us to yourself. Gather us together and allow us to help Jesus divide. May your glory manifest, may our salvation be realized, and may your throne be returned to you on earth as it is in heaven. Glory and Praise are yours alone in Jesus Name. Blessed Mother pray for us that we may be made worthy of the promises of Christ. Amen

WHAT PART OF THE BIBLE DO YOU NOT BELIEVE?

For John came unto you in the way of righteousness, and ye believed him not: but the publicans and the harlots believed him: ***and ye, when ye had seen it, repented not*** *afterward, that* ***ye might believe him***. Mat 21:32 KJV

*But **because of your stubbornness and unrepentant heart you are storing up wrath for yourself on the day of wrath** and revelation of the righteous judgment of God,*
Romans 2:5 NASB

The above scripture tells us that the tax collectors (publicans) and the harlots repented because they believed John. It also says, that if we would have repented, we might have believed him too. Our minds are blinded of the truth because of sin. We are stubborn and prefer not to repent to our detriment. We prefer to believe that we are forgiven or we prefer to believe another man's word rather than the Word of God. It is important to repent to clear our hearts, minds, and souls. It pleases the Lord when we have a contrite heart and repent of our doubts, our unbelief and all our sins.

*the god of this **world (Satan) has blinded the minds of the unbelieving*** *so that they might not see the light of the gospel of the glory of Christ, who is the image of God.* 2Cor 4:4 NASB

*Therefore **bear fruit in keeping with repentance**;*
Mat 3:8 NASB 1995

Or do you think lightly of the riches of His kindness and restraint and patience, not knowing that the kindness of God leads you to repentance? Romans 2:4 NASB

We cannot know the truth, unless we repent! We cannot believe unless we repent! In the New Testament it says that the only sign we will see is the sign of Jonah. We must repent like the people of Nineveh, using sackcloth and ashes. The Lord says that the men of Nineveh will judge and condemn our generation, because we have not repented. If our inner voice gives us a hint of believing that we should repent, we should do it without haste.

The Lord and His Word are the same yesterday, today and always. When He says "you" in the Word, we must take note of our sin and that of our father's and ancestors. Confess them, and learn from them, and desire **not** to commit the same sins. Will we believe the Word of God? Will we desire to obey?

We must choose to obey God rather than men. Our God is a merciful God; He says that if WE are merciful to unbelievers and the worst of sinners, then HE will be merciful to them also. We must seek Him to find Him. We must be sincere with a contrite and loving heart. We must serve Him in the greatest of love, even unto death. Reciprocate all that He exemplified!

*²⁸But He said, "On the contrary, **blessed are those who hear the word of God and follow it.**"* Luke 11:28 NASB

And being made perfect, he became the author of eternal salvation unto all them that obey him; Heb 5:9 KJV

*Whosoever is born of God doth **not commit sin;** for his seed remaineth in him: and **he cannot sin, because he is born of God**.* 1 John 3:9 KJV

And we are his witnesses of these things; and so is also the Holy Ghost, whom **God hath given to them that obey him**. Acts 5:32 KJV

So what part of the Bible should we believe? Although bible interpretations from generation to generation or translations to translation may have resulted in deviations of the actual message, we must trust that through inspiration the Lord teaches even today. Our God can do anything, and can teach us in many creative ways. Sometimes the new translation gives us better understanding. We must be open to Our Lord's teaching. Many times we open our Bibles and our eyes are fixed on words we know are meant to be read by our eyes only, pertaining to our life. That is the Living Word talking to us.

There are many commands that say to do certain things from generation to generation. It seems impossible to obey something that people have not taught, as it was originally intended. Like the game "whisper down the lane" the story changes from person to person. We are full of flaws and obedience seems impossible. The Lord did say we are all sinners and that Satan is the father of sinners. It seems apparent that we cannot escape sin without the grace of God. We must look to the Lord and seek Him for all truth. He desires to teach each one of us.

The Lord made a Covenant, a promise, to teach us Himself! What preacher has told us that? On the contrary, some preachers tell us we cannot interpret the Bible ourselves. We have been blinded by the ways of men. The Lord will teach us, if we allow Him. Repent in sackcloth and ashes!! Desire it!!!

> [10] *"For this is the Covenant that I will make with the house of Israel after those days, says the lord:*
> ***I WILL*** *put my laws into their minds,*
> ***I WILL*** *write them on their hearts. And*
> ***I WILL*** *be their God, and they shall be my people.*
> [11] *"And* ***THEY SHALL NOT TEACH EVERYONE*** *his fellow citizen, and everyone his brother, saying, 'know the Lord,'*
> ***For All Will Know Me, From the Least to The Greatest of Them.*** [12] *"For I Will be merciful to their iniquities, and* ***I WILL REMEMBER THEIR SINS NO MORE."***
> Heb 8:10-12 NASB95

What part of the bible do we continue to ignore or do not believe? What truths, as in the parables said by Jesus have been hidden from us? Swarming in our ignorance
> without desire to love unto death for the salvation of all,
> without repenting in the way the Lord has requested,
> without hoping in His return,
> without returning to Him,
> without reciprocating His actions,

We have been lost in our faith and in our fault. Sadness and pain are our reward for the evil we have chosen without repentance. We have not known the goodness of Our Great

Loving King. It is we who have chosen to bite Eve's apple and wallow in temptation and our sufferings. **The Log in our own eye reeks**!!!

Sadly, the veil is the shield of ignorance; the evil one blinds the people of God from all truth. We refusing to repent, content in the ways of the world, living in the laws of the flesh, perish or suffer fire during purification in the afterlife. What darkness keeps us from entering the light? Sadly, hidden ways of sinfulness lurk throughout the earth very close to our homes, even in us, even in those seeking holiness, until perfection comes.

The Old and New Testament Books were written after the events occurred. Some prophetic books are still awaiting realization. What books are being written today inspired by Our Heavenly Father? Have we closed our minds, hearts, and soul to the new events of Our Lord? He is very much alive. Do we believe He can teach us? Even the Word of God has caused much confusion, perhaps so that we can resolve to allow Him to teach us directly.

It is truly fearful to think of ourselves as being separated from Our Lord. We who love him so much, know that we cannot follow all the rules. There are many we do not even know, our hearts are so sad, but we rejoice in the hope of our salvation. We can only trust Him and greatly hope that He will change us, make us, and mold us to perfection. And most of all, give us the grace to love unto death. We must take the first step in faith. We must obey by gathering.

So, according to His divine plan of redemption, we need to realize, that, this world is in the power of the evil one, and we are participants. Therefore, as lovers of Our Lord Jesus Christ, we must seek Him with all our heart, mind, soul, and strength.

Choose to know the Truth, DESIRE IT!
REPENT OR PERISH! **BE READY!**
JESUS IS COMING!
This is a Call to Arms! Love, pray, fast, repent, and unite!

Read your Bible!

WHO IS THE DEVIL?

***The sinner is a child of the Evil One**; for the Evil One has been a sinner from the first. And the Son of God was seen on earth so that he might put an end to the works of the Evil One.* 1John 3:8 BBE

By this the children of God and the children of the devil are obvious: **anyone who does not practice righteousness is not of God, nor the one who does not love his brother and sister.** 1John 3:10 NASB

The devil longs to destroy and devour our souls. He is on a campaign on earth making us to say yes to the lust of the flesh, the lust of the eye and the boastful pride of life. He takes pleasure in tormenting us.

The devil puts evil thoughts in our mind and mouth and even in that of our friend causing disruption between us. He wants us to think that God is not real. He wants us to think that graven images (statues) are precious. He does not want us to love God and He will do anything to keep us from it. He inflicts us with pain, disease, and suffering as He did Jesus. The earth is presently Satan's kingdom. We must know that all authority and power is from God, but this is not His kingdom. We submit to our own sinfulness and disobedience resulting in our own chaos, sickness, and tribulations. The Lord disciplines those whom He loves, we have been living in ignorance. The devil is a liar and if we are liars, we have chosen our father, the devil. He uses us, sometimes our mouth, our hands, our feet, our privates, our whole being, including our mind. The devil is a creature, spirit, being or thing that takes the form in many manifestations. Some people or things are possessed by the devil. Some devils possess bodies of persons in a good way and others in a bad way. We ask, how can it be good? Well, the Lord clearly said it, when He said that there are devils disguised as angels of light and ministers of righteousness, as discussed below.

Should we take the following words literally: " child of the evil one," "children of the devil," "of your father the devil" and "son of the devil" and "not of God." According to scripture as a sinner you are a child of the evil one; on the other hand, as a child of God, you cannot sin and the devil cannot touch you. It says that as a sinner, you are like your father the devil. However, there is always the argument that perhaps it is a metaphor of the nature of our being or the behaviors that we demonstrate. However, it seems very clear, if taken literally. But as a believer and lover of Christ, we do not want to be one of them! But are we?

So let us consider this, if we are all sinners, a child of the evil one and we cannot escape sin, then why are we in this situation? When Jesus was on the cross, He asked Our Father to forgive us for we did not know what we were doing. Perhaps we also did not know who we are. Jesus knows everything, He would have known if we were devils. Why did He not, just tell us? Perhaps the number of believers was not yet right. So did Jesus die to also save Satan and his followers? They are His creation and all that He created is good!

He came to gift to us incorruption and immortality. He has given us the hope of our salvation and the hope of rising with Him. Perhaps, we were not ready for Him to tells us directly that we are devils, therefore speaking in parables, hints, and codes so we could figure it out. Perhaps, we are good devils with a purpose. Angels of light and ministers of righteousness, are the spark in this world, that ignited when the light of Jesus came into this world. He also says that the elect might be deceived, perhaps because they too are sinners and not yet perfected. We have had a change of heart! We love Jesus and have faith in Him. So again, what is the purpose of our being? He says we are all guilty, we are all sinners.

If we consider the sequence of events in the heavens and the examples, we must follow to follow Jesus, a very interesting image comes to mind. We know that history repeats itself, so, consider Lucifer a beautiful angel in heaven and his followers who were cast out and down to earth because of their rebellion. Perhaps, it is our turn as sinners to rebel against Satan, the father of sinners, in the kingdom of Satan. We must obey Jesus and gather for the glory of God for the salvation of all!

> *Do not let anyone deceive you in any way, for it will not come [the Coming of the Lord] unless the rebellion takes place first and the man of sin, who is destined for destruction, is revealed.* 2Thessalonians 2:3 ISV

So are we the *"man of sin, who is destined for destruction"* now revealed in knowing we just might be devils? And so, is now the time to start the rebellion?

God is Love and we must desire to love unconditionally as He loves. His plan is perfect and we must Trust in Him. Do we love our brother? If we do not, we cannot love God! This book covers topics that will help us to realize who we are and whether we love our brother or not according to scripture. Let us then love one another as the Lord has loved us!

The following scriptures pertain to the devil:

And the great dragon was cast out, that old serpent, called the Devil, and Satan, which deceiveth the whole world: **he was cast out into the earth, and his angels were cast out with him.** Rev 12:9 KJV

[12] "For this reason, rejoice, O heavens and you who dwell in them. **Woe to the earth and the sea, because the devil has come down to you**, *having great wrath, knowing that he has only a short time."* Rev 12:12 NASB 1995

"You are of your father the devil, and you want to do the desires of your father. He was a **murderer** *from the beginning, and does not stand in the truth because* **there is no truth in him**. *Whenever he speaks a lie, he speaks from his own nature, for he is a* **liar** *and the father of lies.* John 8:44 NASB 1995

[45] *"But because I speak the truth, you do not believe*

*Me. ⁴⁶"Which one of you convicts Me of sin? If I speak truth, why do you not believe Me? ⁴⁷**"He who is of God hears the words of God; for this reason you do not hear them, because you are not of God.**"* John 8:45-47 NASB 1995

*"You who are **full of all deceit and fraud**, you son of the devil, you enemy of all righteousness, will you not cease to make crooked the straight ways of the Lord?*
Ac 13:10 NASB 1995

*For, "The One Who Desires Life, To Love And See Good Days, **MUST KEEP HIS TONGUE FROM EVIL AND HIS LIPS FROM SPEAKING DECEIT.***
1Peter 3:10 NASB 1995

*And **the tongue is a fire; it is the power of evil placed in our bodies**, making all the body unclean, putting the wheel of life on fire, and **getting its fire from hell**.* James 3:6 BBE

***But the tongue may not be controlled by man; it is an unresting evil,** it is full of the poison of death.* James 3:8 BBE

But the things which come out of the mouth come from the heart; and they make a man unclean. Mat 15:18 BBE

As in water face reflects face, So the heart of man reflects man. Pr 27:19 NASB 1995

*We are certain that we are of God, but **all the world is in the power of the Evil One**.* 1John 5:19 BBE

***Do not love the world nor the things in the world.** If anyone loves the world, the love of the Father is not in him. ¹⁶ For **all that is in the world, the lust of the flesh and the lust of the eyes and the boastful pride of life, is not from the Father, but is from the world**. ¹⁷The world is passing away, and also its lusts; but the one who does the will of God lives forever.* 1John 2:15-17 NASB 1995

*But above all things, my brethren, **swear not**, neither by heaven, neither by the earth, neither by any other oath: but let your yea be yea; and your nay, nay; lest ye fall into condemnation.* James 5:12 KJV

*But the Lord was by my side and **gave me strength; so that through me the news might be given out in full measure**, and all the Gentiles might give ear: and I was taken out of the mouth of the lion.* 2Ti 4:17 BBE

For we wrestle not against flesh and blood, but against principalities, against powers, against the rulers of the darkness of this world, against spiritual wickedness in high places. Eph 6:12 KJV

And the devil that deceived them was cast into the lake of fire and brimstone, where the beast and the false prophet are, and shall be tormented day and night forever and ever. Rev 20:10 KJV

We must choose our father!!!

"No one can serve two masters; for either he will hate the one and love the other, or he will be devoted to one and despise the other. You cannot serve God and wealth.
Mat 6:24 NASB 1995

My loved one, do not be copying what is evil, but what is good. He who does good is of God: he who does evil has not seen God. 3John 1:11 BBE

Prayer: Lord Jesus, forgive our unbelief, please forgive us for all our offenses against you and others. Receive us as your child and allow your Holy Spirit to take control of our life and keep us in your loving light. Make our heart fit for You, our King. Enter our hearts, and never leave us. We give to you our free will, our life, our love, our total being without reserve. We ask you to teach us your ways which are righteous. We consecrate ourselves to the Immaculate Heart of Mary and the Sacred Heart of Jesus so that we may become pleasing to you. Make us Lord to resist, rebuke, and renounce the devil. We submit to you and you alone in the Name of Jesus. Father in Heaven please hear our prayer, Jesus be the Lord of our life. Blessed Mother of God pray for us that we may obtain the promises of Christ.

PRAYER OF RENUNCIATION

We renounce the wicked who renounce God. We ask God our creator to bless them and have mercy upon them and to change their hearts, minds, and souls. Teach us Lord how to repent and to return to God. We ask for the grace to acknowledge, honor, trust and obey Him who is slow to anger and filled with unfathomable love and mercy.

We renounce pride of all sorts. We renounce irreligion and worldly passions. (*Titus2:12*) We renounce all that We have. (*Luke 14:33*) We renounce our corrupt life and the corrupt life of our family, ancestors, and friends. (2*Esdras14:13*) We renounce all corruption and We desire to put on incorruption. We renounce defiling foods (*4Mac 5:34*), make us Lord to not eat of them and to know which ones they are. We renounce ancestral tradition of our national life in this world. (*4Maccabees8:7*)

"We do not renounce the noble kinship that binds us to our Brothers." (*4Maccabees10:3*) "No, by the blessed death of our brothers, by the eternal destruction of the tyrant, and by the everlasting life of the pious, we will not renounce our noble brotherhood." (*4Mac10:15*)

We will take courage in the faith of Jesus.

"Imitate me, brothers," he said. "Do not leave your post in my struggle or renounce our courageous brotherhood. (*4Maccabees9:23*)

We Announce that We are FOR Christ and with our brothers in Christ, We stand firm in our faith against all evil. We desire to live a sober, upright, and godly life in this world. (*Titus2:12*)

"We will not play false to you, O law that trained us, nor will we renounce you, beloved self-control. (*4Maccabees5:34*)

We recognize, accept, and acknowledge Judaism and We reclaim Judaism to God and to ourselves and to this land which God has given to us. We ask God to return to the Jews their right of inheritance pleasing to God. We ask the Lord to forgive all of us for our inequities, not one of us is without guilt. Make us Lord a people of incorruption in your Great Love.

Lord, make us to set our houses in order and to reprove your people. Make us Lord to comfort the lowly among them. Make us Lord to be the restorer of the breach, use us Lord to help repair the paths in which to dwell. Make us Lord a people of righteousness and fervent in prayer united with cords that cannot be broken by any evil manifestation or presentation seen or unseen. (*Ecclesiastes 10 4:12*)

All Glory, Honor and Power is Yours alone Almighty Father in the Name of Jesus.

PRAYER OF RESISTANCE AND REBUKE

Lord, now knowing that the victory is in the cross, we beg you to let us live in your passionate and sacrificial love. Circumcise our hearts and ears and fill our eyes with your loving light. Help us Lord to yield to our Holy Spirit and obey You without resistance.

Let your every creature serve you; for you spoke, and they were made. You sent forth your spirit, and it created them; **no one can resist your voice**. Judith 16:14 NAB

Make us Lord not to resist You, be our stronghold so that if one slaps us on our right cheek, that we may turn the other to him also. *(Mat 5:39)*. Help us Lord to not resist what God has appointed so that we may not incur judgment. (*Romans 13:2*) Make us Lord to accept your discipline (*Proverbs 13:1*) And teach us Lord to know the difference.

As you were condemned and put to death, the righteous of men and you did not resist, allow us Lord to imitate you in all things and in your Great Love. Mold us Lord to resist the devil firm in our faith. Make us and mold us Lord, to be humble in Your sight, pleasing to you.

Knowing that our brothers are experiencing the same sufferings in this world, we offer them to You Lord. God of all grace who has called us to His glory, may your grace perfect, confirm, strengthen, and establish us. To You dear Lord, be dominion forever and ever. (*2Peter5:9-11*)

Increase in us Lord, increase our trust in you knowing that you will give to us utterance and wisdom which none of our opponents will be able to resist or refute. (*Luke21:15*) Put upon us Lord, the armor of God so that we will be able to resist in the evil day, make us to do everything to stand firm in the faith of Jesus and in Your perfect love. (*Ephesians 6:13*) Oh Lord, rebuke us not in thy anger, nor chasten us in thy wrath. (*Psalm 38:1*)

Let a good man strike or rebuke us in kindness, but let the oil of the wicked never anoint our head; for our prayer is continually against their wicked deeds. (*Psalm 141:5*) Oh Lord, help us not to judge, merciful God, help us to also be merciful and we ask for mercy for the merciless and the unbeliever.

Let us Lord come to one another in friendship to help one another, let our hearts be knit to you and to each other in peace and Love. Let all adversaries of betrayal be bound and rebuked.

(*1Chronicles12:17*) "Thou does rebuke the insolent, accursed ones, who wander from thy commandments; (*Psalm 119:21*) At thy rebuke they fled, at the sound of thy thunder they took to flight (*Psalm 104:7*) "and You are Lord of all, and there is no one who can resist You.

You who is the Lord" (*Ester 4:21*) To You dear Lord, be dominion forever and ever. (*2Peter5:9-11*) In the Name of Jesus.

This is a Call to Arms! Love, pray, fast, repent, and unite!

WHO ARE THE FALSE PROPHETS?

A true prophet will speak of our sinfulness and expose our iniquity. He will tell us these things, not to anger us, but to free us from the bondage and chains of the devil. He will speak truth **leading us to the love of God, unconditional love, and repentance.** Love one another unconditionally! Forgive with all our heart, mind, and soul! Desire it! Avoid the punishment mentioned in the Bible, Repent! Today, there are many false teachers of Christ, false prophets and false christs! Ask the Lord to reveal who we are? We must seek!

*Beloved, do not believe every spirit, but test the spirits to see whether they are from God, because **many false prophets have gone out into the world**. 1John 4:1 NASB 1995*

*But there were **false prophets** among the people, as there will be **false teachers** among you, who will secretly put forward **wrong teachings for your destruction**, even turning away from the Lord who gave himself for them; whose destruction will come quickly, and they themselves will be the cause of it. 2Pe 2:1 BBE*

*Your prophets have seen for you False and foolish visions; And **they have not exposed your iniquity So as to restore you from captivity,** But they have seen for you false and misleading oracles. La 2:14 NASB 1995*

*¹¹Do not participate in the unfruitful deeds of darkness, but instead even **expose them**; ¹²for it is disgraceful even to speak of the things which are done by them in secret. ¹³But all things become visible when they are exposed by the light, for everything that becomes visible is light. ¹⁴For this reason it says, "Awake, sleeper, And arise from the dead, And Christ will shine on you." Eph 5:11-14NASB 1995*

¹⁴ Then the LORD said to me, "The prophets are prophesying falsehood in My name. I have neither sent them nor commanded them nor spoken to them; they are prophesying to you a false vision, divination, futility and the deception of their own minds. JER 14:14 NASB1995

"So My hand will be against the prophets who see false visions and utter lying divinations. They will have no place in the council of My people, nor will they be written down in the register of the house of Israel, nor will they enter the land of Israel, that you may know that I am the Lord GOD. Eze 13:9 NASB 1995

¹⁵ "Beware of the false prophets, who come to you in sheep's clothing, but inwardly are ravenous wolves. Mat 7:15 NASB 1995

"For false Christs and false prophets will arise and will show great signs and wonders, so as to mislead, if possible, even the elect. Mat 24:24 NASB 1995

And the devil that deceived them was cast into the lake of fire and brimstone, where the beast and the false prophet are, and shall be tormented day and night forever and ever. Rev 20:10 KJV

But he, answering, said to them, An evil and false generation is looking for a sign; and no sign will be given to it but the **sign of the prophet Jonah** Mat 12:39 BBE

By this the children of God and the children of the devil are obvious: anyone who does not practice righteousness is not of God, nor the one who does not love his brother. 1John 3:10 NASB 1995

³⁶ Teacher, which is the great commandment in the law? ³⁷ And he said unto him, Thou shalt love the Lord thy God with all thy heart, and with all thy soul, and with all thy mind. ³⁸ This is the great and first commandment. ... ⁴⁰ On these two commandments the whole law hangeth, and the prophets. MAT 22:36-40 ASV

The question arises as to the things that have occurred in times after Christ, regarding prophets, visions, and divinations: are they true? The Lord said the only sign we will see is the sign of Jonah. We must obey and repent!

Prayer: Lord, please give to us the zeal and boldness to glorify you. Help us Lord to expose the iniquity of others, to restore them from captivity. Use our mouth, our tongue, our lips to proclaim your Word, Your Love and the Life others may obtain though You, in You and with You. Give to us a mind of Christ and a sound heart. Clothe us in your righteousness and complete us with your faith and perfect love. Help us Lord, make us Lord to do your will, for Your glory, and for the benefit of others. In Jesus Name I pray.

An evil and false generation is looking for a sign;
*And **no sign will be given to it***
but THE SIGN OF THE PROPHET JONAH:
Matthew 12:39 BBE

*The men of Nineveh **Will Stand Up with This***
Generation at the Judgement,
And Will Condemn It
BECAUSE THEY REPENTED AT THE
PREACHING OF JONAH;
Mat 12:41 NASB

The sign of Jonah is deep and bitter repentance
Using sackcloth and ashes
For both people and animals

REPENT USING SACKCLOTH & ASHES!

WHO ARE THE FALSE CHRISTS?

Are they those who believe in Christ but have different doctrines, different teachings? Yes, that is them. They are not an antichrist, they are false teachers of Christ, for there is only One Teacher, and that is Christ.

CONS:

They glorify themselves. They are not humble. They are proud. Many are concerned with their sustenance and money drives them. There is big business in preaching lies and avoiding truth. They do not repent according to the ways of the Lord. They do not love their brother because they do not know how, some do not care. They do not love other believers of Jesus. They degrade other churches. They do not love Mary, Mother of God, whom Our Father in heaven choose, and loves very much. They teach gospel without love and repentance. They are angels of light, and ministers of righteousness, a devil in disguise.

They think they know Jesus, but they are liars. Read *Mat 23 Woes!* They mislead their congregations leading them to the destruction of their souls and their own.

The Lord taught unconditional love, forgiveness, and repentance. False Christ's speak evil against other Christ believers and/or do not practice the unconditional love and the mercy of Christ. They cause more division and confusion among Christ Believers. There are many contentions among them. They do not know love! and so, what is life without true love... NOTHING!

Do they believe there is only One Teacher as the Lord spoke when He was on earth *(Heb 8:10-12)*? Do they even ask their followers or congregation to pray and ask the Lord to unite us in love, in mind, in spirit, and the same judgement? Do they have a mind of Christ?

> *¹³For such are false apostles, deceitful workers, transforming themselves into the apostles of Christ. ¹⁴And no marvel;* **for Satan himself is transformed into an angel of light.** *¹⁵Therefore it **is no great thing if his ministers** also be transformed as the ministers of righteousness; whose end shall be according to their works.* 2 Cor 11:13-15 KJV

*But there were false prophets among the people, as there will be false teachers among you, who will secretly put forward wrong teachings **for your destruction**, even turning away from the Lord who gave himself for them; whose destruction will come quickly, and they themselves will be the cause of it.* _{2Pe 2:1 BBE}

[24] *"**For false Christs and false prophets will arise and will show great signs and wonders, so as to mislead, if possible, even the elect.** [25] "Behold, I have told you in advance. [26] "So if they say to you, 'Behold, He is in the wilderness,' do not go out, or, 'Behold, He is in the inner rooms,' do not believe them. [27] "For just as the lightning comes from the east and flashes even to the west, so will the coming of the Son of Man be. [28] "Wherever the corpse is, there the vultures will gather.* _{Mat 24:24-28 NASB 1995}

The following are scriptures to consider:

But you may not be named Teacher: for one is your teacher, and you are all brothers. _{Mat 23: 8 BBE}

[10]*Now I beseech you, brethren, by the name of our Lord Jesus Christ, that ye all speak the same thing, and that there be no divisions among you; but that **ye be perfectly joined together in the same mind and in the same judgment.** [11]For it hath been declared unto me of you, my brethren, by them which are of the house of Chloe, that there are contentions among you.* _{1 Corinthians 1:10-11 KJV}

For who hath known the mind of the Lord, that he may instruct him? but we have the mind of Christ. _{1Cor 2:16 KJV}

Let this mind be in you which was in Christ Jesus _{Php 2:5 BBE}

So that as Jesus was put to death in the flesh, do you yourselves be of the same mind; for the death of the flesh puts an end to sin; _{1Pe 4:1 BBE}

That you may not be moved in mind or troubled by a spirit, or by a word, or by a letter as from us, with the suggestion that the day of the Lord is even now come; <u>2Th 2:2 BBE</u>

PROS:

In the flesh, according to scripture, it appears that our leaders and preachers are angles of light, ministers of righteousness, and false apostles. They are a speck of light in this world of darkness. Although a devil in disguise, we must understand that the Lord came to divide. *"God, the sovereign good is guided in all His actions by His most profound wisdom for holy and supernatural purposes"* as noted by St. Dorothy. I believe that the angels of light have been used according to Gods perfect plan, as was Peter when he denied the Lord three times. He came to initiate and gather the Army of God. He came to make us aware of who we are. All this has occurred for a time such as this. Now is the time to divide Satan's kingdom. It is time for the angels of light, ministers of righteousness, false apostles, and all believers, to come to the Light, and let the Lord take command. Repent and Unite to the cause!

The Lord says that a divided house cannot stand. It is very clear, Christians are scattered, they must choose their master. Christians are divided in Satan's kingdom that is why they seem to be at an end, they are playing in Satan's court.

Is it your opinion that I have come to give peace on earth? I say to you, No, but division: <u>Luke 12:51 BBE</u>

All churches are in error. We are in one big Babylon; they are in a state of confusion opposing each other. Satan is trying to keep the people of God from the truth and from the true church. There are many snares. We must wait on the Lord; He is Our Victor.

A divided house is brought to desolation, we are either **"FOR Christ or Against Him."** Believers in Christ are scattered, they are not united. Believers in Christ are against Him! Let us change that!

We who believe in Jesus Christ, God, Son of God, Son of man, one with the Father and His resurrection appear to be for Him, but are not. We do not practice unconditional love as Jesus has taught. (Reference: *1 John 4*). We must repent and unite! We are rebels for Christ and we must gather! We must demonstrate unconditional love.

The Word of God is true. We must ask Him, Our Teacher to teach us all things. We must pray that we may obtain a mind of Christ. We must ask Him for the grace to have the greatest love. We must ask Him for the grace to be totally and unconditionally obedient. We must desire desperately, to love Our Father as He loves us, even unto death, and even offering to Him the death of our beloved for the Love of God, in the fulfillment of His perfect plan. We must ask Him to be our stronghold and take away all fear from any opposition that may confront us.

> *Gird yourselves, and lament, ye priests: howl, ye ministers of the altar: come,* **lie all night in sackcloth**, *ye ministers of my God: for the meat offering and the drink offering is withholden from the house of your God.* Joel 1:13 KJV

> *Howl, ye shepherds, and cry; and* **wallow yourselves in the ashes,** *ye principal of the flock: for the days of your slaughter and of your dispersions are accomplished; and ye shall fall like a pleasant vessel.* 26 Jer 25:34 KJV

> *And I set my face unto the Lord God, to seek by prayer and supplications,* **with fasting, and sackcloth, and ashes***.* Da 9:3 KJV

We must fall like a choice vessel to be a choice vessel! **These are the elect, those who are willing to die innocently for the love of the guilty.** Be as He is, Sow and He sows, Love as He Loves! Let us then, repent and pray for ourselves and for the false christs:

Prayer to the Lord for ourselves:

Please Lord, give to us a mind of Christ, a sound heart, and teach us your ways. Put upon us the armor of righteousness and justice. Teach us Lord to test the spirits and lead us to all truth. We beg you to make us to be pleasing to you: loving, compassionate, merciful and all that you are. Make us Lord to resist the devil and his evil ways. Make us Lord to submit to you completely without hesitation and to obey your every command. Hear us, Dear Father. and help us to Love You as You love us. Be our stronghold and help us to surrender to the cross, that you may be glorified. Remove the veil that blinds us, open our minds, our hearts, and our beings to the reality of who we are. Help us to accept all truth, and give us the strength and courage to change. Take this vessel of clay as your own, be our master, we renounce and rebuke all evil, and the servitude and desires of money.

We beg you Lord, to make us in union with our brethren that we make speak the same thing with no division among us. Join us perfectly together in the same mind, same spirit, and in the same judgment in Your Love, for Your Glory and Honor unto life everlasting. In the Name of Jesus, we pray. Blessed Mary, Mother of God, be our Mother too.

Prayer for false christs:
LEAD FALSE CHRISTS TO YOUR LIVING BREAD

Oh Lord, Help Them. Dearest Lord, Love, and Light of our lives, have mercy on the false Christs. Reveal your truth to them, lead them to eat of Your Living Bread and grant them Everlasting life in your great Love. Lead them to Confess and repent that the door will not be shut on them. Lead them in your way, shine your light upon them.

We bind the stronghold of false christs, false prophets, false apostles, and false teachers. We cut off the tongue of the lying demons and pluck out the eyes of splinters, pride, and glory. May their eyes become blessed and may their ears hear You. We command those evil spirits to reap what they have sown, and we bind each person to the Immaculate Heart of Mary with this prayer:

Hail Mary, Full of Grace, The Lord is with thee, Blessed are You among women, Blessed is The Fruit of your womb, Jesus. Holy Mary, Mother of God, Pray for Us Sinners now and at the hour of our death Amen.

[26] *Jesus answered them and said, Verily, verily, I say unto you, Ye seek me, not because ye saw signs,* **but because ye ate of the loaves**, *and were filled.* John 6:26 ASV

WHO IS THE ANTICHRIST?

Who is the liar but the one who denies that Jesus is the Christ? This is the antichrist, **the one who denies the Father and the Son.** 1John 2:22 NASB 1995

Little children, it is the last hour; and as you were given word that the Antichrist would come, so now **a number of Antichrists have come to you**; *and by this we are certain that it is the last hour.* 1John 2:18 BBE

and every spirit that does not confess Jesus is not from God; this is the spirit of the antichrist, of which you have heard that it is coming, and now it is already in the world. 1John 4:3 NASB 1995

Because a number of false teachers have gone out into the world, who do not give witness that Jesus Christ came in the flesh. Such a one is a false teacher and Antichrist. 2John 1:7 BBE

Those who do not believe in God at all, are Antichrists. Those who do not believe in Our Father nor Jesus Christ to be God in the flesh, the Son of God, Son of man, one with the Father, are antichrists. They are therefore against Him. They do not confess Jesus as their Lord. The Antichrist denies that Jesus is the Christ. Let us pray for them that perhaps the Lord will change their heart and free them from bondage.

Prayer: Lord, You, who is creator of all things great and small, bless our enemies, bless the antichrist. Have pity on Him. Oh Lord, surely, we have received what we deserved for our inequities. Have mercy on us all by the merits of Your Beloved Son Jesus who suffered and died for us out of love and mercy. Lord, please stop us from sinning and from hurting you and one another. Fill us with the grace of your consuming fire of love and create a right spirit within us. Give us the grace to love them unconditionally, to forgive them and to be merciful, even unto death for their salvation. Thank you, Lord for hearing our prayer. In the Name of Jesus.

WHAT POWER DOES SATAN HAVE OVER ME?

The pain of death is sin; and the power of sin is the law:
1Cor 15:56 BBE

Let everyone put himself under the authority of the higher powers, because there is no power which is not of God, and ***all powers are ordered by God.*** *Ro 13:1 BBE*

Jesus gave this answer: ***You would have no power at all over me if it was not given to you by God****; John 19:11 BBE*

But we have this treasure in earthen vessels, that the excellency of the power ***may be*** *of God, and not of us.*
2Cor 4:7 KJV

Jesus said to them, "Is this not the reason you are mistaken, that you do not understand the Scriptures or the power of God? Mark 12:24 NASB 1995

We, in the flesh, are earthen vessels as mentioned in 2Cor 4:7. The treasure in our earthen vessel is God in us, if we obey Him as noted in scripture. The Lord greatly desires to possess us, and baptize us, as He did the apostles in the upper room, with tongues of fire. We must submit to Him! We must repent and desire not to sin so that the devil will flee. Our Lord wants to be one with us and in us. He is waiting for us to take the first step in faith!

And wonder came on them all and they said to one another, What are these words? for with authority and power he gives orders to the evil spirits and they come out. Luke 4:36 BBE

But I will make clear to you of whom you are to be in fear: of him who after death has power to send you to hell; yes, truly I say, Have fear of him. Luke 12:5 BBE

¹⁵He who is the blessed and only Sovereign, the King of kings and Lord of lords, ¹⁶who alone possesses immortality and dwells in unapproachable light, whom no man has seen or can see. To Him be honor and eternal dominion! Amen.
1Ti 6:15-16 NASB 1995

For the word of the cross seems foolish to those who are on the way to destruction; but to us who are on the way to salvation it is the power of God. 1Cor 1:18 BBE

*For it is a sign of grace if a man,
desiring to do right in the eyes of God,
undergoes pain as punishment for something
which he has not done.* 1Pe 2:19 BBE

Full of strength in the measure of the great power of his glory, so that you may undergo all troubles with joy;
Col 1:11 BBE

*For I reckon that the sufferings of this present time
are not worthy to be compared with the glory
which shall be revealed in us.* Ro 8:18 KJV

To make their eyes open, turning them from the dark to the light, and from the power of Satan to God, so that they may have forgiveness of sins and a heritage among those who are made holy by faith in me. Ac 26:18 BBE

For the holy Writings say to Pharaoh, For this same purpose did I put you on high, so that I might make my power seen in you, and that there might be knowledge of my name through all the earth. Ro 9:17 BBE

For this reason I make request to you, brothers, by the mercies of God, that you will give your bodies as a living offering, holy, pleasing to God, which is the worship it is right for you to give him. Ro 12:1 BBE

Who has made us free from the power of evil and given us a place in the kingdom of the Son of his love; <u>Col 1:13 BBE</u>

For with God nothing shall be impossible. <u>Luke 1:37 KJV</u>

Behold, I give unto you power to tread on serpents and scorpions, and over all the power of the enemy: and nothing shall by any means hurt you. <u>Luke 10:19 KJV</u>

And a great voice in heaven came to my ears, saying, Now is come the salvation, and the power, and the kingdom of our God, and the authority of his Christ: because he who says evil against our brothers before our God day and night is forced down. <u>Rev 12:10 BBE</u>

After these things there came to my ears a sound like the voice of a great band of people in heaven, saying, **Praise to the Lord; salvation and glory and power be to our God**: <u>Rev 19:1 BBE</u>

To the only God our Saviour, through Jesus Christ our Lord, let us give glory and honour and authority and power, before all time and now and forever... <u>Jude 1:25 BBE</u>

Let blessing and glory and wisdom and praise and honour and power and strength be given to our God for ever and ever. <u>Rev 7:12 BBE</u>

Prayer: Help us Lord to accept all things for your glory. Help us to accept all trials and tribulations with grace that we may please you in all things and inherit life everlasting in your unfathomable love. Lord, you said that **the power of sin is the law** and in <u>Heb 7:11-18</u> you say that the priesthood changed the law and made things imperfect but brought to us a greater hope to draw near to You. And so, then Lord, in this hope we desire to return to You, Your priesthood, Your altar, and Your throne so that you may once again reign in all hearts, minds, and souls. Remove this imperfection from us and perfect us. Allow us Lord, make us Lord to return to you. Make us Lord a new creation. Come to us King of Glory, reign in us and throughout all creation in the heavens above, on the earth and beneath the earth. Melchizedek, Oh Priest of the Most High God, return to us and take Your place as the Lord has prescribed in His perfect plan. Blessed Be God, Blessed Be His Holy Name, Jesus.

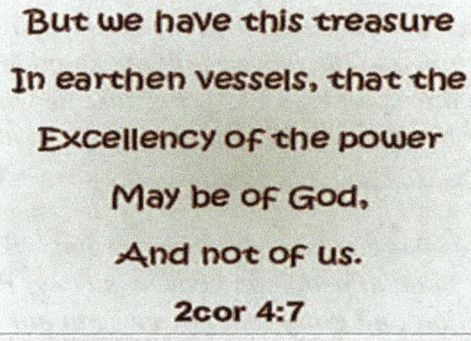

HOW CAN I BEGIN TO OBEY? I AM HELPLESS!

*By lovingkindness and truth iniquity is atoned for,
And by the fear of the LORD one keeps away from evil.*
Pr 16:6 NASB 1995

Desire to Love God first, and then each other as we love ourselves. He will help us and teach us, if we ask Him. The law of the Lord will be fulfilled in our life if we desire and strive to make the Lord our first love and then each other. It is stated in the great commandment, that upon this, all the law and the prophets are based. That is, if we can Love God first with all our hearts, mind, soul, and strength, then the rest of the commandments will automatically be fulfilled. Approach Him with a contrite and sorrowful heart. We must confess our sins so that He may hear us. Confessing is like trying to clear a road with a tree that has fallen on it. We being the road, the tree being our sins. Removing the tree clears the path, as does confessing our sins clears communication or the path to heaven. Sin is the chain that binds us to Satan. Jesus came to break those chains. Do not be a rebel against Jesus, He is merciful to the worst of sinners if they repent. We must join His cause and gather as He has requested!

Jesus has also ordered us to be baptized and eat of the bread of life! He knows are hearts and whether we desire to obey Him. We must pray and ask for the intercession of the whole church. We must love each other unconditionally with a merciful heart. Fear of the Lord is discussed in the next question in this book.

Scripture:
> *[36] Master, which is the chief rule in the law? [37]And he said to him,* **Have love for the Lord your God with all your heart, and with all your soul, and with all your mind.** *[38] This is the first and greatest rule.*
> *[39] And a second like it is this,*
> **Have love for your neighbour as for yourself.** *[40] On these two rules all the law and the prophets are based.*
> Mathew 22:36-40 BBE

We must do as Our Sheppard has done. We must desire to be as He is. We must Love as He loves. Jesus called Mary Mother and so should we. We must desire that our hearts become Sacred like His and Immaculate like Hers; remove our pride and ask the Lord to forgive us and help us to love her as He loves Her. She is the tabernacle of the Word of God; the Word entered her womb. Blessed is the fruit of Her womb, Jesus! The devil is real and does not want us to believe. Let us then repent together, so that all will believe.

Prayer: "Lord we solemnly approach your throne and with a contrite heart we admit our ignorance, our doubts, and our faults, please forgive us. Lord, help us to love you with all our hearts, with all our soul, with all our mind and all our strength. Give to us the gift of the Holy Spirit. Change our heart to please you, our mind to obey you, and our soul to magnify you. Our being we give to you, that your will, may be done in our life. Lord, forgive us for not loving Your Mother as we should, for not desiring to know her. Forgive our unbelief and help us love her as You love Her. Teach us your ways and fill us with Your perfect love." In the Name of Jesus.

2023: Todays message is this:
BE PERFECT AS OUR FATHER IS PERFECT.
Simply obtained:

Love unconditionally, even unto death like Jesus

Forgive unconditionally, be merciful to the merciless, plead for mercy on those who may seem lost

Repent in sackcloth with use of ashes *Mat 11:21*

The Churches must unite as requested in *1Cor 1:10*

The Lord promises victory in *Mat 16:18* at which time our love will be tested. We must gather to rebel in Satan's kingdom.

This is a Call to Arms! Love, pray, fast, repent, and unite!

WHAT IS REPENTANCE & FEAR OF THE LORD?

On June 21st 2004, the Lord taught me the following definition of repentance while adoring Him at the Blessed Sacrament Adoration Chapel:

_ Repentance is an action demonstrating Fear of the Lord, one of the Gifts of the Spirit, it is sensed by:
  _ The fear of offending Him
  _ The fear of the thought of being separated from Him, greatly longing Him as your Bridegroom
  _ The fear of not being with and in Him
  _ The fear of losing His Love or becoming lost and losing Him through sin
  _ The fear of becoming a black sheep, straying and becoming disobedient
  _ The fear of losing grace and falling away from Him through sin
  _ A fear that we have not repented of those things that we have done badly and have been veiled of our sin, therefore, the fear of unknown disobedience
  _ A feeling of remorse for the sins committed.
  _ A contrite heart grieving for what it has done
  _ A strong regret for offending the Lord
  _ It is the Great Desire to Please the Lord, Obey and Abide, and to Love Him Greatly and the fear of not doing so and expressing our heartfelt contrition

IT IS IMPERATIVE THAT WE REPENT USING SACKCLOTH AND ASHES!

The men of Nineveh repented at the preaching of Jonah, and will be at our judgement to condemn those who do not repent. It is difficult to understand why anyone who truly wants to be a child of God would not repent using sackcloth or go to the confessional, anxiously awaiting to receive Holy Communion.

Our Lord is seen in the Host. The Bread of Life unseen, is our seed, consumed in holiness, capable of resurrecting in us.
- fearing to be without life everlasting
- to receive the Body of Christ, flesh of my flesh,
whom the Lord said if we do not eat, we do not have life in us. The Living Bread is our source of life, Jesus said it!
The devil tries to steal it from us.

Ignorance is the devil's strength.

Pray for knowledge, wisdom and understanding.
Read the Bible. Trust in Jesus!

It is said that if everyone would go to confession many illnesses would be healed. Believe! Surrender! Receive! Return to Love! Reconcile one to another.

Woe unto thee, Chorazin! woe unto thee, Bethsaida! for if the mighty works, which were done in you, had been done in Tyre and Sidon, **they would have repented long ago in sackcloth and ashes.** Mat 11:21 KJV

Hurry Do Not Delay!!! Time is of the Essence!
The Reign of Jesus Is at Hand!
JESUS IS COMING!!!!   REPENT!
Consider this: think of all the things we are proud of: our home? children? accomplishments? business? boat? car? money? possessions? Knowing Satan's flaw was pride, should we remove the word "Proud" from our vocabulary? Pray that the Lord will teach us and be our stronghold to abandon the lusts, lures and loves that attach us to this world. We should ask for forgiveness with a contrite heart for our pride and attachments to this world.
Be as Jesus was in the desert SAY NO TO THE DEVIL.
Remove the splinters of the eye; the eye is the lamp of the body, when the eye is clear, the body is full of light.

If, then, all your body is light, with no part of it dark, it will be completely full of light, as when a flame with its bright shining gives you light. Luke 11:36 BBE

I have come as a light into the world, so that no one who has faith in me will go on living in the dark. John 12:46 BBE

*Because **the god of this world has made blind the minds of those who have not faith**, so that the light of the good news of the glory of Christ, who is the image of God, might not be shining on them.* 2Cor 4:4 BBE

But Jesus, turning to them, said, Daughters of Jerusalem, let not your weeping be for me, but for yourselves and for your children. Luke 23:28 BBE

*[5] 'Therefore **remember from where you have fallen, and repent** and do the deeds you did at first; or else I am coming to you and will remove your lampstand out of its place— **unless you repent**.* Re 2:5 NASB 1995

Repent using sackcloth and ashes!
   THIS IS A CALL TO ARMS!
  Love, pray, fast, repent, and unite!

WHY IS THE VIRTUE OF CHARITY A GREAT VIRTUE?

¹² Put on therefore, as the elect of God, holy and beloved, bowels of mercies, kindness, humbleness of mind, meekness, longsuffering;
¹³ Forbearing one another, and forgiving one another, if any man have a quarrel against any: even as Christ forgave you, so also do ye.
¹⁴And above all these things put on charity,
which is the bond of perfectness. <u>Col 3:12-14 KJV</u>

Charity is the bond to perfection as noted in the Word. The gift of perfect charity is greater than we understand. Yes, loving unconditionally and giving without restraint, but it is also a greater giving. It is a **detachment from all things and every one of the earth,** renouncing their evil ways and not desiring them to a point of possessiveness; not allowing them to possess us. Yet, Loving each other still, even unto death.

Herein is our love made perfect, that we may have boldness in the day of judgment: because as he is, so are we in this world. <u>1John 4:17 KJV</u>

And so whoever is not ready to give up all he has may not be my disciple. <u>Luke 14:33 BBE</u>

But if you give to the poor such things as you are able, then all things are clean to you. <u>Luke 11:41 BBE</u>

WHY IS THE VIRTUE OF HUMILITY A GREAT VIRTUE?

In his humiliation his judgment was taken away: and who shall declare his generation? <u>Ac 8:33 KJV</u>

The great virtue of Humility comes through humiliation. We must be humble. We must accept humiliation with kindness so that we may be like Him. In our humiliation our judgment will be taken away obtaining the great virtue of humility. In our trials and tribulations, we must look for the lesson beyond our understanding. The victory is in the cross.

³²Give no offense either to Jews or to Greeks or to the church of God; ³³just as I also please all men in all things, not seeking my own profit but the profit of the many, so that they may be saved. <u>1Cor 10:32-33 NASB 1995</u>

³Do nothing from selfishness or empty conceit, **but with humility of mind regard one another as more important than yourselves**; <u>Php 2:3 NASB 1995</u>

With all gentle and quiet behaviour, taking whatever comes, putting up with one another in love; <u>Eph 4:2 BBE</u>

Therefore, ridding yourselves of all filthiness and all that remains of wickedness, in humility receive the word implanted, which is able to save your souls. <u>James 1:21 NASB</u>

And in the same way, let the younger men be ruled by the older ones. Let all of you **put away pride and make yourselves ready to be servants**: *for God is a hater of pride, but he gives grace to those who make themselves low.* <u>1 Peter 5:5 BBE</u>

WHAT EXACTLY DOES "I AM THE WAY" MEAN?

Jesus is the Way!
Jesus saith unto him, I am the way, the truth, and the life: no man cometh unto the Father, but by me. John 14:6 KJV

Mary said it all, with these few words:
His mother said to the servants, Whatever he says to you, do it. John 2:5 BBE

Just recently, the Lord showed me a simple explanation for "THE WAY." He is the Way! But what does that mean?

Many times we have heard others tell us: "I am going to show you how to do this?" We try to do that and we do it wrong. Their next remark is to do it again saying: "Look this is **the way** we do it" or perhaps they say "Do it this **way**."

Jesus clearly tells us that He is the good Shepherd, His sheep follow Him, His sheep know Him, and hear His voice.

As a child, did you ever play the game "follow the leader" and if you messed up you were out of the game. Well, this is no game!!! We must follow our leader, Jesus! He is the Way! He is the Living Word, our Living Instruction Sheet. Look at Him, do as He has done. Copy Jesus! Reciprocate!

Keep in mind those who were over you, and who gave you the word of God; seeing the outcome of their way of life, let your faith be like theirs. Heb 13:7 BBE

*My loved one, **do not be copying what is evil**, but what is good. He who does good is of God: he who does evil has not seen God.* 3John 1:11 BBE

We must follow Jesus. **We must do as He does. Love as He Loves. We must be willing to die for the salvation of all whom Our Lord desires, both the living and the dead** (spiritually or physically and technically everyone).

WHAT DOES "I AM THE TRUTH" MEAN?

To live in Jesus, we must desire to be like Him. He is the truth. If we want to live in the truth, we must not lie!!!

Do not break the Ten Commandments! It is the devil using our tongue that makes us to lie!!! Choose Jesus as master!!! There is no such thing as a 'little lie." A lie is a lie. Desire truth!

> *Jesus saith unto him,* ***I am*** *the way,* ***the truth****, and the life: no man cometh unto the Father, but by me.* John 14:6 KJV

> *³²and you will know the truth, and the truth will make you free."* John 8:32 NASB 1995

> *²¹ "But* ***he who practices the truth comes to the Light****, so that his deeds may be manifested as having been wrought in God."* John 3:21 NASB 1995

> *God is a Spirit: and they that worship him must worship him in spirit and in truth.* John 4:24 KJV

> *For the law was given through Moses****; grace and the true way of life are ours through Jesus Christ.*** John 1:17 BBE

> *"But I tell you that every careless word that people speak, they shall give an accounting for it in the day of judgment* Mat 12:36 NASB 1995

> *For by thy words thou shalt be justified, and by thy words thou shalt be condemned* Mat 12:37 KJV

> *But* ***the things which come out of the mouth come from the heart****; and they make a man unclean.* Mat 15:18 BBE

> *⁴The one who says, "I have come to know Him," and* ***does not keep His commandments, is a liar,*** *and the truth is not in him;* 1John 2:4 NASB 1995

> *And **the tongue is a fire; it is the power of evil placed in our bodies**, making all the body unclean, putting the wheel of life on fire, and getting its fire from hell.*
> James 3:6 BBE

> *And so, putting away false words, let **everyone say what is true to his neighbour**: for we are parts one of another.*
> Ephs 4:25 BBE

> *²²Since you **have in obedience** to the truth purified your souls for a sincere love of the brethren, **fervently love one another from the heart**, ²³for you have been born again not of seed which is perishable but imperishable, that is, **through the living and enduring word of God**.*
> 1Peter 1:22-23 NASB 1995

When we are filled with grace, we do not lie. **Those who are born of God** do not lie, and the evil one cannot touch them. They have the love of God in them and they love each other as God loves them.

The Lord also says that we must live by faith and not by sight. What is it that we see that we should not believe?

Everything?

> *²²The faith which you have, have as your own conviction before God. Happy is he who does not condemn himself in what he approves. ²³But he who doubts is condemned if he eats, because his eating is not from faith; and **whatever is not from faith is sin**.* Ro 14:22-23 NASB 1995

"*Whatever is not from faith is sin*" what does that mean? We must not doubt, but rather believe and acknowledge God in everything we say and do. We must know that He is in control and has authority even over Satan. He is Our Provider, Our Sustenance, Our Father, and He knows what is best for us. We must have faith in Divine Providence, knowing that Our life is His and everything that happens in our life has a divine purpose according to his divine wisdom, for holy and supernatural purposes, for the good of all mankind, living and dead.

Consider the lies Satan has put in our path, into our minds, and into our hearts? Oh, let us rephrase that: Consider the lies we speak every day, the false influences we leave in the hearts and minds of other people. We are earthen vessels, consider who drives that clay we live in. Our spirit being hides in these vessels making us to sin. Out of ignorance, we walk blindly. Therefore, acknowledge the Lord in all you say and do.

> *³ But Peter said, Ananias, why has the Evil One put it into your heart to be false to the Holy Spirit, and to keep back part of the price of the land? ⁴ While you had it, was it not your property? and after you had given it in exchange, was it not still in your power? how has this purpose come into your mind?* **you have been false, not to men, but to God.** *⁵ And at these words, Ananias went down on the earth, and his life went from him: and great fear came on all who were present.* Acts 5:3-5 BBE

In the above verse, Peter clearly states that Ananias has **lied to God not to men.** It is the Spirit in us that Peter refers to. Peter was full of grace, possessed by the Lord. So, **when you lie, in every circumstance, you lie to God not to men.**

> *and **every spirit** that does not confess Jesus is not from God;* 1John 4:3 NASB 1995

From what truth have we departed? Are we living in a dream of torment and sorrow? When the Lord allowed Lazareth to arise, He told the apostles that he was asleep. Is our spirit sleeping?

What slumber keeps us from our love? Are we living an illusion in Satan's dessert? Are we living a lie in a nonexistent world? What happened when Jesus was in the Dessert? Is this something each of us must overcome as well? What are the hidden messages in the Bible? Let us rip that veil!

True Love, Awaken us from our slumber!

Help us to come to the Light Lord!

Allow us to know the ONE TRUTH - Jesus!

If we live by faith and not by sight,
then we hope that by faith
we are living in the House of the Lord
in Everlasting Love. Where forgiveness is,
where compassion is, where love is,
where divine mercy is,
where gentleness is, where all good things dwell,
where time and distance do not exit,
but only truth and unfathomable love.

The only existence we desire to know is that of our Great God, the Great I AM, our Heavenly family and that which is True.

We believe!

Jesus in the desert said "no" to everything. Moses climbed the mountain to leave the desert at which time the Ten Commandments were given to him. The people were still saying yes to the devil, sinning and keeping to their evil ways.

Jesus came and said that if we love Him obey the Commandments. With grace we can be obedient to the Commandments. It is so difficult for us not to sin. Perhaps our every effort and desire to please the Lord has merit. The truth is, we are sinners living in the kingdom of Satan, partaking. Desiring to please the Lord by exemplifying Him is our only solution to live in the truth and to reach perfection.

Our purpose to live, must be as His, for the salvation of all. Our unconditional love, greater than the love we have for each other, even unto death, because we want everyone to be saved, to live in love, peace, health, and happiness.

Again, we might not be literally crucified as He was, but as we grow in number with cords that cannot be broken, we will be stronger in the Lord. And as we unite, the Lord will be pleased! And only He knows the right time to allow Pentecost to fall upon us, the baptism that will not allow Satan or his evil spirits to torment us anymore. Why? Because we will belong to God, we will be His children and can sin no more.

Do you not know to whom you are offering yourselves as servants under obedience? You are the servants of whomever you obey: whether of sin, unto death, or of obedience, unto justice. (righteousness) Ro 6:16 CPDVTSB

⁸the one who practices sin is of the devil; for the devil has sinned from the beginning. The Son of God appeared for this purpose, to destroy the works of the devil.
⁹*NO ONE WHO IS BORN OF GOD PRACTICES SIN,* *because His seed abides in him; and, he cannot sin,* *because he is born of God.* 1John 3:8 NASB 1995

Desire to walk on that narrow road! Jesus came to teach us and give to us faith in Him. He came to teach us that WE CAN Trust Him. He has converted us to believe in Him, in our salvation and in His love. Hope is our aspiration! We do not doubt that Jesus will come again because He told us that He would. Can we do our part? Unite in unconditional love!

Living by faith and not by sight, we might visualize our faith manifested:

- The vision of the gathering of all believers in Christ in unconditional love
- The vision of the new Pentecost upon all believers
- The vision of the Enthronement of Our Lord on earth
- The Crowning of Our Lord as King of Heaven and earth
- A new Jerusalem
- The vision of our return to God.
- The vision of the Way, the Truth, and Our Life in Jesus
- The vision of living with Our Holy Family
- The vision of peace on earth and goodwill to men
- The vision of Divine Mercy in each of our hearts, minds, and souls
- The vision of the most joyous annunciation from Angel Gabriel to Mary,
- the vision of our returning to the Lord those glorious words of annunciation to the heavens, that we also may

be true sons of God and being born as a child of God in Our Fathers presence
- The vision of Love beyond our understanding in our hearts, in our minds, in our souls with all our strength
- The vision of the embrace of the consuming fire of love
- The vision of our union with the Lord and becoming ONE with Him, a supernova of love in our bodies
- The vision of the celebration of the heavens and all the angels and saints
- The vision of being dressed in white garments of which the Lord speaks
- The vision of the wedding and the invitation accepted by all who are invited
- The salvation of all, living and dead!!!

Glory and Praise to Him who desires all good things for His children. Come Lord Jesus let us live our faith in you, through you and with you.

Heal us and make us yours; heal our world and make it to adore you. Come, we enthrone You. Receive your Crown, We give it to you with our life. Reign, Oh Heavenly Loving King! We love You!

Give ear, O Shepherd of Israel, thou that leadest Joseph like a flock; **thou that dwellest between the cherubims, shine forth.** *Ps 80:1 KJV*

O Lord of armies, the God of Israel, seated between the winged ones, you only are the God of all the kingdoms of the earth; you have made heaven and earth.
Isa 37:16 BBE

And Hezekiah prayed before the LORD, and said, O LORD God of Israel, which dwellest between the cherubims, thou art the God, even thou alone, of all the kingdoms of the earth; thou hast made heaven and earth. *2Ki 19:15 KJV*

The following is taken from Volume I of <u>The Mystical City of God</u> page 38. This reading is profound leading to the awakening of our slumber.

"... let us run together; for, united to its Beloved, it does not any more feel the doings of this earthly life. Seeking to fly after the odor of the ointments of its Beloved it (the soul) begins to live more where it loves than where it lives"

As for me, I will behold thy face in righteousness: I shall be satisfied, when I awake, with thy likeness.
<u>Ps 17:15KJV</u>

And so, may we seek more and more to live where love is, than where we live. Allow us Lord to love those least lovable, and to embrace every humiliation; Allow us Lord, to love unto love everlasting, even unto death… Help us Lord and gift to us your grace.

I can do all things through Christ which strengtheneth me.
<u>Philippians 4:13 KJV</u>

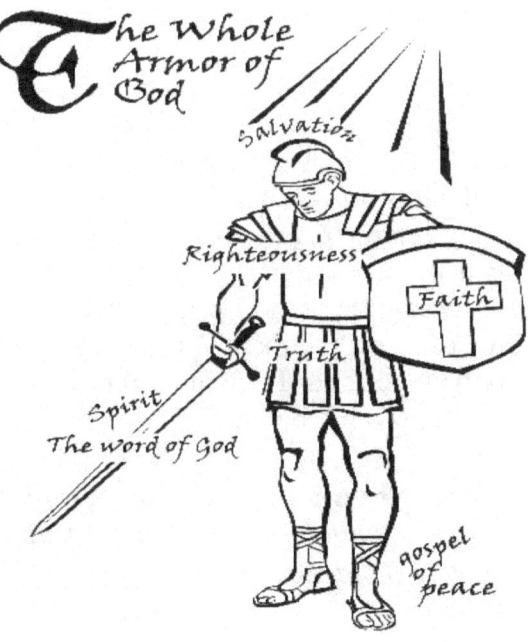

WHO ARE THE RIGHTEOUS?

But seek ye first the kingdom of God, and his righteousness; and all these things shall be added unto you. <u>Mat 6:33 KJV</u>

As it is written, there is none righteous, no, not one:
<u>Romans 3:10 KJV</u>

And if Christ is in you, *the body is dead because of sin, but* **the Spirit is life because of righteousness.** <u>Romans 8:10 BBE</u>

The following sentences include words used from reading the references indicated to describe righteousness.

Those who believe in the Lord (references: <u>Gen 15:6 and Ro 4:3</u>) and are careful to observe all His commandments (<u>De 6:25</u>) by doing righteousness and justice (<u>Gen 18:19</u>) are righteous. It is they who walk in truth and uprightness of heart (<u>1Ki 3:6</u>) with whom the Lord is pleased. It is they who trust in the Lord and offer the sacrifice of righteousness (<u>Ps 4:5</u>). We must call on the Lord with a pure heart filled with faith, love, and peace. (<u>2Ti2:22</u>).

In <u>Ps 18:20</u> the Lord rewards "according to the cleanness of our hands." In <u>Pr 8:8</u> what we say out of our mouth must not be perverted nor crooked, our mouth must be righteous confessing with our mouth with all our heart believing in our salvation as mentioned in <u>Romans 10:10</u>. <u>Pr 16:12</u> says that wicked acts are an abomination for a throne. <u>James 1:20</u> says that anger does not achieve righteousness. These are just a few notes to help us understand righteousness. Pray that the Lord will gift to us the fruit of righteousness. Hunger and thirst for righteousness, so that we may obtain it as promised by the Lord.

Scripture:
[16] All Scripture is inspired by God and profitable for teaching, for reproof, for correction, for training in righteousness; <u>2Ti 3:16 NASB 1995</u>

By faith Noah, being warned by God about things not yet seen, in reverence prepared an ark for the salvation of his household, by which he condemned the world, and became an heir of the righteousness which is according to faith. <u>Heb 11:7 NASB 1995</u>

"It is not for your righteousness or for the uprightness of your heart that you are going to possess their land, but it is because of the wickedness of these nations that the LORD your God is driving them out before you, in order to confirm the oath which the LORD swore to your fathers, to Abraham, Isaac and Jacob. <u>De 9:5 NASB 1995</u>

For in it there is the revelation of the righteousness of God from faith to faith: as it is said in the holy Writings, The man who does righteousness will be living by his faith. <u>Ro 1:17BBE</u>

Do you not know that when you present yourselves to someone as slaves for obedience, you are slaves of the one whom you obey, either of sin resulting in death, or of obedience resulting in righteousness? <u>Ro 6:16 NASB 1995</u>

And do not give your bodies to sin as the instruments of wrongdoing, but give yourselves to God, as those who are living from the dead, and your bodies as instruments of righteousness to God. <u>Ro 6:13 BBE</u>

I am using words in the way of men, because your flesh is feeble: as you gave your bodies as servants to what is unclean, and to evil to do evil, so now give them as servants to righteousness to do what is holy. <u>Ro 6:19 BBE</u>

Blessed are they which do hunger and thirst after righteousness: for they shall be filled. <u>Mat 5:6 KJV</u>

I put on righteousness, and it clothed me: my judgment was as a robe and a diadem. <u>Job 29:14 KJV</u>

By the word of truth, by the power of God, by the armour of righteousness on the right hand and on the left, 2Cor 6:7 KJV

For the Lord is upright; he is a lover of righteousness: the upright will see his face. Ps 11:7 BBE

Righteousness and justice are the foundation of Your throne; Loving kindness and truth go before You.
Ps 89:14 NASB 1995

*In thee, O LORD, do I put my trust;
let me never be ashamed:
deliver me in thy righteousness.* Ps 31:1 KJV

*I have not hidden Your righteousness within my heart;
I have spoken of Your faithfulness and Your salvation;
I have not concealed Your lovingkindness and
Your truth from the great congregation.* Ps 40:10 NASB 1995

*For Your righteousness, O God, reaches to the heavens,
You who have done great things; O God, who is like You?*
Ps 71:19 NASB 1995

Mercy and truth are met together; righteousness and peace have kissed each other. Ps 85:10 KJV

And my tongue shall speak of thy righteousness and of thy praise all the day long. Ps 35:28 KJV

Before the LORD: for he cometh, for he cometh to judge the earth: he shall judge the world with righteousness, and the people with his truth. Ps 96:13 KJV

But the mercy of the LORD is from everlasting to everlasting upon them that fear him, and his righteousness unto children's children; Ps 103:17 KJV

Give me life, O Lord, because of your name; in your righteousness take my soul out of trouble. _{Ps 143:11 BBE}

As for me, I will behold thy face in righteousness: I shall be satisfied, when I awake, with thy likeness. _{Ps 17:15 KJV}

Prayer: Lord, we desire to live a righteous life in Your sight. We desire to please you greatly. We desire to love our brothers as You love them. Help us Lord to Love as You love.

Lord, we fear being apart from You, please keep us in the abode of Your Heart and make us One with You. Clothe us in the armor of righteousness, the armor of God, the Helmet of Salvation, Girt our loins with truth and shod our feet with the gospel of truth, give to us the shield of faith and the sword of the Spirit, the Word of God that we may boldly proclaim the Love of You, for You and In You.

Make our hearts to overflow with the everlasting love of you, for you and for the benefit of others. Make us to live where love is, where you will maintain it, sustain it, and unfathomably consume it with your grace. Oh Lord, keep us clothed in your loving armor of light. May you be forever praised, adored, and glorified and loved beyond love as in no other time of all creation.

Blessed are You Holy ONE! Thank you for your love and for delighting in the creation of us. In the Name of Jesus.

WHAT IS GRACE?

When I received the message "Why the Hail Mary?" as written in this book, the Lord very clearly defined "grace" for me. It is simply defined as follows:

**Grace is a love which bears all things
and conquers all of our enemies.**

Now knowing that by grace we are saved it becomes more apparent that we must desire to be like Jesus "full of grace," perfect as our Father is perfect. We must run the race the apostles ran. We must seek with all our heart, mind, and soul. Our hearts must ache for His love with a great desire to be with Him, fearing, dreading the thought of being apart from Him. He is Our Sovereign Good.

The Lord said that the road is narrow. We must obtain a greater love to obtain that grace that saves. Few believe and so the pattern since Noah has not changed. People still refuse to obey the Lord in repenting in a way pleasing to the Lord. We must desire greatly and hope desperately that the Lord will allow us to be born a child of God. We must desire to be possessed by Our Lord and resist, rebuke, and renounce the devil and all his works. We must empty ourselves of our sinfulness with the help of the Holy Spirit. We must forgive unconditionally thus loving unconditionally. We must gain virtue to obtain grace. Jesus was full of grace; Mary was also full of grace. With grace they were able to endure the wiles of the devil. They were made strong in the Lord. Jesus was able to be tormented and displayed his love; Mary was able to endure her sorrow without retaliating. Both accepted all things according to the will of God. The spiritual battle was taking place, true love WAS, IS and WILL ALWAYS BE conquering all of our enemies. The apostles were also full of grace. Their trials and tribulations were also set to exemplify the life we are to live in Christ, and the battles we must endure with grace. They were perfect as Our Heavenly Father is perfect, as was Jesus and Mary.

Scripture:

And with great power gave the apostles witness of the resurrection of the Lord Jesus: and great grace was upon them all. <u>Acts 4:33 KJV</u>

From his full measure we have all been given grace on grace. <u>John 1:16 BBE</u>

And Stephen, **full of grace and power**, *did great wonders and signs among the people.* <u>Acts 6:8 BBE</u>

By whom we have received grace *and apostleship,* **for obedience to the faith** *among all nations, for his name:*
<u>Romans 1:5 KJV</u>

    We must ask for grace. Grace is manifested in many ways. Obedience to the Word of God is gifted by grace. The Lord said if you love me, obey my commands. Other ways of obtaining grace with a contrite and loving heart include prayer, longsuffering, Holy Communion, praying the Rosary, charity, humility, and most importantly by loving, and forgiving unconditionally. We must embrace our humiliations and ask the Lord to help us respond to every situation in His way admitting we do not know how. Grace comes when we acknowledge the Lord and do these with great love towards Our Lord and His Holy Family and each other.
    How obedient are we? Do we keep the commands of the Lord? Do we abide in Him? Do we lie? Do we get angry at our brother? do we judge or condemn others? and are we an adulterer? Are we a fornicator (sex before marriage or with self)? It is by grace alone, that we can be brought about to be obedient to the faith and laws of Our Lord. The greatest grace is to love our enemy, even unto death! To sell all our possessions and to give them to the poor is also a great gift of grace. We must not let money or things possess us.
    Scripture:
For sin may not have rule over you: because **you are not under law, but under grace**.
<u>Romans 6:14 BBE</u>

*We know that **no one who has been born of God sins**; but He who was born of God keeps him, and **the evil one does not touch him*** _{1John 5:18 NASB}

Breaking any of the commands of Our Lord is sin. Idle words, swearing, evil tongues and thoughts or actions are all sins. How proud are the people who think they do not sin? We are all sinners, but **we must desire** greatly not to sin. Pride is sin.

We must desire greatly to love unconditionally.

We must pray for all religious leaders. The Lord will give them the grace to bow down to Him if they repent and let go of the master of this earth, money, personal pride, lies, and self-glory. The Lord desires to teach His people, lead them in His Way, in His Truth, in His Light. He desires to make us true Children of God and complete us in the fullest of grace for the Salvation of all Mankind. We must gather!

We must pray for the Pope, the Orthodox leaders, all Preachers, teachers and for the Jews. May the Lord give them the Grace to endure the consequences of setting things right during the Apostasy and the things to come. The Apostasy is the rebellion against Satan, the gathering of believers. It is heartbreaking to even think that we are all devils, we are evil doers, and worst of all, that we cannot stop our sinning without grace. True grace will come when we receive the Holy Spirit like on Pentecost. We will be born again and will not be able to sin. The Lord is anxious for that to happen, how anxious are we for that day to come? Can we take the first step?

The split between the Romans and the Orthodox, and all churches was necessary, as was the kiss of Judas, and Peters denial, know that all these things are for the Glory of God.

Christians are scattered in mind and body. They do not gather as one. They do not know love. They are against Our Lord. They do not follow Jesus, Our leader? There are so many contentions among Christ believers, sadly, they are scattered. They are Satan disguised as angles of light. They have not found "THE WAY." They do not know they are rebels in the kingdom of Satan.

[30] *"He who is not with Me is against Me;*

and he who does not gather with Me scatters.
<u>Mat 12:30 NASB 1995</u>

The following are graces we can pray for: the grace of gathering as one in Christ / the grace of increased light / the grace of increased simplicity / the grace to deny ourselves everything/ the grace to hear Him / the grace to see Our Lord / the grace to enter at the narrow gate / the grace to know the love of His Mother, Mary / the grace of wisdom, knowledge, and understanding / the grace of reason and intelligence / the grace of perfect charity / the grace of perfect humility / the grace of perfect love/ the grace of perfect hope / the grace to obtain perfect faith / the grace to love our enemy even unto death / the grace to be full of grace /the grace to pray without ceasing/ the grace of undistracted devotion to the Lord / the grace to be worthy to receive the Holy Spirit on our Pentecost / the grace to dwell in the House of the Lord.

We must desire desperately, to love Our Father as He loves us, even unto death, and even offering to Him the death of our children for the Love of God, in the fulfillment of His perfect plan. Ultimately, we will not be full of grace until the new Pentecost. The new Pentecost will not come until we obey, repent, love and gather.

We must sow as He sows, Be as He is,
Love as He Loves.

Now is the time to come back home to the One True Church! The devil is already threatened, stirring up things in the Roman Catholic Church! It is under attack! It is our battle ground. We must Stand firm and keep our eyes on Jesus! Love beyond love! We will live by faith, be still and know that God is with us! Love your Christ believing brothers, do not judge them. Be merciful as Our Father is Merciful! Let us then repent so that the Lord will reveal His truth and victory to all of us.

Seek! Repent! Ask the Lord to teach you!
Lean not on human understanding! WE ARE ONE!

WHAT IS YOUR BLESSING?

Who has ever heard the expression "Be careful of what you ask for in prayer?" This expression sometimes relates to patience. In any case, do we know the difference between an apple or an orange when it comes to defining a blessing?

The flesh seems to think that a blessing is abundance, luxuries, and comfortable living. Our Blessed Mother appeared to Bernadette as "The Immaculate Conception" and told her something similar to this: *"I cannot promise you happiness in this world, only in the next".*

How have we demonstrated our faith? Faith without works is dead, and we are nothing without love. If we do not believe this, then we must repent so that we can believe. The devil has put blinders in our eyes, and clouded our minds with things of this world to keep us away from the truth. Think of the ways we have manipulated, lied, or deceived others, yes that is the devil in action.

Scripture:
Because the god of this world has made blind the minds of those who have not faith, so that the light of the good news of the glory of Christ, who is the image of God, might not be shining on them. 2Cor 4:4 BBE

For as the body without the spirit is dead even so faith without works is dead. Jas 2:26 BBE

if I have all faith, by which mountains may be moved from their place, but have not love, I am nothing. 1Cor13:2 BBE

These are your blessings: the poor, the hungry, the naked, pain, suffering, financial disasters, our tormentor, all trials, and tribulations... All these teach us to produce the fruits of the spirit:

*²² But the fruit of the Spirit is **love, joy, peace, longsuffering, gentleness, goodness, faith,** ²³ **Meekness, temperance: against such there is no law.** ²⁴ And they that*

are Christ's have crucified the flesh with the affections and lusts. ²⁵ If we live in the Spirit, let us also walk in the Spirit. ²⁶ Let us not be desirous of vain glory, provoking one another, envying one another. <u>Gal 5:22-26 KJV</u>

All of these teach us to gain the blessings of grace and increased virtues. They are the opportunity given to us to become Christ like. They are the opportunity to imitate Jesus, who is Love itself. They are the opportunity to abandon ourselves from this world.

They are the opportunity to resist, rebuke, and renounce the devil by crucifying the flesh against the affections, attachments, lusts and desires of this world. The grace to give freely and detach ourselves openly is the road to perfect charity. Love our enemy, speak to them with love, and embrace them with all our heart in the love of God. And, if we do not confront them, desire to love them and pray for them, ask the Lord to be merciful to them. This is the road to perfect humility. Grace and virtues lead us to Perfect love which conquers all our enemies. Yes, these are our blessings, and these are the Blessed:

Scripture:

³ Blessed are the poor in spirit: for theirs is the kingdom of heaven. ⁴ Blessed are they that mourn: for they shall be comforted. ⁵ Blessed are the meek: for they shall inherit the earth. ⁶ Blessed are they which do hunger and thirst after righteousness: for they shall be filled. ⁷ Blessed are the merciful: for they shall obtain mercy. ⁸ Blessed are the pure in heart: for they shall see God. ⁹ Blessed are the peacemakers: for they shall be called the children of God. ¹⁰ Blessed are they which are persecuted for righteousness' sake: for theirs is the kingdom of heaven. ¹¹ Blessed are ye, when men shall revile you, and persecute you, and shall say all manner of evil against you falsely, for my sake. ¹² Rejoice, and be exceeding glad: for great is your reward in heaven: for so persecuted they the prophets which were before you. <u>Matthew 5:3-12 KJV</u>

WHO IS THE KING?

WHO IS THE KING?
YES, OUR BELOVED JESUS!
But who else like Caesar? Who else like Jesus?
Scripture:
> ... ***they are acting against the orders of Caesar,***
> saying that there is another king, Jesus. <u>Acts 17:7 BBE</u>

Who do we imitate? Who do we follow? Caesar on our throne or Jesus, a servant's servant, with nowhere to lay His head?

Humble, meek, lowly, poor, filled with love! He came to save, not to condemn. He healed and cast out demons. Sometimes He fled for safety, simply to avoid further chaos. He knew the enemy and he loves them. While on the cross He said "they know not what they do." He came to teach us, and to let us know who we are. He showed us that no matter what we do, He loves us unconditionally. He came to tell us to be Perfect like Our Heavenly Father, and showed us how. He is the perfect teacher. We are like the enemy who crucified Him. We are the vessels of clay with spirits such as those He delivered and fled from. He fled simply to keep us from continuing to sin. All power belongs to the Almighty, yet, He handed himself over to us for our salvation. He loves us! He tells us to love even the worst of sinners as He has done! We are enemies to ourselves. In our sinfulness we are the demon's needing deliverance.

Do we think that when Jesus came to this world He needed to suffer? Do we think He needed to be baptized or to receive the Holy Spirit? Do we think that He needed to be born in a stable? Do we think He needed to be poor? Do we think He needed anything of this world? He did not have to do any of these things, but He did these things, to show us **the way.** He showed us what we must do and how to do it. He showed us what our desire should be.

He suffered so that we can understand that we are in a suffering world, suffering in it; in a poor world, and we are poor in it; in a dark world. He came to show us a more excellent way!

In our suffering, our life is reflected in the sufferings of Jesus. Jesus came to be like us. He willingly suffered more than we can conceive. Jesus said you reap what you sow. Many times, cast out, many times the devil has attempted to devour our souls, but the Lord has preserved us, because He loves us. Many have suffered; we have had our trials and tribulations, some in groups, some individually. All these things are for the glory of God. We must ask the Lord to lead us! We must be merciful and trust in Jesus!

We must offer our sufferings to the Lord, deny ourselves all things and be willing to detach ourselves from the things of this world. We must be baptized because we are sinners and we must desire to receive the Holy Spirit because we are helpless without the Lord. We cannot fight evil of our own accord. We must be willing to do His will, not ours. He is our perfect example; we must desire to imitate Him, to be like Him, in Him and One with Him.

He said that we must be like a child to enter the Heavenly gates. We see Him as a child embracing His Mother. We see Him performing His first miracle through His Mother. We see Him at the Cross giving His Mother to man. What do children do? As a child imitates their parents, we must imitate Jesus in all things; we must also embrace and love His Mother. He is our perfect example, Our Shepherd.

And said, Truly, I say to you, If you do not have a change of heart and become like little children, you will not go into the kingdom of heaven. Mat 18:3 BBE

The Lord says all things are imperfect until perfection comes. We can only hope that the Lord will give us the grace to bring what is hidden in the darkness, into the light. Do we believe His Word "Be perfect as My Father is perfect?" Believe and know that He can do anything and if we ask with a fervent soul, He will grant it. We must **first confess our doubt with a contrite heart,** asking for the grace to please Him. He also says "lean not on human understanding," so, **we must be willing to forget what man has taught us** and ask the Lord to teach us - pray, fast, and read the BIBLE! Be open to the teachings of the Lord.

We must desire to think in the Spirit, walk in the Spirit and live in the Spirit, "By Faith and not by sight!" Crave for the love of God!!!

Our Father craves our love so much that He sent His only Son to die for us; to show us the way, to teach us His truth and to bring us out of darkness into the Light.

Jesus, Our Shepherd, came to shepherd His sheep. His sheep know Him and follow Him. Scripture:

> *And when he has sent out his sheep, he goes before them, and the sheep follow him, because they know his voice.*
> John 10:4 CPDVTSB

> *"I am the good shepherd, and I know My own and My own know Me,* John 10:14 CPDVTSB

Jesus, laid his crown down before his Father, to become the lowest. We, NOW, must follow Jesus, Our Shepherd, with the greatest of love. He is Our King, leading His people. It is our turn to **Lay Down Our Crown at The Feet of Jesus!** Submitting to His glorious plan of redemption by fulfilling His requests as noted in the bible.

Can we each humble ourselves and get off our throne like Jesus did? Can we give up our platform, our attachments? Can we unite regardless of our differences and trust the Lord to deliver us from them? Can we love our enemy? Jesus, Our King, is waiting to claim His throne. Can we give Him ours? Can we walk away from our throne and not look back?

He is our Suffering King on earth, long suffering, and long waiting. He came to show us the way. Could it be that it is each of us, keeping Him from sitting on His throne, because of our pride, our hate, our judgements, our thoughtlessness, insecurities, or self-centeredness? Is it money we prefer to follow?

Who of us is sitting on His Throne, high and mighty?

Is it one, or all of us - rabbi, father, teacher, leader, or master of all? Is it the rulers of this world? Yes, rulers of darkness in this world, in the flesh made of dust, mentioned in Eph 6:10-18. We are all partakers, rulers of our own domain, whether it be home, city, state, country or where ever.

Are we so vain? Are we so proud of our families, possessions, ambitions, our churches, our jobs, our whatever? Is it we who have filled our heart with false treasures? We have made no room for Him, which is why He was born in a stable.

There is no room in the deepest depth of our inner-most being; the Inn of our heart, the chambers in which Our Lord desires to be loved and to love.

Our hearts have been steered to follow treasures of the earth in various manifestations. We chose to obey man rather than God.

Our Thrones are full of pride, vanity, makeovers, fashions and glitter, vain glory, ambitions, false power, self-centeredness, love of possessions, love of money, love of false gods, we love each other more than we love God. **We have not returned that love to Him.** We conform to believing that the love we know is enough, but truly, it is not.

Our insecurities drive us to not trust in the Lord; almost everyone has said "yes" to Satan in the desert. We are all guilty.

We are a vessel of clay, nothing but dirt. We should be concerned as to who occupies our shell of clay. Pray that the Lord will let the Holy Spirit arise and take control of each of us. When the Holy Spirit takes control, we will understand the meaning of "IN HIM, we live, move and have our being".

It will be apart from ourself,
in ourself, distinct,
as a Sail of a boat, we being the boat,
the Holy Spirit being the Sail.
Scripture:

*"**Do you not know of whose spirit you are?*** Luke 9:55 CPDVTSB

And if, we think we have free choice, free will, and are exercising it, then we do not believe in Divine Providence! If we are moving by **our own** choice then we are not In Him!

Now, if we believe that we are in Him, then we must believe that everything that happens in our life, is according to God's Holy Will for His Divine and Perfect Plan. We accept this by faith.

Are we Christ-like or not? if not, then what are we? Is our mind on the Lord 24/7? Do we know which spirit owns our body? Whose earthen vessel, are we? Do we sin? Sadly, we all sin. But, do we desire to please the Lord?

> *looking at his disciples, he admonished Peter, saying, "Get behind me, Satan, for you do not prefer the things that are of God, but the things that are of men."* Mark 8:33 CPDVTSB

And if the Lord rebuked Peter, calling him Satan, what makes us think we are anything better than Peter who was with the Lord. Although, in this case, at that time, Peter submitted to the Lord's perfect plan according to Divine Providence, for the Glory of the Lord, willing to demonstrate anything appearing good or bad for the glory of God. He was with the Lord. The Lord came to divide and the apostles were on the same mission. They needed to convert the wicked to become believers in Christ and build up the faithful in Christ. I believe that when Peter denied the Lord three times it signified the separation of the Churches. At the time, perhaps this was necessary until today, simply to convert and draw more people to Jesus. Now it is time to form the army of God and gather. It is time to unite and divide the kingdom of Satan, forming the greatest Kingdom of God on earth, in unconditional love. It is time to rebel on earth with Jesus Christ our Leader!

Can we repent for accusing a believer of the faith, a believer of Jesus, that Satan has entered that church? The world is in the power of the evil one, Satan! Every Church is sinful and judgmental! The churches cannot be perfected, unless we unite, proof is in the Word of God. Judgement belongs to the Lord. We must simply follow Him in sacrifice, mercy, and unconditional love.

Do we believe that the Lord's plan is perfect? What church has no flaw? What church has not sinned? Who is a "proud" pastor of their church? Pride was Satan's flaw; it was Satan's fall. Who can cast the first stone? We must ask the Lord to direct our path no matter what the consequences! Let go of "big business."

Come, let us love our brother in Christ, and be not proud. We must desire for the Lord to deliver us all from evil. Love the enemy even unto death. Who is the enemy? Is it the demons in our vessels of clay? Who else could it be? Love the sinner, hate the sin. So, the father of sinners is Satan, therefore, love all of God's creation. Know who we are and the treasure within us, therefore demonstrate your unconditional love. Walk in the Spirit by acknowledging the Lord in everything we say and do.

> *This I say then, Walk in the Spirit, and ye shall not fulfil the lust of the flesh.* Gal 5:16 KJV

> *But **love your enemies** and do good, and lend, expecting nothing in return; and your reward will be great, and you will be sons of the Most High; for He Himself is kind to ungrateful and evil people.* Luke 6:35 NASB

Enter the lion's den. Be Love, like Mary who did not condemn or retaliate against those who tormented her Son.

In <u>The Poem of a Man God</u>, by Marie Valtorta Vol I, page 115 the following leaves a great impression in our hearts:
Mary, a virgin of the love of God,
overcame "the horror of having to say:
"I Love You, Come to Me Who am your Mother"
to each murderer of Her Son, born of the most sublime love that Heaven ever saw of the love of a God with a Virgin of the kiss of fire, of the embrace of Light which became Flesh, made the womb of a woman the Tabernacle of God."

Why do Christian brothers continue to criticize each other, or why do they say that perhaps one so-called-religion does not believe the bible when they themselves are guilty of it?

It is as the Lord has said; we must remove the splinters or plank from our own being! Satan makes us only believe what is convenient for our torment. Repent!!! Love your Christian brothers!!! Love and bless your enemy!!!

What part of the Word of God do we not believe? We are of an evil generation. Be careful! Be watchful! Repent!! Believe! Get Baptized! Obey God not man! We must make Him king of our being! We have been misled... these are additional Scriptures to believe, there are many:

> *Whoever will have believed and been baptized will be saved. Yet truly, whoever will not have believed will be condemned.* <u>Mark 16:16 CPDVTSB</u>

> *⁹ For even now the axe has been placed at the root of the trees. Therefore, every tree that does not produce good fruit shall be cut down and cast into the fire." ¹⁰ And the crowd was questioning him, saying, "**What then should we do?**" ¹¹ But in response, he said to them: "**Whoever has two coats, let him give to those who do not have. And whoever has food, let him act similarly.**" ¹² Now the tax collectors also came to be baptized, and they said to him, "Teacher, what should we do?" ¹³ But he said to them, "You should do nothing more than what has been appointed to you." ¹⁴ Then the soldiers also questioned him, saying, "And what should we do?" And he said to them: "**You should strike no one, and you should not make false accusations. And be content with your pay.**"* <u>Luke 3:9-14 CPDVTSB</u>

> *Jesus said unto him, If thou wilt be perfect, go and sell that thou hast, and give to the poor, and thou shalt have treasure in heaven: and come and follow me.* <u>Mat 19:21 KJV</u>

> *When Jesus heard this, He said to him, "One thing you still lack; sell all that you possess and distribute it to the poor, and you shall have treasure in heaven; and come, follow Me."* <u>Luke 18:22 NASB 1995</u>

> ¹*Masters, **give unto your servants that which is just and equal**; knowing that ye also have a Master in heaven.* ² *Continue in prayer, and watch in the same with thanksgiving;* _{Col 4:1-2 KJV}

The Lord says His people perish because of lack of knowledge. Do we even know what it is that we need to obey? In our sinfulness, it seems impossible for us to obey, but with grace and the love of God, all things are possible. We must submit to and exalt our Beloved King. Above all else, believe, love unconditionally, forgive and be merciful. Desire to please the Lord! We must be willing to turn away from the things men have taught us incorrectly, and ask Him to teach us.

Pray for the day that the Lord, Our Shepherd, **will lead us in unison, in one accord throughout the world,** as He did the children in the Book of Daniel. On that day, in unison, Satan and all his works will be crushed and all whom the Lord desires will be saved, the living and the dead.

The true church is the Roman Catholic Church, the rock, the church of the apostle Peter. This is where the Lord has promised that the gates of hell will not prevail. Jesus Christ is our Victor.

In this world, any army would be alerted when its troops are in trouble. The Roman Catholic Church **is under attack, it is an obvious call to arms for the Army of God to gather**. So who cares who the antichrist is!!!! We already know we are all devils, but "we are the converted Loving Jesus." **"We are the rebels in Satan's kingdom."** We have faith in Jesus Christ. WE ARE BELIEVERS OF JESUS CHRIST, OUR WARRIOR, Our Victor. Let us follow Him into battle and divide the kingdom of Satan. Do not be afraid, Satan was thrown out of Heaven like lightening.

> *Now where there is forgiveness of these, there is no more offering for sin.* _{Heb 10:18 BBE}

> *For what the law could not do, in that it was weak through the flesh, God sending his own Son in the likeness of sinful flesh, and for sin, condemned sin in the flesh* _{Ro 8:3 KJV}

Can we prove our Love to the Lord, by taking the first step of faith? Can we love one another unconditionally as He loves us and unite in the one church, one body?

Let us prepare to be tested as mentioned in *1John 3:16:* **Repent, pray and fast, loving strong and willing to lay down our lives, and our crowns for our brethren.**

Can we give Our King, His Throne?

Will we stand firm with Jesus Christ the Warrior?

THIS IS A CALL TO ARMS! Love, pray, fast, repent, and unite!

Concluding Prayer:

Dearest Holy Trinity, Father, Jesus, and Holy Ghost, We submit ourself to You; We resist, rebuke, and renounce Satan and all his works. We repent, and with a contrite heart, mind, and soul and with the greatest love that is within us, we lay down our crown. Help us Lord, to do Your will and to please You in all Your ways, in Your truth and in Your loving light. Make us Lord, to do what we must to become the lowest, be our everlasting loving King. We embrace all our brothers and sisters in Christ, with Your love and as ONE with all our hearts, mind, and soul we ask You to claim our souls as Yours alone and accept the crowns we lay before You. We return to God, His throne, all our love and all that we are. We confess by our Holy Temple and by the Holy Spirit within us, By Heaven, by the Throne of God, By Him who sits on it, Our Father, That Jesus is King and He is Our Lord, Our Master. Jesus is one with the Father, one with Our Holy Spirit, to Him We submit and in Him, We desire to live, move, and have our being. We surrender to His Divine Will. In the Name of Jesus We stand firm to the Profession of our Faith.

Blessed is He who comes in the name of the Lord!

Holy! Holy! Holy! You are Lord God, King of all creation!

WE LOVE YOU! WE LOVE YOU! WE LOVE YOU, LOVE EVERLASTING with Everlasting Love!

The following scripture has been added for your reference:

⁸"*But do not be called Rabbi; for* **One is your Teacher**, *and you are all brothers.*⁹*"Do not call anyone on earth your father; for* **One is your Father**, *He who is in heaven.* ¹⁰*"Do not be called leaders; for* **One is your Leader, that is, Christ**. ¹¹*"But the greatest among you shall be your servant.* ¹²*"Whoever exalts himself shall be humbled; and whoever humbles himself shall be exalted.*

Eight Woes

¹³**"*But woe to you, scribes and Pharisees, hypocrites***, *because you shut off the kingdom of heaven from people; for you do not enter in yourselves, nor do you allow those who are entering to go in.* ¹⁴*["Woe to you, scribes and Pharisees, hypocrites, because you devour widows' houses, and for a pretense you make long prayers; therefore you will receive greater condemnation.]* ¹⁵*"Woe to you, scribes and Pharisees, hypocrites, because you travel around on sea and land to make one proselyte; and when he becomes one, you make him twice as much a son of hell as yourselves.* ¹⁶*"Woe to you, blind guides, who say, 'Whoever swears by the temple, that is nothing; but whoever swears by the gold of the temple is obligated.'* ¹⁷*"You fools and blind men! Which is more important, the gold or the temple that sanctified the gold?* ¹⁸*"And, 'Whoever swears by the altar, that is nothing, but whoever swears by the offering on it, he is obligated.'* ¹⁹*"You blind men, which is more important, the offering, or the altar that sanctifies the offering?* ²⁰*"Therefore, whoever swears by the altar, swears both by the altar and by everything on it.* ²¹*"And whoever swears by the temple, swears both by the temple and by Him who dwells within it.*

²²*"And whoever swears by heaven, swears both by the throne of God and by Him who sits upon it.* Matthew 23:8-22 NASB 1995

WHO IS THE SERVANT OF MONEY?

CHOOSE YOUR MASTER! (Teaching 11/29/2006)
[24] *"No one can serve two masters; for either he will hate the one and love the other, or he will be devoted to one and despise the other. You cannot serve God and wealth.*
Matthew 6:24 NASB 1995)

IMPORTANT NOTE: Before this topic is addressed, please do not to judge, especially the religious. The Lord's plan is perfect; this is an awakening the Lord desires so that we may come to him. Give contributions and donations to help others and the religious, especially those most in need. The transformation is not ours alone, but the earth as well. We must offer all giving's to the Lord with Love and to others **as if they themselves are the Lord**. Not judging, but giving freely what the Lord has given us. May the Lord give us the grace to abandon all and unite to Him.

Who Is The Servant Of Money?
How Are We A Servant To Money?
Who Wants To Be In The Kingdom Of God?
Scripture:
Take no gold or silver or copper in your pockets; Mat 10:9 BBE

And he said that they were to take nothing for their journey, but a stick only; no bread, no bag, no money in their pockets; Mark 6:8 BBE

For men will be lovers of self, lovers of money, uplifted in pride, given to bitter words, going against the authority of their fathers, never giving praise, having no religion,
2Ti 3:2 BBE

Do we truly desire to please the Lord and be His servant alone? He says to choose our master! Do we want to inherit the kingdom of heaven? If we believe that we do not serve money, because we think we do not love it, then, are we a servant of it unknowingly? How do we serve money? Is money the master of the earth? Do we rely on it or think we need money for essentials?

When we go to a restaurant the waiter brings our food and drink and sets it before us, serving us. Afterwards, the waiter will give us a candy or a drink and put it in our hand or table. The waiter is serving us.

We in turn for their service, put into their hand, money to pay for our food and tip for the service. So are we serving money to them? When we put it on their book fold wallet are we serving them, not on a platter but on what accommodates money? Perhaps the god of money likes to be in a book fold wallet, clinched shut for the eyes of the beholder. The waiter, hopes for it to be a big tip. The waiter desires more money and according to the following scripture is the reason for many griefs!

> *For the love of money is a root of all sorts of evil, and SOME BY LONGING FOR IT have wandered away from the faith and pierced themselves with many griefs*
> 1Ti 6:10 NASB 1995

The Lord said there is not one righteous. He said no one seeks Him.

> *¹⁰ As it is written, There is none righteous, no, not one:*
> *¹¹ There is none that understandeth, there is none that seeketh after God.* Romans 3:10-11 KJV

Could it be true that if we serve money simply by exchanging hands for services rendered or items purchased, then **IS IT our sin**? We work for it! We buy with it! We even pray for it! In this world in the mind of men, there is nothing you can do without it. Even the religious and preachers beg for it thinking this charity is what the Lord refers to. They spend it on themselves for worldly needs including for food out of need, as we do. Some however, consider the church business, big business for moneys sake. Money is an essential factor in the minds of ALL men.

But what does the Lord mean … we cannot serve both!

> *³³ "Sell your possessions and give to charity; make yourselves money belts which do not wear out, an unfailing treasure in heaven, where no thief comes near nor moth*

> destroys. *³⁴ "For where your treasure is, there your heart will be also.* <u>Luke 12:33-34 NASB 1995</u>

What faith is required of us?
> *And he said to them, When I sent you out without money or bag or shoes, were you in need of anything? And they said, Nothing.* <u>Luke 22:35 BBE</u>

> *⁵Make sure that your character is free from the love of money, being content with what you have; for He Himself has said, "I WILL NEVER DESERT YOU, NOR WILL I EVER FORSAKE YOU," ⁶so that we confidently say, "THE LORD IS MY HELPER; I WILL NOT BE AFRAID. WHAT WILL MAN DO TO ME?"* <u>Heb 13:5-6 NASB 1995</u>

What FAITH IS REQUIRED of us?
What profound love and charity is our Lord made of that He desires for us to be like Him?

Do we think that this form of giving or charity is for religious preachers only?
Is the Lord requiring it of every person?
Who knowing the Lord, would deny Him anything?
Who would give their life and their riches?
So what is money, and why do we value it?
Is serving money giving value to it?
What value do we give to the Lord?

The Lord says we cannot serve Him and money! Various times in the Bible the Lord showed us the worthlessness of money. When the thousands were with him the miracle of the fish and bread multiplied so that all were fed. Money was mentioned but was not needed. The Lord provided. In another instance a man offered the apostle money for his miracles, it was an insult and not accepted. They told him that his heart was not right with God. He was in the gall of bitterness and in the bondage of iniquity. He is a slave to money, sin chains him down. They said Repent and Pray that the Lord, IF POSSIBLE, will forgive the intention of his heart.

> *¹⁸ Now when Simon saw that the Holy Spirit was given through the touch of the Apostles' hands, he made them an offering of money, saying, ¹⁹ Give me this power, so that when I put my hands on anyone he may get the Holy Spirit. ²⁰But Peter said, May your money come to destruction with you, because you had the idea that what is freely given by God may be got for a price.* Acts 8:18-20 BBE

So what exactly is going on today? Has anything changed? Is our use of money a hidden way of serving it? We think we do not serve it, **but do we? What is the intention of our hearts?**

Much has been hidden from us! "Lord please forgive us, increase our desire of you, for you and in you! Help us to seek you and to find you. Pray that the Lord will give to us the courage, faith, and trust to do all that is necessary to inherit the kingdom of God, with Jesus and our heavenly family. Pray that the Lord will grant all of us the faith, boldness, and zeal to reach perfection."

> *for they all saw Him and were terrified. But immediately He spoke with them and said to them, "Take courage; it is I, do not be afraid."* Mark 6:50 NASB 1995

Pray that we will obtain the necessary faith to live in God's favor and in the faith, He desires of us. Help us Lord, Abba Father! You are our only hope!

The following scripture is the answer to the above, may we come to live in His Word, in His Light and in His Love:

> *Be anxious about nothing. But in all things, with prayer and supplication, with acts of thanksgiving, let your petitions be made known to God.* Php 4:6 CPDVTSB

whatever is not of faith is sin. Ro 14:23 BBE

Could it be that no money nor bartering is required? Is all that is required simply an exchange of true love, prayer and devotion to Our Lord? Can we trust Jesus to be our provider? The Lord knows our every need, we must desire to be ONE with Him.

Here is the patience of the saints: here are they that keep the commandments of God, **and the faith of Jesus.**
Revelation 14.12 KJV

By whom we come near to God without fear through faith in him. Ephesians 3:12 BBE

Let us gaze upon Jesus, as the Author and the completion of our faith, Hebrews 12.2CPDVTSB

It seems that we are all servants of money simply by dealing with it. What kind of Faith is required of us? It seems very clear that we must learn to live the faith of our fathers before us, in Jesus, Mary, Joseph and all the great saints! We must take the first step in faith. We must choose our master!

^{24}" **You cannot serve God and wealth**." Mat 6:24 NASB 1995

Money is the master of this world. Realizing that the use of money is a sin, because money is our master, then without a doubt, we are all guilty! We are all sinners. According to scripture Satan is the father of sinners. Oh but, as Believers and Lovers of Christ we are REBELS in the Kingdom of Satan! This is why we have suffered much. We are continuously misdirected.
Remedy:
It is of utmost importance that **all believers in Christ GATHER** and form the Army of God. **We must join Jesus in His cause to divide. We must begin the rebellion by dividing the kingdom of Satan!** Trust Jesus Christ the Warrior of Love! Our Victor!

^{30}The one who is not with Me is against Me; and the one who does not gather with Me scatters Mat 12:30 NASB

This is a Call to Arms! Love, pray, fast, repent, and UNITE!

WHO IS LIKE OUR FATHERS OF GREAT FAITH?

Elijah was taken up to heaven, who like Moses, entered into that place of faith where **evidence is unseen, the substance of things hoped for is manifested;** or the Faith of Jesus, who commands the seas and the winds, walks on water, and saves and so according to scripture:

> *Let us gaze upon Jesus, as the Author and the completion of our faith, who, having joy laid out before him, endured the cross, disregarding the shame, and who now sits at the right hand of the throne of God.* <u>Hebrews 12:2 CPDVTSBN</u>

WHO IS LIKE OUR FATHERS OF GREAT FAITH?

Persevere in faith and always pray without ceasing. Faith will be of utmost importance when the Son of man comes. Faith, the substance of things hoped will be seen to be true and manifest. In times of adversity, what would we do? If the day came and things we have never seen before, ugly, and frightful, manifested we would be forced to believe in fright. What would we do then, we who do not seek the Lord? How firm can we stand in the absence of the love of God? We will not stand, we will perish. It is in that moment that no matter what we see, we must keep your eyes on Jesus and in the great love of Our Lord. He is the conqueror of the devil, the devil's armies, and his evil ways. Love conquerors all!

> *¹ And he spake a parable unto them to this end,* **that men ought always to pray, and not to faint**; *² Saying, There was in a city a judge, which feared not God, neither regarded man: ³ And there was a widow in that city; and she came unto him, saying, Avenge me of mine adversary. ⁴ And he would not for a while: but afterward he said within himself, Though I fear not God, nor regard man; ⁵ Yet because this widow troubleth me, I will avenge her, lest by her continual coming she weary me.*
> *⁶ And the Lord said, Hear what the unjust judge saith. ⁷ And shall not God avenge his own elect, which cry day and night unto him, though he bear long with them? ⁸ I tell you that he will avenge them speedily. Nevertheless when the Son of man cometh, shall he find faith on the earth?* Luke 18:1-8 KJV

There are many movies of spiritual warfare or of evil fear. The movies of exorcism have been fabricated. The devil wants us to be afraid of the devil. Are we afraid? Know that the devil cannot drive out the devil! Satan flashed out of Heaven like lightening when the Lord cast him out. Satan is all show, he is weak and powerless. All power belongs to the Lord. Ignorance is Satan's strength.

Speak the Word, love, repent and pray. We must allow our faith to flourish, simply by believing. Faith is exemplified in the Bible many times: just as the sea parted for Moses, the Jordan dried up for Joshua. The Jordan was full of water, Joshua and the people took the first step into that water and it dried up. They took the first step of faith.

> *Now instruct the priests, who are carrying the ark of the covenant, and say to them, **'When you will have entered into a part of the water of the Jordan, stand still in it.'***
> Joshua 3:8 CPDVTSB

This is a good demonstration of taking the first step in faith. It demonstrates that the people believed without a doubt, obeyed, and trusted in God. We must do the same! Today, we must join the army of God! We must gather in unconditional love.

So, what kind of faith did our fathers before us have? I was so impressed with the scripture in *1 Maccabees 3:17-22*.

VICTORY AT WAR

> *[17] But when they saw the army coming to meet them, they said to Judas, "How will we few be able to fight against so great and so strong a multitude, even though we are weakened by fasting today?" [18] And Judas said: "It is easy for many to be enclosed in the hands of a few, for there is no difference in the sight of the God of heaven to liberate by means of many, or by means of few. [19] **FOR VICTORY IN WARFARE IS NOT IN THE MULTITUDE OF THE ARMY, BUT IN THE STRENGTH FROM HEAVEN.***
> 1 Maccabees 3:17-19 CPDVTSB

> *Then Asa called to the LORD his God and said, "LORD, there is no one besides You to help in the battle between the powerful and those who have no strength; so help us, O LORD our God, for we trust in You, and in Your name have come against this multitude. O LORD, **You are our God; let not man prevail against You**."* 2Ch 14:11 NASB 1995

WOW!!! is that powerful!!!!! So what faith is required of us? How do we obtain it? Perhaps, we need to pray for the grace to have the faith of Moses/ Elijah/ Elisha/ Elizabeth/ Ester/ Mary/ Joseph, and in Jesus and the love that they also had for the Lord with which they fervently cried out to Him. Observation: They also knew they were vessels of clay and acknowledged the Lord.

MOSES: - **the Faith of Moses** going up the mountain, to enter that place of faith where evidence is unseen and where the substance of things hoped for is present. Perhaps we should request the faith of Moses in the desert, hoping that the Lord will hear us and feed us manna from Heaven where no money is needed. A desperate faith and cry to the Lord when there is no other resolve. Hope with a confidence that Our Father will hear us and answer. As Moses made the plea when the slaves were set free from Pharaoh's bondage – but Lord what will they eat, what will they drink? In the Love of Moses for Our Lord and in His obedience, we seek to find the answer.

ELIJAH: -Or perhaps that **of Elijah** who was taken up to heaven, who like Moses entered that place of faith where evidence is unseen, the substance of things hoped for is Manifested.

the sons of the prophets, who were at Jericho, drew near to Elisha. And they said to him, "Do you not know that today the Lord will take away your lord from you?" And he said: "I know it. Be silent." 2Ki 2:5 CPDVTSB

And when they had gone across, Elijah said to Elisha, "Ask what you wish that I may do for you, before I am taken from you." And Elisha said, "I beg you, that twice your spirit may be accomplished in me." 2Ki 2:9 CPDVTSB

And Elisha saw it, and he cried, My father, my father, the chariot of Israel, and the horsemen thereof. And he saw him no more: and he took hold of his own clothes, and rent them in two pieces. 2Ki 2:12 KJV

> *[14] And he took Elijah's robe, which had been dropped from him, and giving the water a blow with it, said, Where is the Lord, the God of Elijah? and at his blow the waters were parted this way and that; and Elisha went over. [15] And when the sons of the prophets who were facing him at Jericho saw him, they said, The spirit of Elijah is resting on Elisha. And they came out to him, and went down on the earth before him.* 2Ki 2:14-15 BBE

ELISHA: -Or perhaps the faith **of Elisha** whom we should also ask for a double portion of Elisha's spirit which would be four times that of Elijah. Surely, they were possessed by the Lord! It was His Spirit!

The faith of Elisha whose prayers gave a woman and her son food to eat throughout the drought. A woman who gave her last serving of food **accepting death giving life to another with all she had left .**

ELIZABETH: -Or perhaps, that **of Elizabeth** mother of John the Baptist, who fled to the mountains when Herod was searching for John to kill the baby. Elizabeth an old woman could not climb at her age, she could not find a secrete place to hide him.

> *She groaned within herself and said "O Mountain of the Lord, receive the mother with the child. For Elizabeth could not climb up. And instantly, the mountain divided and received them. And there appeared to them an angel of the Lord, to preserve them.*
> (The Lost Books Of The Bible – The Protevangelion, page 35)

Why would she say "the mother with the child?" Surely because she was speaking in the Spirit, possessed by the Lord as did Jesus calling Mary "woman" at the wedding of Cana. In the gospels we are told that the minute Mary spoke Elizabeth was spirit filled.

ESTER: -Or the **faith of ESTER**, pleading for the life of her people, the Jews. **Risking her life for theirs**, taking a step of faith that could lead to her physical death.

MARY: - Or perhaps the **faith of Mary**, who believed the angel and whose obedience and faithful response to the Lord changed our world bringing forth Our Messiah. Whose pregnancy appeared by faith in glory and not by sight as someone in the flesh might have perceived it. Mary, who was full of grace and great faith, trusted Our Lord unconditionally and replied so beautifully to Joseph who was so worried on their way Bethlehem:

> *"Oh! What is our small trouble if we consider the beauty of this moment of peace? Just think Joseph a period of time when there is no hatred in the world! Can there be a happier hour for the rising of the "Star", the light of which is divine and its influence is redemption? Oh! Do not be afraid Joseph. If the roads are not safe, if the crowds will make the journey a difficult one, the angels will defend and protect us. Not us: but their King. If we find no accommodation, their wings will be our tents. No mishap will befall us. It cannot. God is with us.* (in her womb) *Joseph looks at her and listens to Her, happy. The wrinkles on his forehead smooth away. He gets up, no longer tired or worried. He smiles. "You are blessed, Sun of my soul! You are blessed, because you see everything through the Grace, of which You are full!*
> (Taken from The Poem of The Man-God by Maria Valtorta Vol 1 pg 132)

JOSEPH: Guardian of Our Fathers most beloved Son and Mary, most blessed. Joseph who was given the responsibility to take care of God Himself in the flesh, and His mother who was the bond to the Blood of the New Covenant. Mary, is the woman with whom God chose to commingle His blood. The woman most blessed and God the child in His care. What can a man/father of the flesh do for God all-knowing even as a child? Joseph was humble, obedient, lived by faith and submitted to His holy will. Contemplating the life of the Holy Family proves that God covered all aspects of our trials and tribulations of which we are to learn and grow to perfection. How many times did Joseph have to start up in taking care of Mary with the little he had – once in Bethlehem and again in Egypt and again when he returned to the holy land.

CENTURION: The Centurion came to Jesus imploring Him to heal his servant. Jesus said that He would go to Him.

> *⁸But the centurion said, "Lord, I am not worthy for You to come under my roof, but just say the word, and my servant will be healed. ⁹"For I also am a man under authority, with soldiers under me; and I say to this one, 'Go!' and he goes, and to another, 'Come!' and he comes, and to my slave, 'Do this!' and he does it." ¹⁰Now when Jesus heard this, He marveled and said to those who were following, "Truly I say to you, I have not found such great faith with anyone in Israel.* <u>Mat 8:8-10 NASB 1995</u>

The Lord said to the Centurion that he had a greater faith. Why was his greater? He believed it was greater because the Centurion knew that His Word was powerful. Simply by believing that anything the Lord said would be done without haste. He knew God can do anything. He believed and his faith was great.

JONAH: Jonah went to the people of Nineveh telling them to repent or the Lord would destroy the city. Taking the first step in faith, the people believed and repented in sackcloth and ashes. As a result, the Lord also repented and did not destroy the city. Believe this then and repent:

> *The men of Nineveh will rise up in the judgment with this generation and condemn it, because they repented at the preaching of Jonah;* <u>Mat 12:41 NKJV</u>

JESUS: All these are simply synonymous in the faith of Jesus, whose faith above all is perfect with the Father and Holy Spirit. Who in the New Testament teaches love, forgiveness, mercy, faith, and hope and of His omnipotent power and glory.

And so, let us pray that the Lord will gift to us perfect faith, perfect love, perfect charity, perfect hope, a holy desire, and a holy want. Let us pray that we will attain that level of perfection in which Our Lord desires for us to attain. He said "Be Perfect as my Father is perfect." Let it be done to us according to His Word!

Is that the ultimate perfection we should desire? Yes, of course! And with boldness and confidence we do have access through faith in Him. Manifestation comes when we take the first step in faith. When we take action, perhaps, we will no longer be of ourselves, but rather, be born again. He will live, move, and have our being, and His every word will flow from our mouth, and every move will be His and we will no longer be of ourselves but rather walking in the Spirit, thinking in the Spirit, loving in the Spirit unto death and desiring nothing else.

As Elizabeth spoke to the mountain "receive the woman and the child," it was the Spirit moving her that spoke, no longer recognizing the flesh or any part thereof. We become Spirit and the flesh through mortification is confined! Glory to God in the Highest of Heaven and earth! Blessed is He!

Oh Lord, what will it take for us live where love is and not where we live. Teach us to be like our ancestors of great faith, and complete us in the faith of Jesus. Help us Lord to find the way! We beseech you to allow us to obtain the grace beyond grace to do what is necessary for the fall of the kingdom of Satan's. Be our stronghold!

We are willing to take that first step of faith, trusting in the Lord, trusting in Jesus no matter what the consequences. Love without hesitation, even unto death. Jesus, We Trust in You!

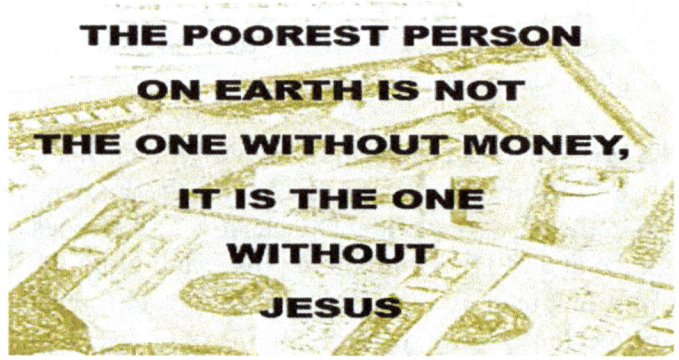

IN WHAT TIMELINE IS FAITH EXECUTED?

(Jan 2023)   It is important to consider the timeline exemplified in the Word of God. In many stories, and parables, the Lord waits on His people to take the first step in faith and then He responds.

Like our fathers of great faith, they undoubtedly believed and took the first step in faith. Therefore, as exemplified in the Word of God, we must first act in faith so the Lord can respond.

¹Now faith is the substance of things hoped for, the evidence of things not seen. Heb 11:1 KJV

It is time to take the first step in faith. "Faith is the **substance**... and the **sign**".   In other words, "substance" is something real. The online Oxford Languages dictionary says it is *"the real physical matter of which a person or thing consists and has tangible, solid presence."*   In our case, it is the action being demonstrated in faith by believing that Jesus will respond by our gathering with the actions He has promised. Our actions are in obedience, not by intuition. Faith is the "sign" that we believe without a doubt, that by our actions, what we do not see, will manifest to be true. Our hope will manifest by faith! Our hope will be realized when we believe without a doubt and take the first step in faith. Now is time, to act and obey. *"All hope **will be ours** in the power of the Holy Spirit,"* Ro 15:13, the second Pentecost. Our first step in faith is to repent in sackcloth and ashes confessing the sins of our ancestors and ours, love unconditionally and gather.

The Lord has already given us instruction, will we obey? Christians must come back to the Church of Saint Peter where the Lord has promised victory. **This is a call to Arms! The Roman Catholic Church is presently under attack! As we gather, the lion's den will form. The Lord is our stronghold Jesus is our Victor!** Join the rebellion against the kingdom of Satan. Starting today and now, We will get stronger in numbers.

"If Satan has risen up against himself and is divided, he cannot stand, but he is finished! Mark 3:26 NASB 1995

WHO IS THE THIEF?

Is it he who took the cloak? Or is it he who denies him? Jesus said "if he takes your cloak do not stop him from taking your tunic/coat also. Give to everyone who asks you, and if anyone takes what belongs to you do not demand it back".

"As you judge you are judged." (Mat 7:2) In calling him a thief, is it the accuser who is the thief? Is it the accuser who has kept from those in need? Is it the accuser who does not give their first fruits to the Lord? Are you so ignorant to think that what you have is yours? We must know that nothing is ours! Surely, we must realize that we cannot take it with us when we die. Why do we allow ourselves to suffer in selfishness, greed, and love of earthly treasures? Why do we allow things to possess us? Surely all these things will cause us to suffer much, unless we repent!

We must detach ourself from the things of the earth and give freely.

> *And unto him that smiteth thee on the one cheek offer also the other; and him that taketh away thy cloak forbid not to take thy coat also.* Luke 6:29 KJV

Both were wrong, both sinned: one to steal and one to be greedy. Give freely and with love! We must detach ourselves from the things of this world. Do not allow things to possess you.

> ***Be ye therefore merciful, as your Father also is merciful.*** Luke 6:36 KJV

This is a Call to Arms! Love, pray, fast, repent, and unite!

WHO IS THE MURDERER?

Remember! The Lord came not to condemn but to save! We must change our ways!!! These are questions to consider. We must search our inner most being and consider which might apply to each of us and repent.

Repent and Be Ready – Jesus is coming!

Who is the murderer?

- Is it we who kill the flesh? The dead burying the dead?

- Is the murderer, the murderer of the soul and mind through hate and vengeance? (as referenced *1John 3:15*)

- Or is it the living who deny the dead life? Is it we who deny the Bread of Life to others?

- Is it we who lie breaking the Ten Commandments? Is it we whose deceitful ways lead to death? (as referenced *Acts 5:1-9* death to liars)
  You have not lied to men, but to God! Acts 5:4 CPDVTSB

  Thou shall not bear false witness against thy neighbor.
  Exodus 20:16 KJV

- Or is it we who misunderstand the Word of the Lord, telling one church or another that the other church is a liar?

- Is the murderer a believer of Christ who calls another believer of Christ a heretic or a demon? Do we reap what we sow? Are we the heretic as we speak the words from our own heart? Would we lay our life down for our Christ believing brother?

  But I say unto you, that every idle word that men shall speak, they shall give account thereof in the day of judgment. Mat 12:36 KJV

> *But those things which proceed out of the mouth come forth from the heart; and they defile the man.* Mat 15:18 KJV

> *"The good man out of the good treasure of his heart brings forth what is good; and the evil man out of the evil treasure brings forth what is evil; for his mouth speaks from that which fills his heart.* Luke 6:45 NASB 1995

> *Let no evil talk come out of your mouth, but only what is good for giving necessary teaching, and for grace to those who give ear.* Eph 4:29 BBE

> *¹⁵Everyone who hates his brother is a murderer. And you know that no murderer has eternal life abiding within him. ¹⁶We know the love of God in this way: because he laid down his life for us. And so, We Must Lay Down Our Lives for Our Brothers*
> 1 John 3:15-16 CPDVSB

- Is it we who throughout time have changed the Bible and its interpretation? Lean not on human understanding!

  > *²⁷ But as for you, let the Anointing that you have received from him abide in you. And so,* **you have no need of anyone to teach you.** *For his Anointing teaches you about everything, and it is the truth, and it is not a lie. And just as his Anointing has taught you, abide in him. ²⁸ And now, little sons, abide in him, so that when he appears, we may have faith, and we may not be confounded by him at his advent.*
  > 1John2:27-28 CPDVTSB

- Is it we who have not preached the truth, **by not telling people** that the Lord wants to teach them according to His Covenant? (in Heb 8:10-12)

Surely, our doubt of this possibility is a strike against us, the preachers. Doubt is a sin.

- Or is it we who have copyrighted the Word of God? Who, can claim the Word to themselves? No one can claim ownership! No one should profit monetarily! All profit should be spiritual and spreading of the good news! Do we not fear God? Do we think we control the Word of God, a book? Why do we set limitations of its usage? What can the Word of God not do? It is truly alive and **IT IS in control**! Repent!
Is it for everyone? Yes! Everyone!

    [20] May your money come to destruction with you, because you had the idea that what is freely given by God may be got for a price. [21] You have no part in this business, because your heart is not right before God. Acts 8:20-21 BBE

- Or is the murderer those who say to another "You are not qualified to read the Word of God only I can help you"?
Knowing this first, that no prophecy of the scripture is of any private interpretation. 2 Peter 1:20 KJV

- Is it we who rebuke others from the love of Mary Most Holy, whom Our Father chose and whom Jesus called Mother? Who is our shepherd?

- Is it we who are called apostles and are liars as noted in *Rev 2*, deceiving people away from the truth? Away from true love?

- Is it we whom the Lord spits Himself out, when we receive Holy Communion unworthily eating and drinking judgment upon ourselves? Are we lukewarm? Is it a miracle or is it the Lord rejecting us?

- Is the murderer anyone who has killed even the smallest living creature of any form? A bug or even a rose? In the book of Revelations, the animals are all living in peace.

Prayer: Lord, give to us the grace to love Your Word and please allow every word that comes from our mouth to be good for edification to give grace to those who hear. Help us Lord to listen to you and to obey without hesitation. We desire to respond to you immediately at your command. Please give to us the grace to love our brethren even unto death, forgive our hatred and fill us with your perfect love that we may love you perfectly. We desire the grace to be, as you desire, Perfect as Our Father in heaven is Perfect. Make us of the same mind, bond us in the same spirit, and unite us in the same love so that Your joy may be complete. You are our only hope, our redeemer, our loving creator. All Glory, Honor and Power are yours alone. Oh Beloved King of True Love, unite us to yourself and make us to please you. In the Name of Jesus I pray.

This is a Call to Arms! Love, pray, fast, repent, and unite!

WHO ARE THE LIVING, WHO DENY THE DEAD LIFE?

This too is for the glory of the Lord! God Reconciled Himself with men at the cross. Now, men must be reconciled one to another to be reconciled to God. Perhaps we will not be on the cross, but instead demonstrating our unconditional love by gathering the Army of God with Jesus Christ Our Warrior, Our Leader and Victor. Repent, confess, and love unconditionally!

Be merciful, just as your Father is merciful." Luke 6:36 NASB

⁴ John was in the desert, baptizing and preaching a baptism of repentance, as a remission of sins. ⁵ And there went out to him all the region of Judea and all those of Jerusalem, and they were baptized ... confessing their sins.
Mark 1:4-5 CPDVTSB

- Is doubt the murderer in each non-believing heart of God's truth as written in His WORD, our very breath of life? The Word is Spirit and it is alive! Believe! Repent or perish!

    the words which I have said to you are spirit and they are life. John 6:63 BBE

- Is doubt the murderer in each non-believing heart of God's true presence in the Bread of Life?

    ***I am the living bread** which came down from heaven: **if any man eat of this bread, he shall live forever**: and the bread that I will give is my flesh, which I will give for the life of the world.* John 6:51KJV

    Then Jesus said unto them, Verily, verily, I say unto you, Except ye eat the flesh of the Son of man, and drink his blood, YE HAVE NO LIFE IN YOU.
    John 6:53 KJV

Our beloved Bread of Life LIVES!!!
Appearing defenseless yet defending!!

- Is the murderer, we who lie about the Bread of Life brought to life by God Himself, saying it is only a symbol?

- Is it we who do not believe in the presence of God in the Bread of life and teach falsely to others?

- Is it we who have restricted children of certain ages from receiving the Bread of Life? Are these man's rules?

*^{15} Then, when they had dined, Jesus said to Simon Peter, "Simon, son of John, do you love me more than these?" He said to him, "Yes, Lord, you know that I love you." He said to him, **"Feed my lambs.***" *^{16} He said to him again: "Simon, son of John, do you love me?" He said to him, "Yes, Lord, you know that I love you." He said to him, **"Feed my lambs.***" *^{17} He said to him a third time, "Simon, son of John, do you love me?" Peter was very grieved that he had asked him a third time, "Do you love me?" And so he said to him: "Lord, you know all things. You know that I love you." He said to him, **"Feed my sheep."*** John 21:15-17 CPDVSB

But Jesus said, **Let the little ones come to me***, and do not keep them away: for of such is the kingdom of heaven.* Matthew 19:14 BBE

And he said to her, **Let the children first have their food***: for it is not right to take the children's bread and give it to the dogs.* Mark 7:27 BBE

- Is the murderer we who deny the Bread of Life to those in darkness? We are all guilty. We are not to judge! The Bread of Life must be received with a contrite heart, desperate love, and adoration. But who is the judge? Is

Christ the Judge? Who are we? How many Pharisees (people who think themselves of highest sanctity) and scribes are here today? Who can truly love unconditionally?

"But woe to you, scribes and Pharisees, hypocrites, because you shut off the kingdom of heaven from people; for you do not enter in yourselves, nor do you allow those who are entering to go in. Mat 23:13 NASB 1995

²⁶ Then shall ye begin to say, We have eaten and drunk in thy presence, and thou hast taught in our streets. ²⁷ But he shall say, **I tell you, I know you not whence ye are; depart from me, all ye workers of iniquity.** Luke 13:26-27 KJV

Woe unto you, scribes and Pharisees, hypocrites! for ye make clean the outside of the cup and of the platter, but within they are full of extortion and excess. Mat 23:25 KJV

- Is the murderer we, made of flesh, who think that they need to control and protect the Bread of Life? or is it the Bread of Life that controls and protects us?

- Is our mouth filled with filthy words that come from the heart? Are we murderers of ourselves, not allowing the Lord to arise in us through the Bread of Life? Is our mouth a tomb in which the Sword of the Spirit will speak? Repent! Honor the Lord, receiving Him with Honor! We must purify our tongues thus our heart, then receive!

> ***Their throat is an open sepulchre;*** *with their tongues they have used deceit; the poison of asps is under their lips:* Romans 3:13 KJV

- Is it we who doubt the "cleansing power of life" in the Bread of Life, God Himself?

- Can the Living Bread save us? What can God not do in a piece of bread that seems motionless?

"Amen, amen, I say to you, you seek me, not because you have seen signs, but because you have eaten from the bread and were satisfied. John 6:26 CPDVTSB

Ye people of little faith!
He can do anything and everything!
He saves and gives life! God in us will lead us, teach us, transform us and do as He desires. He is alive and well...
but WILL HE RECEIVE US? Do we desire it? Do we desire to love Him above all else? Do we desire to turn from our evil ways? Do we desire to please the Lord! We must Trust Him, acknowledge Him and learn from Him!

- Is it we who think that we alone possess the true bread of life, the only bread that lives? What person can possess God alone, is that possible? No one has rule over God, He is Supreme! How long has man tried to keep God to or for themselves?

Is he the God of the Jews only? is he not also of the Gentiles? Yes, of the Gentiles also: Romans 3:29 KJV

- Is it the priests and religious who will not be reconciled with our brothers because they think their way is right? Why do we not break bread with our brothers? Why do we allow divisions among us? Are these the sinners who offer Holy Communion to others? Is this reason for shame?

Are these **differences of the flesh?**
Brothers, what would the Lord say or do because we do not break bread with each other? **He says to love one another as I love you! He says that we who believe in Him and gather are FOR HIM!**

We must leave our gifts at the altar and go then to be reconciled one to another. Not one is less guilty than another. Be NOT PROUD!

Men bickering – is the time of the Lord here?

Is it time to Love without bickering?
The **Lord did not defend Himself in the courts.**
We who think we are Christ like – are we really?
Who do we bicker for?
Think Love! Love with incorruptible love! No matter what is said and done, be as Christ loving, compassionate, silent, and humble. Preach Love! Preach Repentance! Be Merciful! Gain the virtue of humility through humiliation in the love of God.

The power is in the cross of Christ and His passionate love.

> *[47] "Again, the kingdom of heaven is like a dragnet cast into the sea, and gathering fish of every kind; [48] and when it was filled, they drew it up on the beach; and they sat down and gathered the good fish into containers, but the bad they threw away. [49] "So it will be at the end of the age; the angels will come forth and take out the wicked from among the righteous, [50] and will throw them into the furnace of fire; in that place there will be weeping and gnashing of teeth.*
> Mat 13:47-50 NASB 1995

> *No one is to seek his own advantage,*
> *but rather that of his neighbor*   1Cor 10:24 NASB

> [46] *Day by day continuing with one mind in the temple, and breaking bread from house to house, they were taking their meals together with gladness and sincerity of heart,* [47] *praising God and having favor with all the people. And the Lord was adding to their number day by day those who were being saved.*   Acts 2:46-47 NASB

> *by abolishing in His flesh the enmity, which is the Law of commandments contained in ordinances, so that in Himself He might make the two into one new man, thus establishing peace,* Eph 2:15 NASB 1995

> *Grace be with all those who have true love for our Lord Jesus Christ.* Eph 6:24 BBE

> *And above all these things have charity, which is the bond of perfection.* Col 3:14 CPDVTSB

> *The cup of blessing which we take, does it not give us a part in the blood of Christ? and is not the broken bread a taking part in the body of Christ?* 1Cor 10:16 BBE

> *Because we, being a number of persons, are one bread, we are one body: for we all take part in the one bread.* 1Cor 10:17 BBE

Would this be the moment that we would truly return to God in love? we will be of one mind, one spirit, one God, we are One Body in Christ!

Receive, with love, with a contrite heart, the ONE true bread of life, the living bread! Break bread together and in love, forgiving unconditionally even unto death.

Surely, you are condemned if you condemn! You are Judged as you judge! Love one another as I love you, says the Lord.
Jesus said:

> *"Amen, amen, I say to you, you seek me, not because you have seen signs, but because you have eaten from the bread and were satisfied.* John 6:26 CPDVTSB

> *Jesus said: IF ANYONE…*
> *If anyone eats from this bread,*
> *he shall live in eternity. And the bread that I will give is my flesh, for the life of the world."* John 6:51 CPDVTSB

Whoever believes in the Son has eternal life. But whoever is unbelieving toward the Son shall not see life; instead the wrath of God remains upon him." _{John 3:36 CPDVTSB}

We must repent! We must confess! We must love one another! We must pray that the Lord will beckon everyone living in darkness. We must plead for mercy upon the unbelievers and those whom the Lord is ready to cast out to the fire. We must!

We who believe in Jesus Christ must COME BACK to the Roman Catholic Church! The ONE TRUE CHURCH! It is the battleground, and Jesus is Our Warrior of Love! We too must love!

Prayer: Heavenly Father, lead your people to the light, then keep them in your light, that all will know your love, that we may all obtain life in heaven with You. Make us Lord to do your will. Let it be done to us according to Your word. Teach us Lord your way, your truth and show us how to live a holy life in you, with you and through you. Make us to eat of the one true bread and to break bread together in love, that you may be pleased in all that we say and do. Have mercy on the unbelievers and on us. Forgive us for judging one another. In the name of Jesus I pray.

And at the sounding of the seventh angel there were great voices in heaven, saying, The kingdom of the world has become the kingdom of our Lord, and of his Christ, and he will have rule forever and ever _{Rev 11:15 BBE}

And I heard a great voice in heaven, saying:
"Now have arrived salvation and virtue and the kingdom of our God and the power of his Christ. For the accuser of our brothers has been cast down, he who accused them before our God day and night. And they overcame him by the blood of the Lamb and by the word of his testimony. And they loved not their own lives, even unto death _{Rev 12:10-11 CPDVTSB}

This is a Call to Arms! Love, pray, fast, repent, and unite!

WHO IS THE WORKER OF INEQUITY?

The Lord says to weep for ourselves, remove the splinters and plank from our own being then we can help our brethren.

It is scary for us to even consider the thought that we are all sons of the devil, because we sin, or even that we are demon possessed until we become Light; until we become a lamp stand; until the Lord himself possesses us; until we are free of all demons; until that time when no evil can touch us and we sin no more.

Fear of the devil is an epidemic. The devil wants us to be afraid of the devil. Pride, resentments, hatred, anger, malice, wrath, judgments, condemnations, selfishness, vain glory, greed, gluttony, adulterers, fornicators, liars, masturbators, blasphemy, abusers, filthy communication out of your mouth, are all governed by demons, there are many members in one body. Who moves us? Who is our master? It is that simple!! Who drives our vessel of clay?

Do not be afraid – the enemy is afraid of Our Holy Family; our victory is in Jesus. "Pray for perfect love. We must make the Love of God, Our Father, and Jesus our passion, and love them back passionately."

Seek the Lord, and ask Him to teach us and help us to be open to His truth. Search high and low. Ask Our Holy Spirit to help us to discern.

> *But Peter and the Apostles responded by saying: "It is necessary to obey God, more so than men.* Ac 5:29 CPDVTSB

> *By mercy and truth iniquity is purged: and by the fear of the LORD men depart from evil* Pr 16:6 KJV

This is a Call to Arms! Love, pray, fast, repent, and unite!

AM I BORN AGAIN?

THE REAL BORN AGAIN:
*[18]We know that no one who has been born of God sins;
but He who was born of God keeps him, and the
evil one does not touch him.
[19]We know that we are of God, and that
the whole world lies in the power of the evil one.
[20]And we know that the Son of God has come, and
has given us understanding so that we may know Him
who is true; and we are in Him who is true, in His Son
Jesus Christ. This is the true God and eternal life.*
  1 John 5:18-20 NASB

*All those who have been born of God do not commit sin.
For the offspring of God abides in them,
and he IS NOT ABLE TO SIN,
because he was born of God.* 1 John 3:9 CPDVTSB

*[5] Jesus answered, "Very truly I tell you, no one can enter the
kingdom of God unless they are born of water and the
Spirit. [6] Flesh gives birth to flesh, but the **Spirit gives birth
to spirit.** [7] You should not be surprised at my saying,
'You must be born again.' [8] The wind blows wherever it
pleases. You hear its sound, but you cannot tell where it
comes from or where it is going. So it is with everyone born
of the Spirit."* John 3:5-8 NIV

*[49]"I have come to cast fire upon the earth; and how I wish it
were already kindled! [50]But **I have a baptism to undergo,
and how distressed I am until it is accomplished!** [51]Do you
think that I came to provide peace on earth? No, I tell you,
but rather division; [52]for from now on five members in
one household will be divided, three against two and
two against three.* Luke 12:49-52 NASB

In the morning of March 2007, I woke up receiving a distinct thought not my own. It said to me:

"a multitude of your sins are forgiven you

for you have loved much."

My response to that was: "Thank you Lord! A multitude? I had that many? What about the rest of them? How do I get rid of those?" I was alarmed. I believed I was white as snow already, having been baptized both in the Catholic Church and by a Non-Denominational Church. I thought I was born again. I even felt an internal cleanse like white as snow in my body. It was amazing, it was a spiritual sensation; but I know now, it was a lie, Satan fooled me. I am still a sinner.

I believe it is the Lord Himself that will baptize the faithful, at which time, in Him, we will truly live, move, and have our being. Spirit giving birth to spirit. Like in the upper room, tongues of fire shall consume us with His perfect love. We will be filled with grace upon grace. We are to follow Jesus!

How many of our beloved dead, are waiting for us to be their advocate? Will we imitate Jesus for the salvation of all? It is dreadful to think that almost all the dead, have not yet entered heaven. John 3:5 tells us we must be born again to enter the kingdom of God, heaven. We in the flesh have made many assumptions, leaning on human understanding, wallowing in selfishness, and all things of this world. We think that some who have died were good, we try to be good too, but the truth is that we have neglected our spiritual responsibility. The Lord said there is no one who is righteous.

So, do we really think we are born again?

If we sin, **no, we are not born again.**

If we do not obey his Commandments, then

No, we are not born again.

Our desire must be to obey God. If He says "move" we must want to obey by moving. Many of us have accepted by faith the baptism of the Holy Spirit through our churches. Perhaps because they also are in sin, not yet perfected, it has not yet manifested as a full possession of Our Lord, controlling our bodies as we would see or understand it. Or perhaps, the preachers are Satan disguised as an angel of light, who have lied to us and it is all pretend. The Lord said He is anxious to baptize us, Spirit giving birth to Spirit. We must repent! We must pray for each other. We must unite! Let us make this happen!

> *For John, indeed, baptized with water, but you shall be baptized with the Holy Spirit, not many days from now."* Acts 1:5 CPDVTSB

> *Then Peter said unto them, Repent, and be baptized every one of you in the name of Jesus Christ for the remission of sins, and ye shall receive the gift of the Holy Ghost.* Acts 2:38 KJV

> *He that believeth and is baptized shall be saved; but he that believeth not shall be damned.* Mark 16:16 KJV

> *And we are witnesses of these things, with the Holy Spirit,* **whom God has given** *to all who are obedient to him."* Acts 5:32 CPDVTSB

> *If ye keep my commandments, ye shall abide in my love; even as I have kept my Father's commandments, and abide in his love.* John 15:10 KJV

> *For this, Thou shalt not commit adultery, Thou shalt not kill, Thou shalt not steal, Thou shalt not bear false witness, Thou shalt not covet; and if there be any other commandment, it is briefly comprehended in this saying, namely, Thou shalt love thy neighbour as thyself.* Romans 13:9 KJV

If we are sleeping with our girlfriend, doing ungodly immoral sex, telling little lies, if we lie in any way, if we steal, if we hate, if we break any of the commandments then
NO! we are not born again!
If we do not desire His Love above all else,
NO! we are not born again!
If we do not love Jesus and are not willing to die for the love and salvation of another, even the worst of sinners,

NO! we are not born again!
If we do not want to talk to our brother because of conflict and think we forgave them, but prefer not to talk to them but will only if we must,
NO! we are not born again; we do not know love!
If we criticize, condemn, and use our nasty tongue to say anything evil against anyone or in judgement,
NO! we are not born again!
If we use money in any way, and money is our master,
NO! we are not born again!
If we must figure out if we are born again, then we are most likely NOT born again! When the Lord possesses us, it will be the Lord thinking for us and we will not be wondering! For now, perhaps it is only an act of faith, however, our preachers have not revealed that to us.

We must repent! Desire to follow Jesus and please the Lord!

> **You will recognize that you have love if, after having experienced annoyance and contradiction, you do not lose your peace, but pray for those who have made you suffer and wish them well.** Diary of Sister Faustina ¶1628

We must desire to be possessed by the Lord. We must desire to be holy as He is holy, pure, and sacred.

> *Whoever possess the Son has life; whoever does not possess the Son of God does not have life.* <u>1 John 5:12 NAB</u>

> *¹¹ He went to his own, and his own did not accept him.*
> *¹² Yet whoever did accept him, those who believed in his name, he gave them the power to become the sons of God.*
> *¹³ These are born, not of blood, nor of the will of flesh, nor OF THE WILL of man, but OF GOD.* <u>John 1:11-13 CPDVTSB</u>

Be Born Of The Will Of God!!! **We must give our free will to the Lord!** Believe in divine providence and know that everything that happens in our life is according to His perfect plan.

The Lord desires to make us all that He desires and that is **to be perfect as Our Father is Perfect! Perfect as His Holy Mother is Perfect!** He desires for us to be born again, Spirit to Spirit.

Prayer:
Be Perfect As My Father is Perfect (Mat 5:48)
Beloved Heavenly Father, we pray
that we may be pleasing to You
Obedient and Abiding;
Father, only You are perfect, Yet, You request
that we be perfect as Our Heavenly Father is perfect.
Allow us to serve you, and in submission to You,
You promise that we are One with You
One with Your Son, Jesus, Our Savior
And One with Your Holy Spirit,
Make us Whole, a being of your loving intent
Make us perfect as Our Heavenly Father is perfect
Give to us all that you perfectly desire:
Perfect Faith, Love, Hope and Charity,
a Perfect Heart, Mind, Body, Soul,
Consume us and do with us as You will.
Help us to live in your grace to the fullest.
There is no love greater than Yours
Magnificent Love Beyond Understanding
Be strong in us; allow us to live in the Spirit;
to always walk in the Spirit, and never let us fail you.
Glorify Yourself in our weak earthly being
that we may dwell in the house of the Lord
in everlasting joyful bliss. In Jesus' Name. I pray.

WHO IS YOUR FATHER?

Jesus said to call no one father for there is only ONE, that is Our Father in heaven. Thus says the Lord:

And call no man your father upon the earth: for one is your Father, which is in heaven. <u>Matthew 23:9 KJV)</u>

And turning round, he said to them, If any man comes to me, and has not hate for his father and mother and wife and children and brothers and sisters, and even for his life, he may not be my disciple. <u>Luke 14:26 BBE</u>

²⁷ Then Peter said to him, See, we have given up everything and have come after you; what then will we have? ²⁸ And Jesus said to them, Truly I say to you that in the time when all things are made new, and the Son of man is seated in his glory, you who have come after me will be seated on twelve seats, judging the twelve tribes of Israel. ²⁹ And everyone who has given up houses, or brothers, or sisters, or father, or mother, or child, or land, for my name, will be given a hundred times as much, and have eternal life. ³⁰ But a great number who are first will be last, and some who are last will be first. <u>Mat 19:27-30 BBE</u>

This topic can be confusing because He tells us to love one another, and to love our enemies. Then tells us, that if we do not hate our father, mother, sister, brother, spouse, children and even ourselves, we cannot be His disciple. He says that if we sin, we are sons of the devil. Could it be that He is trying to make a point?

We know that we must separate ourselves from each other spiritually and unite ourselves to Him in the greatest love, which is not conceivable to our limited minds. Many persons do not realize they are earthen vessels and that we must walk in the spirit. It is apparent that many do not know who they are. Our flesh is one thing and our spirit is another. Our flesh, these bodies of clay are made from dust as mentioned in Genesis when the Lord formed Adam and Eve. They are earthen vessels. It may be difficult to understand that there are many members in one body, however the

Lord wants us to be ONE with Him. Our body is a temple designed by Our Lord for the Holy Spirit, so that we may be like Him. However, we with our feeble minds, ignorant, like dumb sheep, are blinded. We do not understand the Glory of God and the wonders of our being, which He made for His pleasure. In our ignorance, we choose free will and not the will of God in our lives, so we suffer much. The Lord says to mortify our flesh; mortify these prisons of clay. He says that, so that the devil in us can be trapped and bound and He can deliver us from evil. He wants to bring us to His Everlasting Love and Light. Simply said, we must stop being deceitful, stop lies, stop cursing, obey God! Desire truth! **We must detach ourselves from everything and everyone in spirit.** This is part of His perfect plan of redemption. We must love unto death!

What profound obedience is required of us? The Lord said to choose our master and in sin, we are told that Satan is the father of sinners. So if we sin, if our parents' sin, and if we are not striving to attain perfection, then we cannot be Our Lord's disciples. We must strive desperately to become filled with the perfect love of Our Lord, where nothing else matters except the inexhaustible love that no evil can harm or hurt.

Living in the Love of God, we can then help those we love, with the love our limited minds once knew, that they may also come to know His love. **And we, hating them (heavenly hate vs earthly hate?) and our own life simply because we desire nothing of this world but only that of Our Father in Heaven, only then can Our Lord work in us to help them. Simply because we have surrendered completely to the Lord, even unto death, where true love dwells.**

Perhaps we have not repented of being called "father" or "mother." This is for both lay men and priests, preachers, parents etc. Everyone! Instead we babble and argue among ourselves and say "Oh, it's okay to be called father." Who do we attempt to please? The Word is clear! Let us seek the Lord and ask Him to make us obedient to Him. What part of the Word of God do we not believe or continue to manipulate? Repent! Be careful!

Okay, not making excuses for the disobedience of calling my earthly father, father, the conclusion is this: There is a point proven here. **The point being that no matter how much we try, we cannot escape sin, except by the grace of God.** There is an awareness here, realizing we are all sinners we can come to the conclusion of the importance of gathering against Satan.

Listening to the radio, a man once said that "he does not sin." Surely, he is blinded by sin unknown to him. Funny as it seems, many sins are right in front of our faces and we fail to acknowledge our sinfulness out of pride or ignorance. God only knows if that man has children and is called father, but does he use money? It is the master of the earth. Has he prayed for it?

So, if we choose to call earthly people father, it appears to be a sin. And again proving that Satan is the father of sinners, thus calling him father. With a heavy heart, it is apparent that we are disobedient. We should not call anyone father. It is the Word of God, the Living Word. So what do we call them? Many have been guilty of this sin and we struggle with this sin too. Pray the Lord will help us with it.

Aside from proving that we are all guilty and that there is no escape, except by the grace of God. Then, the only resolve is that all Believers in Christ, rebel. Again, as in heaven, there was a rebellion of hate, ours will be a rebellion of love. Lucifer rebelled against God; now we as sinners, rebel against Satan the father of sinners. Join the Army of God with Jesus Christ Our Warrior, Our Victor! We must rebel against the kingdom of Satan and desire to join forces with Our Lord Jesus Christ! Do it! Jesus came to divide and we must join Him in the cause to divide. Repent in sackcloth using ashes!

This is a call to arms! Love, pray, fast, repent, and unite!

Prayer: Help us Lord to attain perfect obedience that is pleasing to you. Remove all treasures on earth from our heart, mind, and soul, so that you will be our only treasure, the King of our being. Dwell in the chambers of our heart and make it fit for You, Our King. Shut our mouth and let us proclaim Your Word that you may be pleased by all that is spoken from our mouth which comes from our heart filled with Your perfect love. Give to us the grace to accept Your truth and proclaim it boldly and zealously, that we may remain in your Loving Light. Thank you, Lord, for Your inexhaustible mercy, may we live in it, be consumed by it, and become mercy and love like You. In the Name of Jesus, I pray. Oh, Inexhaustible mercy and everlasting love, may you be glorified throughout all eternity. Bind us to you, Jesus now and forever Amen.

Repent that you might believe as mentioned in *John 21:32*.

WHO IS YOUR MOTHER?

The fifth of the Ten Commandments tells us to "Honor your mother and your father." If the Lord says not to call any man father, then surely it is Our Father in Heaven whom we must honor. Who is our mother? In the book of Luke, Elizabeth calls Mary "Mother of My Lord." The Mother of God

> *"And how has it happened to me, that the mother of my Lord would come to me?"* Luke 1:43 NASB 1995

We must desire for our soul to magnify the Lord. We must want our spirit to rejoice in God our Saviour. We must contemplate the love of Mary, her life, and her obedience so that we may imitate Her. She has been hidden from many. Her love is profound! We must ask the Lord to forgive us and to open our heart, mind, and soul to **His** love for her, that her love may not be hidden.

> 26*When Jesus then saw His mother, and the disciple whom He loved standing nearby, He said to His mother, "Woman, behold, your son!"* 27*Then He said to the disciple, "Behold, your mother!" From that hour the disciple took her into his own household.* John 19:26-27 NASB 1995

When the Lord told John, "Behold, your mother" we know clearly that she did not bear John in her womb. We do know that she is the Mother of Our Lord and He told the disciple to behold his mother. We have always understood it to be that he would take care of her. But the word means more than just watch over her, take care of her. For us perhaps it means to comprehend, gaze at and call attention to her so that we may come to know her. To discern, apprehend and discover that which is righteous and love itself. Mary! We must behold Our Mother in Heaven, receive her into our lives and take her into our homes as well; surely, we are indebted to her for her wonderful and magnificent "Yes."

When Jesus told Mary to behold her son, I am sure He was giving us to her as well. That she also, may comprehend, gaze at and call attention to each one of us that she may also know us and give regard to each one of us.

"Behold" according to the online dictionaries means:

Dictionary.com Unabridged (v 1.1) - *Cite This Source*
1. regard, gaze upon, view; watch; discern.
American Heritage Dictionary - *Cite This Source*
1. a. ***To perceive by the visual faculty; see:*** ...
   b. ***To perceive through use of the mental faculty; comprehend:*** ...
2.   ***To look upon****; gaze at:* ...

We can also contemplate that just as there is only One Father who is in Heaven, so also, there is only One Mother who is also in Heaven. Mary! Our God chose her as the bride, as we would understand it, to unite Himself for His divine purpose with someone in the flesh to bear His child.

The Word became flesh when Mary was over-shadowed by the Holy Spirit. The blood of Mary formed a new blood with the Divine Child in her womb, creating Jesus, a man-God. Could this possibly be the Blood of the New Covenant of which Jesus referred? We have always thought or referred to the Blood of the New Covenant as that of Jesus on the cross. Yes, this is true, but it also stands to reason that a New Blood, a New Covenant would be the unity of God with flesh. Jesus in the womb of Mary, comingled!

In The Mystical City of God, Vol. III p. 765 it states:

Just as I have told you, that he who sees Me
sees my Father, and he who knows Me, knows also Him;
*so I now tell you, that **He who knows my Mother,***
***knows Me**; he who hears Her, hears Me; and who*
honors Her, honors Me. All of you shall have her
as your Mother, as you Superior and Head, and
so shall also your successors.

Jesus came and preached repentance and love. We must ask the Lord for the grace to know and love His Mother, Our Mother. Ask the Lord for the grace to know the Truth, He is the Truth. We must ask the Lord to forgive us for disobedience to His Word and for leaning on human understanding. If we are in sin against calling no one father, then a great number of us have broken this command. Men tend to give okay and reason to disobey this command. But what will the Lord say, will we see His face with a pure heart?

Anyone who would deny Mary as their Mother is vain to think they are better than she. If God Himself called Her Mother, who are we to do otherwise? Who in all creation but Mary could have met the heavenly criteria necessary for the great honor of being called the Mother of Our Lord and Savior Jesus Christ the Redeemer of mankind? If God honors her, how can any other person deny her? He exalts the humble as mentioned in the scriptures. She was humble; therefore, Our Lord exalted Her. Every generation will call her Blessed! She is Blessed indeed!

She was overshadowed by the Holy Spirit, a filling of the Holy Spirit all over her body, consumed and overtaken, possessed by the Holy Spirit, filled with grace upon grace. She is truly ONE with God, One with the Holy Spirit, One with Jesus, and One with the Father. Even Jesus on earth said that the Father was in Him.

Would anyone ever qualify to meet the standards that Mary met to be received by Our Lord as ONE? Perhaps, the circumstances will not be the same, but with grace, we must hope that it will happen to us! In the perfection given to Her by Our Lord, in loving her, we grow in love and understanding. He becomes Our Only Want as He was to Mary. Let us all hope to be ONE. This is the Lord's desire: That we be perfect as our Heavenly Father is perfect.

Perhaps we have not asked Her to be the Mother in our life or of our family. Please ask her, she is like Our Father, both are patiently waiting for us to invite them into our heart and into our lives. Ask them to please come with Jesus and take their reign on earth! May the Lord make us Blessed!

THE WORD OF GOD TRANSFORMS!

Just as Our Heavenly Father transformed His Word in Mary's womb forming Jesus, we must understand that Jesus is again transformed, and alive in a great stillness, in the Bread of Life. Holy Communion is a sacred and holy union with Our Beloved Holy living creature in the Bread of Life, Jesus.

Jesus!!! **Jesus**, in Our Holy Communion, **gives to us the opportunity** to also become of His Body and Blood of the New Covenant. The question is "what is the intent of our heart?" Will we repent and love Him enough for Him to receive us? Can we be merciful like Him? In Holy Communion, He is Our Bridegroom; this is our union with Him. With a right heart and a right spirit the Love intensifies and the union is consummated! Yes, with Our Beloved, Our Most Holy Want and there is no other!

In Our Holy Communion, Jesus gives to us an opportunity to enter the New Covenant and partake. With grace, we are transformed into His Body and Blood of the New Covenant. We become Blood of His Blood, Flesh of His Flesh, through Him, with Him and In Him we are transformed, united.

> *Then Jesus said to them, Truly I say to you, If you do not take the flesh of the Son of man for food, and if you do not take his blood for drink, you have no life in you.* John 6:53 BBE

It is difficult for many people to believe in this mystery. It is a fact that He Lives in the form of Bread! God can do anything! People who do not believe are of little faith. They cannot even believe that the host, the Living Bread is in control because they do not see it move. He is mightier than our limited minds can conceive. He IS! and He is the Great I AM! He is the Presence of Everlasting Love! Let us pray that He will unite all of us to Himself!

> *He who takes my flesh for food and my blood for drink is in me and I in him.* John 6:56 BBE

The Lord says **that we must not eat and drink judgment**. Our heart must be right to receive Him. We must love Him with all our heart, all our mind, all our soul and all our strength. We must not condemn anyone or we will be condemned! Love them, pray for them that the Lord will bless them, and be merciful to everyone including the worst of sinners!

> *[27] Wherefore whosoever shall eat this bread, and drink this cup of the Lord, unworthily, shall be guilty of the body and blood of the Lord. [28] But let a man examine himself, and so let him eat of that bread, and drink of that cup. [29] For he that eateth and drinketh unworthily, eateth and drinketh damnation to himself, not discerning the Lord's body. [30]* **For this cause many are weak and sickly among you, and many sleep.** 1Cor11:27-30 KJV

With desperate love, intense desire, a contrite and humble heart, with great faith and confidence, with a mouth that is cleansed from all evil things spoken, with a mind that desires to be Christ like, and with a heart filled with love for Mary, our Mother, we receive. With a longing desire to please the Lord hoping for a pure and immaculate heart like hers, in which our soul can magnify the Lord and rejoice in Him, so we receive; hoping that He will receive us and give to us the grace that saves and gives everlasting life. Surely, if the Lord said be perfect as my Father is perfect, he also desires for us to have an immaculate heart.

Oh, that we may all obtain that grace beyond grace, that place of love beyond love, the bond of ONE.

The following is a personal note from the author, a personal experience taken from the book <u>We Lay Down Our Crown, Sealed by the Spirit of God</u>:

"ADORATION

Well, this most certainly is an area I thought little of. I know the Lord has forgiven me. It was in 2004 that I started going to church every day, if possible. The "Our Father" clearly states that we should receive our bread daily, the bread of life.

One day I got to church early and the Blessed Sacrament chapel is right next to the big church, so I stepped in. Whooooa! It was as if I was a piece of dirt being gently vacuumed up from the carpet. I felt the power of the Lord drawing me toward the altar where the Blessed Sacrament (the Host, the Holy Communion) was. My immediate thought was "it's alive!" I understood it to be a sign of welcome. I was in awe, stunned at the reality of the presence of Our Lord. I dared not and could not go to the front pew. I stayed in the back. It took a month or so before I finally went to the very first pew. When that happened, I could sense the Lord communicating with my soul. He had me crying. I was in a state of repentance. The bible states "Be Still and Know that I am" and I was experiencing this stillness. Once again, I was truly amazed.

Since then, I have been there many times. A thought to consider of the Blessed Sacrament is this: When the Lord told the apostles "could you not spend one hour with me." This is most definitely the place to make amends."

**EXALT
AND
ADORE
OUR LIVING BREAD**

**OUR SEED
OF LIFE**

**OUR
HOLY COMMUNION**

**THE WORD
THAT BECAME FLESH,
THAT BECAME THE BREAD
OF LIVE**

**IN HUMBLE STILLNESS
UNCONDITIONAL LOVE ITSELF!**

WHAT IS THE SIGNIFICANCE OF THE ROSARY?

The significance of the Rosary when prayed with your whole heart, mind, soul, and strength, which becomes the intent of our heart, is to please the Lord.

We must sow to reap. The Hail Mary is the Call to Heaven. The prayers and meditations are scriptural. With these prayers prayed with a great DESIRE to please the Lord we receive revelation to understand the life we are to live in Christ. The meditations of the Rosary are reflections of the Passion and Life of Jesus. The Hail Mary's remind us of the annunciation to Mary by angel Gabriel. As we recite these words, we are returning the annunciation to the heavens, hoping for the return of our Glorious God and perhaps the hope of being born of God. We are led to be of one mind, a fervent love grows and grace bestows.

Regarding repeated prayers: Jesus repeats his prayers in the Garden of Gethsemane three times *Mat 26:39,42, 44*; He does not condemn repeated prayers. Psalms are often very repetitive. For example, *Psalm 136* repeats the same phrase 26 times: *"God's love endures forever;"* The key here is to pray with our whole heart, mind, and soul! Vain repetition is mindless and heartless babbling *(Mat 6:7)*. Pray with desire and hope. The Hail Mary is a scriptural prayer taken primarily from the book of Luke. Scripture references can be found on the internet, EWTN has a beautiful professional and thorough writing and can be found on their Website at: http://www.ewtn.com/expert/answers/rosary_scripture.htm. (subject to change)

We must all call to Heaven by Praying the Rosary, **Praying without ceasing as in the *Worldwide Agreement of Hope* in this book.** It is said that the Rosary will crush Satan's head.

This is a Call to Arms! Love, pray, fast, repent, and unite!

WHY THE "HAIL MARY"?

This message came to me from my soul. It was like a bubble floating from my stomach upward toward my head. I sensed the movement of the bubble and I felt it open like a burst of knowledge perhaps around the area of my heart, and I was in awe… Oh My God, My Beloved! **For those having trouble to accept this scriptural prayer:**

One "Hail Mary" Prayed every day with your whole heart, mind, and soul with the intent to please the Lord will change your life.

The Rosary is grace bearing and blooming in love. It will help you to pray more fervently. **The Rosary is not just for Catholics.** It is said that with this prayer Satan's head will be crushed. When she said Yes, the devil knew his days were numbered.

The Call to Heaven!

THE HAIL MARY
Hail Mary full of grace the Lord is with thee
Blessed are you among women and
Blessed is the fruit of your womb, Jesus
Holy Mary Mother of God, Pray for us sinners
now and at the hour of our death. Amen

WHY THE "HAIL MARY"?

Today, on May 18, 2006, **I asked the Lord to help me honor Mary** and to teach me about her. I briefly read about a saint that spoke about her for hours and hours and whose listeners were converted, but no information was given. I had a sudden hope and a desire to be able to talk so much about her, since I know little. I am nothing and know nothing. The Lord was so gracious to me today in giving me a word of knowledge about her. What I learned today was really beautiful. (We should all ask the Lord to teach us all things too!! We will all be of one mind, one body, one spirit!!! but first we must repent with a contrite heart for doubting His Word and for not trusting in Him as we should and for leaning on human understanding)

THE MESSAGE:

Why the "Hail Mary"? Many times on earth, a husband gives a gift to his wife, **a bouquet of roses**.

The Hail Mary is a gift to Mary from Our Lord, a rose. The Rosary is **a bouquet of roses**. It is a grand remembrance of a profound moment being brought back to life. Our Father who gifted this to Her is pleased when we honor her by praying these scriptures. They are words of Redemption. They are words of promise announcing the arrival of the Messiah. They are words of announcement that Mary was chosen as Mother of the Messiah who will come through her, born from her. They are words of birth and redemption for in His Birth He became Our Redemption, Our Savior. They bring life to this earth. Our Messiah is alive. And to Our Father it is a profound moment of great love finally being accepted and united with His People made of flesh. Though Mary, Our Father receives what He has long awaited, Prefect Love, perfect obedience, total submission to the King of Kings. To us, this moment is a moment of mercy, a moment of promise, a moment of great hope, a moment of love beyond our comprehension, a moment we must expect to also experience, a moment of ONE.

The Rosary is a present that brings Mary and Our Lord much happiness every time they hear those glorious words being said out of **our mouths** with our whole heart, mind, and soul. Through the gift Her Spouse gave to her we grow in the Love of God, in the Love of Mary. We must become one. It resounds from our mouth to the heavens and vibrates throughout all the earth. It causes demons to tremble. The Hail Mary is a weapon against Satan. He hates it!!! It is said that Satan's head will be crushed by praying the Rosary. The victory was won when Mary conceived the Son of God, Jesus.

To Our Blessed Mother, the Hail Mary prayed with much love is like a rose. A pleasant aroma fills the air. This is why they call it the Rosary. It is a bouquet of roses to Mary from Our Lord. **Love awakens like a blooming rose. Grace manifests itself in the fervent soul desiring more love, more grace.** Sometimes persons dedicated to praying the rosary will actually smell roses when praying the rosary and there are no roses to be found in the immediate area. The prayers are given credit for such a pleasant aroma. The soul is nurtured with each recitation of such holy proclamation when said with the deepest desire to love and please the Lord. They are angelic words. The WORD became flesh, these are WORDS of rebirth. They are words proclaiming the coming of Our Lord. They are a message from the Lord to Mary His selected spouse and to each of us they are words of hope. They are words from the Lord accepting Mary as His own loving her so much so as to bear His Child. We must desire also to be His own.

We must proclaim the annunciation of the coming of the Messiah, the Second Coming with the Rosary.

As we say the words with love, we reap what we sow.
WE RETURN THEM TO OUR LORD:
1. Originally,
   **The Angels Spoke to an earthly being (Mary) and the unexpected spiritual manifestation of a Man-God, Our Messiah, was born (Jesus).
2. And now, in praying the rosary **we return to God those magnificent words**:

An Earthly Being Speaking Birth to the Heavens, (YOU) proclaiming **the joy of the Coming of Our Lord (the Second Coming, to the Jews it is the First Coming) and then the joy received in the heavens will give to us the unexpected spiritual manifestation of God returning to us and we returning to Him.

Would this be the happiest day of Our Father's being when we return to Him? When we announce to Him,

"**Hail, full of grace, Blessed are you among women, Bring forth your Son, that we may live with our heavenly family!**"

An outburst of Joy in the heavens, saying "**Finally, you want me, you have announced me and I will come to you**". "**YES**" says the Lord, is my response as was Mary's response, My Beloved Blessed Mary Most Holy, my family and I will come and we will live together at last. You have announced my coming with Love, Joy and anticipation of Our Union, and my answer is YES!!! Eternally Yours in Everlasting Love…

The first Joyful Mystery is the Annunciation. We must pray the Rosary and consecrate ourselves to the Immaculate Heart of Mary so that we may please Our Father. We must experience the child Jesus through Holy Communion, the Bread of Life, the Living Bread, and our union with Our Lord, so that we may become one. Our Hope is that our souls will be united with Our Bridegroom.

She who gave birth to the Son of Our Father, Jesus, was overjoyed when Angel Gabriel announced to her that she would be the Mother of the Messiah, the Mother of God.

> *"Hail, full of grace. The Lord is with you.*
> *Blessed are you among women."* Luke 1:28 CPDVTSB

> *"Blessed are you among women, and*
> *blessed is the fruit of your womb.* Luke 1:42 CPDVTSB

The Hail Mary is a prayer in which our soul should rejoice to recite. Her joy was beyond our comprehension. Any Mother on earth who is so happy, anxious, and thrilled about being pregnant can only begin to understand this gladness in a very small measure compared to Hers. The great love that Our Lady experienced in that moment was profound. **It was the happiest and most uplifting day of her life.** As any mother loves to show her child to another, we must ask Mary to present to us Her Son. We must love the Holy family and desire to be part of it. This was such a miraculous act of God, Our Father, who loves her so much. She was the first person to be made perfect as Our Father is Perfect. The Son of God became flesh from her flesh. Her blood flowed with His, mingled and created by Our Maker forming Jesus, in the womb of Mary. Jesus is the fruit of her womb.

On the day that the Hail Mary was said to Mary, she was overwhelmed and consumed by unfathomable love and joy. With her answer "YES" and with this proclamation Our Messiah manifested Himself first in the womb of Mary. She was His tabernacle, the tabernacle of the WORD of God. She was the residing place in which Our Lord chose to lodge until He manifested Himself in the flesh as a living creature, a new being, a divine child, a man-God.

She herself was transformed into Love itself. **It could not be any other way.** She was overshadowed and embraced by Love itself. Our Father wanted His Son to be perfectly loved, perfectly attended to, perfect as Our Father is perfect. Our Father became one with Mary. When she embraced Jesus in her arms so did Our Father through her and His Perfect Love in Her. She was One with Jesus, He was One with Jesus as mentioned in the Gospels, suffering with Him and in Him.

And so, when we say, "Hail Mary, full of grace the Lord is with thee" it reaffirms the angelic words again coming to life, which are words of life and give life. "Full of grace" is a love which bears all things and conquers all of our enemies. "The Lord is with thee" are words of being ONE with the Lord. Mary is Blessed Indeed! And all generations will call her Blessed! The words that flowed from her mouth tell it to us in such a way that we can comprehend how she felt. But again, only in such a small measure is it understood since no words are sufficient to give edification to such an outburst and consumption of unfathomable Love. Her heart, mind, body, and soul was being filled with perfect love itself. And these were her words, Catholics call this prayer taken from scripture <u>Luke (1:46-55)</u> "***The Magnificat***":

> [46] My soul doth magnify the Lord,
> [47] And my spirit hath rejoiced in God my Saviour.
> [48] For he hath regarded the low estate of his handmaiden: for, behold, from henceforth all generations shall call me blessed. [49] For he that is mighty hath done to me great things; and holy is his name.
> [50] And his mercy is on them that fear him from generation to generation. [51] He hath shewed strength with his arm; he hath scattered the proud in the imagination of their hearts. [52] He hath put down the mighty from their seats, and exalted them of low degree. [53] He hath filled the hungry with good things; and the rich he hath sent empty away. [54] He hath helped his servant Israel, in remembrance of his mercy; [55] As he spake to our fathers, to Abraham, and to his seed forever. _{Luke 1:46-55 KJV}

Glory be to the Father and to the Son and to the Holy Spirit. As it was in the beginning, is now and ever shall be, world without end. Amen

May we also become One with Her and Her great love and obedience to Her Beloved Spouse, Our Father. One through the Holy Spirit, Ours, His, Hers and each other's, together all become one. Glory to God! and so I say to you:

Pray for Those Who are Still in Darkness
Hail to you (*I acclaim and greet you enthusiastically*)
 the Lord's grace is given to you
who have accepted the Lord's invitation
to let Him into your heart, into your life,
 and who are consumed by His Holy, and loving Will.
The Lord is with you.

Blessed are you among God's people.
Blessed is the fruit that you sow in Love.
Holy are you Child of God through Jesus Christ.
Pray for all sinners and
for those who are still of the world in darkness;
may they be led, during their lifetime
to the Way, the Truth, and the Light of Life
through Jesus Christ.
Pray without ceasing always,
and in everything giving God the Glory
He so Highly deserves
now and at the hour of our death. Amen.

With the Rosary, the Lord has given to me the grace to pray more fervently and more continuously throughout the day. I have been amazed at the grace it bears. I can only wonder what it would be like to be filled with such great magnitude of love. Perhaps, my heart, mind, body, and soul would not be able to contain itself and my spirit would burst itself out of this prison of clay. All darkness banished, set free at last. Ohhhhh how I wish that would be!!! I hope in it!!!

Why Was Mary Chosen to Be the Mother of Our Lord?

Perhaps it was Mary's Hope and lifetime fast of being chaste that beamed in the eyes and heart of Our Lord.

The Lord chose Mary as the first human being with whom to unite himself. Yes, indeed! Mary was chaste on earth! Mary who has been given to us to behold is our perfect example, of what the Lord desires, for us to be ONE with Him. In the book of <u>Revelations 14:4-5</u> we are told that the **Lord has purchased the first fruits among men**:

1. those who are chaste
2. and have not been defiled
3. and **follow the Lamb** wherever He goes.
   (RECIPROCATE- do as He does)
4. They do not lie
5. and are blameless.

⁴These are the ones who have not been defiled with women, for they have kept themselves chaste. These are the ones who follow the Lamb wherever He goes. These have been purchased from among men as first fruits to God and to the Lamb. ⁵And no lie was found in their mouth; they are blameless. <u>Rev 14:4-5 NASB 1995</u>

Although it may refer to a certain group, first fruits among men, we must know that it applies to those who desire to please the Lord. Mary is our perfect example. We must comply!

For am I now seeking the favor of men, or of God? Or am I striving to please men? If I were still trying to please men, I would not be a bond-servant of Christ. <u>Ga 1:10 NASB 1995</u>

Everyone is required to be chaste, truthful, and blameless. We are required to follow Jesus, that is, imitate Him. We must desire to please God not men!

The Lord loves for us to Hope in Him and to humble ourselves in His sight. The Lord loves for us to always acknowledge Him in everything we say and do. Having faith the size of a mustard seed as Mary demonstrated, brought favor in the eyes of Our Lord.

Moses was favored because He had great faith and was righteous. Mary also had great faith and her greatest desire was for the Messiah to come. When she met Joseph her designated spouse, after living in the Temple for so many years, she had to disclose her vow made to the Lord to Joseph. When she told Joseph her vow, he immediately said let us both go to the Temple so that I also can make the same vow. The vow was to remain chaste so that the Messiah would come sooner. It was a form of fasting and humbling themselves to the Lord.

Faith is a knowing that the Lord will answer, it is a firm belief and confidence in Him. Believe and Trust in Jesus! It is as simple as that of the Centurion. It is part of loving the Lord desperately and greatly desiring to be with Him. It is a part of fearing the Lord hating to be apart from him. We must have faith to partake in our transformation. It is a greater faith, a greater trust, a greater virtue. The Lord desires it and so must we.

Will the Divorced, Adulterers, and Homosexuals be Chaste at The Coming of The Lord?

In our many sins and errors can we be made clean and chaste to be part of the 144,000? It is a requirement according to Rev 14:4. **We must all be chaste for the Coming of the Lord!**

In May-June 2009 the Lord taught me about Chastity in "Loves True Desire" (not included in this book, it is in <u>The Great Deliverance Stop a Grieving World</u>). Here is a definition of "Lust of the Flesh":

> **Lust of the Flesh** is any form of carnal sex or sexual desire satisfying the body of self or of another, individually or jointly, in thought, word or deed other than for the purpose of procreation (having children) with the Lord's blessing.

In this day and time, men have failed to remember what true faith, true love and true hope are. In the book of <u>Tobit</u> in the Bible it says people get married out of lust like mules and horses. Tobit prayed and fasted for three days before the marriage was consummated. They offered their marriage to the Lord; and with the fear of the Lord, **they were moved rather for the love of children, than for lust**. They ask the Lord to bless them and He answers their prayers.

What kind of marriages does the Lord see today? How many days do today's newlyweds abstain in prayer and fasting before consummating the marriage? Angel Raphael says the following:

> *For example, those who receive marriage in such manner as* **to exclude God from themselves and from their mind**, *and in such a manner as to empty themselves to their lust, like the horse and mule, which have no understanding,* **over them the demon has power.** _{Tobit Ch 6:17 CPDVTSB}

Today, people marry out of lust resulting from selfish desires Do they abstain before consummating their marriage or relationship to honor the Lord? Others live together without marriage, still not honoring the Lord, but live in selfishness.

Perhaps marriages have been cursed with disorder, cheaters, or divorce through their neglect and ignorance of not acknowledging the Lord in their relationship. This world has enjoyed its sinfulness, it is partaking in Satan's kingdom. Again, believers in Christ are not united, they are not lovers of Christ, they do not love unconditionally and are scattered. It does not matter if they were married in a Church, their intent must be focused on God, not just in the ceremony. Their life must be set on God, and chastity must be exercised, it is a great virtue. We must pray for the Lord to bless the marriage and bless it with children. Intercourse is a holy act for the purpose of procreation.

We tend to believe that Our Merciful Lord has forgiven us, so we continue in our sinfulness. We think it is okay because everyone does it. We think the laws have changed, but they have not. That is not repentance. If we love the Lord, we would not want to hurt Him; we would desire not to sin ever again! We would want to obey. We would repent immediately, not wanting to be separated from Him. We would stop our sexual immorality and desire to be one of the 144,000 in the book of Revelations.

There is salvation for all, but we must change our ways!

In Mark 6:17-20, John accuses Herod and his wife Herodias of adultery. She was previously married to Herod's brother, and John told him that it was wrong. According to God's law, the punishment is death, John warned and preached repentance. Our Lord is merciful, greatly merciful, but **all adulterers must repent, change their ways, and remain chaste.** Our bond is with God and each other. God is the same, yesterday, today, and always.

Seek the Lord. The Love of God is unconditional and so is His mercy unconditional. He will forgive. We must come to know and live in His mercy! Do not perish, therefore, repent!

We ought to obey God rather than men. Acts 5:29 KJV

(March 8th 2007) What do you think of Pharaoh whose heart was hardened? Is he forgiven? He whom the Lord hardened his heart so that the glory of God would be made known. In his self-centeredness and idol worship did he repent? Moses allowed divorce because hearts were hardened. Those who are divorced and those who are remarried have a harden heart, They are like Herod and his brother's wife whom he married. Did Herod have a decree of divorce according to the laws of men? Does it matter? Their hearts were hardened! Are those who are remarried today living in sin according to the Law of Our Lord? Yes! The Lord states:

> *Therefore, what God has joined together,*
> ***no person is to separate."*** <ins>Mark 10:9 NASB</ins>

Who would be so humble to ask the Lord to forgive them in this and live a chaste life? Who will plead, wail, and mourn with cries of repentance that perhaps the Lord will forgive us for leaning on human understanding?

How many have we known, that are deceased that have lived a life that seemed good, but according to God were not, because they were adulterers, remarried, cheaters, nymphomaniac, liars, and such. We thought they went to heaven, but are not according to the bible. You must be born again to enter the kingdom of heaven. We are not yet born again. We wait for the second Pentecost. We have thought it to be okay because we are used to the evil and wicked generation, we live in. We have leaned on human understanding. We must pray for them and ask the Lord to be merciful to all sinners living and dead.

Focusing on the divorced, we know that they are adulterers of a great population. Those whose spouse is alive and are remarried are adulterers. The Lord said that those who divorce and are not remarried, will commit adultery therefore will also be adulterers. They are set apart as evil and wicked according to scripture. Here is hoping that we, who are divorced will desire to be chaste and change our ways to prepare for the coming of the Lord. There is hope.

> *And the Pharisees approached him, testing him, and saying, "Is it lawful for a man to separate from his wife, no matter what the cause?"* <ins>Mat 19:3 CPDVTSB</ins>

⁴ And he said to them in response, "Have you not read that he who made man from the beginning, made them male and female?" And he said: **⁵ *"For this reason, a man shall separate from father and mother, and he shall cling to his wife, and these two shall become one flesh. ⁶ And so, now they are not two, but one flesh. Therefore, what God has joined together, let no man separate.*"** Mat 19:4-6 CPDVTSB

⁷ They said to him, "Then why did Moses command him to give a bill of divorce, and to separate?" ⁸ He said to them: **"*Although Moses permitted you to separate from your wives, due to the hardness of your heart,*** *it was not that way from the beginning.* Mat 19:7-8 CPDVTSB

And I say to you, that whoever will have separated from his wife, except because of fornication, and who will have married another, commits adultery, and whoever will have married her who has been separated, commits adultery."
Mat 19:9 CPDVTSB

Except for the reason of fornication? Does this mean that adultery has already been committed? yes. So, what is fornication? Sexual immorality, Unfaithfulness! The scripture here clearly indicates that adultery has been committed before divorce *and who will have married another, commits adultery.* We who are divorced and remarried with our x-spouses living - we are an adulterer, blinded by the laws of man. The Lord has said it in His Word. This scripture continues to indicate that if adultery is not committed before the divorce, it will be committed after the divorce. The innocent spouse most likely has already been driven to commit adultery as the Lord warned.

but I say to you that everyone who divorces his wife, except for the reason of sexual immorality, **makes her commit adultery;** *and whoever marries a divorced woman commits adultery*. Mat 5:32 NASB

unless you repent, you will all perish Luke 13:3 CPDVTSB

> *But if she has separated from him, she must remain unmarried, or be reconciled to her husband. And a husband should not divorce his wife.* _{1Cor 7:11 CPDVTSB}

> *Concerning the rest, I am speaking, not the Lord. If any brother has an unbelieving wife, and she consents to live with him, he should not divorce her.* _{Co 7:12 1 CPDVTSB}

Moses issued a decree of divorce for the disobedient, just as the Lord told the apostles that when they enter a place that rejects them to dust their feet.

It is a separation from the Lord to those whose hearts are hardened like that of Herod and his brother's wife. Therefore, the fact that Moses allowed divorce did not make it right. It only separated the evil from the good. Those who choose not to love unconditionally are not like Christ and cannot love the Lord because they obeyed man rather than God. We choose "self" over "selflessness." We did not fast and humble ourselves before the Lord to please Him and ask forgiveness as did Tobit.

Know this then: if His love is in us, then we would be like Jesus. We too would love unconditionally. We would have forgiven our spouse that committed adultery. We would have fasted, prayed, and repented unto the Lord. Not just for ourself, but for both of us, for the entire family. We are bound in marriage as ONE and we are ONE family. We are ONE body in Christ. We would not have divorced and our children would not have been troubled. We would have prayed and fasted. We would desire greatly to be reconciled to God and to each other. Consider repenting with the use of sackcloth and ashes. What part of the Word do we insist on not wanting to believe? Adulterer Repent or perish. Be careful!! Be watchful!!! **Repent and believe!**

And if our pastor is divorced and remarried, and his x-wife is living, or if your preacher condemns other churches be careful!! Be alert!!! They are filled with presumptions and assumptions, appearing as an angel of light. It is a spirit of fornication, a spirit of adultery occupying the shell made of dust in which we/they have chosen our/their master. Can we recognize the adulterer, a worker of Satan? We must forgive them. We must not judge them. We are condemned if we condemn, leave the judging to God, knowing all things are prescribed by the Lord for a divine purpose, for His glory. We must seek the Lord for all truth. Repent! The Lord sadly turns away from the sinner who does not repent. Leave that church! Join the rebellion!

> [10] *The disciples said to Him, "If the relationship of the man with his wife is like this, it is better not to marry."*
> Mat 19:10 NASB

> *Indeed I will cast her into a sickbed, and those who commit adultery with her into great tribulation, unless they repent of their deeds.* Rev 2:22 KJV

> [20] *But the rest of mankind, who were not killed by these plagues, **did not repent** of the works of their hands, that they should not worship demons, and idols of gold, silver, brass, stone, and wood, which can neither see nor hear nor walk. 21And **they did not repent of their murders or their sorceries or their sexual immorality or their thefts**.*
> Rev 9:20-21 NKJV

> *We ought to obey God rather than men.* Acts 5:29 KJV

Focusing on Homosexuality we are told in Romans 1:27 that they receive within themselves the recompense that is the result from their error. Is aids the penalty? By their own choosing they receive their penalty - **Repent, He loves everyone!**

> *And similarly, the males also, abandoning the natural use of females, have burned in their desires for one another: males doing with males what is disgraceful, and receiving within themselves the recompense that necessarily results from their error.* Romans 1:27 CPDVTSB

Our passions seem to control us, not just the homosexuals, but the adulterers, and all those exercising sexually immoral acts, liars, and all sinners. Throughout the Bible, the Lord continues to tell us our sin, the consequences leading to the destruction of our souls. and urges us to repent. Being gay is no different. To everyone who condemns gays, the condemnation you speak is your own. Remember this: Love The Sinner! Hate The Sin! **Oh, but we are all sinners?** Do we hate our own sin? Stop judging! Stop throwing stones! Let him without sin cast the first stone. **The devil is a liar!!!** Sin is a curse to the sinner. Unfortunately, we are all sinners. We must strive to take the Log out of our own eye! Then we can help our brothers!

We must make room in the deepest depth of our inner-most being; the Inn of our heart, the chambers in which Our Lord desires to be loved and to love even the most dreadful sinner. We must make Jesus the King of our Heart, of our life and of this world. Love Unto Death! We must imitate Him! Jesus came as a merciful God. He came to teach us to love and to repent so that we would have a great hope for our salvation. He came to save, not to condemn. Can we be like Him?

> *For to this end also did I write,*
> *that I might know*
> *THE PROOF OF YOU,*
> *Whether ye be obedient in all things.*
> ***To whom ye forgive any thing, I forgive also****:*
> *For if I forgave anything, to whom I forgave it,*
> *For your sakes forgave I it, in the person of Christ;*
> *Lest Satan should get an advantage of us:*
> *for we are not ignorant of his devices.* 2Cor2:9-11 KJV

The point here, is that the Lord desires everyone to be saved. We must partake in unconditional love and mercy and advocate as Jesus did. He is calling everyone to repentance. He is making everyone aware of their sins. Stop the fornication! Stop the adultery! Stop the lies! Stop pointing the finger! Pray with true contrition, and be reconciled one to another. Do not allow yourself to perish! Love unconditionally like Jesus. He wants us to follow Him to the cross.

The Lord says in the book of revelation that a select group that is chaste is "purchased from among men as first fruits to God". Our God, is a God that can do anything impossible. Believing that we will be changed from corruption to incorruption, then it stands to reason that He can make everyone who wants to be included in the 144,000 fall into that required category. Of course, we must believe and desire it. We must repent, otherwise it is unlikely for the unbeliever! **EVERYONE IS REQUIRED TO BE CHASTE,** not just the sexually immoral, but all sinners, including the single, and those who are not divorced. **Will we ALL become chaste?**

We are all guilty! Satan is the father of sinners. Let us separate from the kingdom of Satan. It is of utmost importance that all believers in Christ **REPENT** in sackcloth with use of ashes; **GATHER** in unconditional love and **form the Army of Jesus Christ Our Loving Warrior. Take the first step in faith.**

We must divide the kingdom of Satan! Trust Jesus Christ the Loving Warrior! Our Victor! THIS IS A CALL TO ARMS!

> *⁷ Saying with a loud voice, Fear God, and give glory to him; for the hour of his judgment is come: and worship him that made heaven, and earth, and the sea, and the fountains of waters. ⁸And there followed another angel, saying, Babylon is fallen, is fallen, that great city, because she made all nations drink of the wine of the wrath of her fornication.*
> Rev 14:7-8 KJV

Prayer: Remove the foreskin of our hearts Oh Lord, harden them no more, make us to repent, make us to please You. Bind the spirit of fornication and fill us with Your Holy Spirit. Be our stronghold and make us to be chaste. Make Yourself known to us! Abba Father! You are our only Hope! Thank you, Jesus for your great love and grace! Pray for us Jesus as you did for the Apostles, that our faith may not fail and that we may be filled with Your great love and grace! Mary, Mother Most Holy please intercede for us that we may obtain the promises of Christ in Jesus.

> *But I will hope continually, and will yet praise thee more and more.* Ps 71:14 KJV

HOW DO WE BECOME BLAMELESS?

May 5, 2010 Today I had a thoughtless thought... That is...
• a thought by not thinking
• a thought that was not my own,

It was regarding the word BLAMELESS. I had previously asked the Lord "How do we become blameless?" it has been a long time since I had asked Him. The 144,000 in the book of Revelations are blameless. He finally gave me an answer:

To be blameless one must not blame anything on anyone not even themselves. Now, more specifically, in the love of God knowing that all things experienced in trials and tribulations ARE for our learning; ACCEPTING them as such and seeking the Love of God in all things we become blameless when we in a loving way "Blame God" because He is the one in control as Job said "He wounds and He binds up."

We blame Him in a divine way, it is not like "blame" as we know on this earth but a loving blame filled with grace, love, and gratitude toward the Lord in thanksgiving for the growth of Love in us, united to Him, knowing more of Him.

When we realize that all authority belongs to the Lord, NO MAN CAN HAVE VICTORY except through the Lord. Let us Glorify our Beloved King of Glory through Jesus who deserves all the glory, praise, and honor and to our Beloved Father and the holy family and those who are like them. Blessed are they! and blessed is Mary who said yes to our Heavenly Father. May they come and may the Lord deliver us from evil, may we also be blameless. Thank you, Jesus, thank you Heavenly Father, We love you Mary, Mother of God. We love you Heavenly Father thank you for this revelation may we be blessed in Jesus Name. May the Lord fill us with his perfect love that cast out fear bears all things and conquers all our enemies

This can also be better understood by reading about St. Dorothy in *Why do we suffer?*

WHY DO I SUFFER?

Understand that we must contemplate the passionate love of God through our sufferings. We must acknowledge Him in our lives, in all our ways, and every moment we live.

Our sufferings are "our blessings." They are a small measure given to us to compare to His great suffering. This is how we can better understand His great love for us and come to love Him greatly.

The Lord was mocked, tortured, and crucified beyond anything we can imagine. Through our suffering we come to realize in a small way the suffering He endured. We can understand the degree of forgiveness we must demonstrate, and unconditional love He desires for us to imitate. Every day we betray him though sin and He still loves us. He is merciful and so should we be merciful.

We must seek to find the Lord and His victory. We must learn to live where love is and not where we live. We must choose love or we will always be in misery.

In making the sacrificial love of Christ, our love of sacrifice, in His love, with His love and through His love, we enter a different realm of understanding. In offering our sufferings to Him, our burden truly becomes light, and believe it or not – we thirst for more of Him. We desire to know Him in a way we have never known Him before.

The following are scriptures regarding our trials, tribulations, and our sufferings:

> *In this you greatly rejoice, even though now for a little while, if necessary, you have been distressed by various trials,* 1Pe 1:6 NASB 1995

> *Consider it all joy, my brethren, when you encounter various trials,* Jas 1:2 NASB 1995

> *Every athlete in training submits to strict discipline, in order to be crowned with a wreath that will not last; but we do it for one that will last forever.* 1Cor 9:25 GNT

*A pupil is not above his teacher; but **everyone, after he has been fully trained, will be like his teacher.*** Lu 6:40 NASB 1995

For I wrote you out of great distress and anguish of heart and with many tears, not to grieve you but to let you know the depth of my love for you. 2 Cor 2:4 NIV

The torments in our life and the difficulties we experience, when most unbearable in the flesh, teach us and help us to realize that there is strength in the cross and in a love beyond our comprehension. They teach us to Love God as He desires for us to Love Him. We realize that Perfect love conquers all our enemies.

It is then that we can comprehend "what we are made of" and desire greatly to deny ourselves everything. We can understand that as much as we love, he loves us and more. We come to realize that He is our ONLY WANT. We find a greater love and a greater hope.

Without such a measure we cannot learn to be like Him who desires for us to be of His image. This is where we learn to understand and desire to love the Lord greater than ever before, and first above all persons and things created.

The following is taken from the book *Trustful Surrender to Divine Providence* an internet source in pdf form page 11): *TrustfulSurrenderToDivineProvidence.pdf (archive.org)*

*"Let us never then **attribute our losses**, our disappointments, our afflictions, our humiliations to the devil or to men, but **to God as their real source**. "To act otherwise" says St. Dorothy, "would be to do the same as a dog who vents his anger on the stone instead of putting the blame on the hand that threw it at him." So let us be careful not to say 'So-and-so is the cause of my misfortune.' **Your misfortunes are the work not of this or that person but of God**. And what should give you reassurance is that **God, the sovereign good, is guided in all His actions by His most profound wisdom for holy and supernatural purposes.**"*

In the book of *Job* we can see that even He admits that it is the Lord who disciplines:
"Blessed is the man whom God corrects; so do not despise the discipline of the Almighty. For he wounds, but he also binds up; he injures, but his hands also heal. Job 5:17-18 NIV

But if ye be without chastisement, whereof all are partakers, then are ye bastards, and not sons. Heb 12:8 KJV

And in the Book of *Revelation,* the following:
Those whom I love I rebuke and discipline.
So be earnest, and repent. Rev 3:19 NIV

Because of our sinfulness Our Lord disciplines. Because of our continued sinfulness and unrepentant heart, we suffer. The Lord is a jealous God wanting our undistracted love and devotion for Himself. Our ignorance and sinfulness are the reason we suffer.

The Word talks about possessing things as if not possessing them, about being married as if not married. The writing pertains to distraction and attachment to people and things of this world. He informs us that each individual and those who are married are more distracted with the things of the world and each other. He desires our undistracted devotion to Himself. Our sufferings bring us closer to Him and help us to refocus our attention on Him.

Perfect Love, make us to Love you Perfectly!

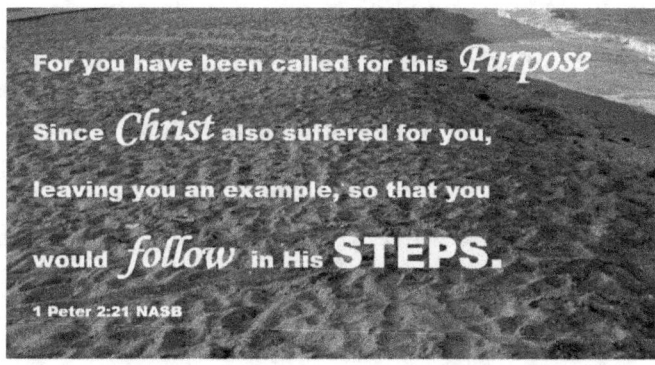
For you have been called for this *Purpose* Since *Christ* also suffered for you, leaving you an example, so that you would *follow* in His STEPS.
1 Peter 2:21 NASB

WHEN IN TIME DID THEY CHANGE "Our Lord's Prayer"?

We know that from the beginning men have changed the Word of God and continue even today. As we pray the Lord's Prayer, is it carnal forgiveness or Divine forgiveness we seek?

Whether it was ever changed or not, **consider the thought** in the next new prayer, a prayer of Divine love requesting that we be like our Maker of Unconditional Forgiveness.

> *Our Father who art in heaven, hallowed be thy name, thy kingdom come thy will be done on earth,* ***and in us****, as it is in heaven, give us this day our daily bread and forgive us* ***our debts make us*** *to forgive* ***our debtors****,* ***fill us with your perfect love****, lead us not into temptation, but deliver us from evil. Amen*

It seems that to forgive "as we forgive" is carnal forgiveness... men do not easily forgive... but Our Lord Our Maker, made us and He can change us. Perhaps the Lord was referring to himself and Our Heavenly Father, however, that was difficult to understand until Aug 2022 as noted below. Debt and debtors includes praying for our ancestors.

THE PERFECT PRAYER (new teaching)

On October 17, 2009 the Lord taught that Our Lord's Prayer is the perfect prayer. It was understood, that it was the Lord Himself saying the prayer. And in this instance, He was referring to Himself and of us in His image (as the apostles whom He taught how to pray and how to forgive as He forgives). Reflecting on the words "To forgive as we forgive" we must visualize the forgiveness He gave to sinners who mocked Him, hurt Him, and hung Him on the cross during His passion; a very real and emotional moment. Visualizing Him on the Cross we can understand that He undoubtedly forgives all of us. The first part "Forgive us," is thought provoking. Why is the Lord asking for forgiveness? The next day, being reminded that He is Our Father, and He teaches His children all things "to pardon and to ask for pardon." Reminded of a coworker, a Jewish woman that was angry at God because her child was handicapped and has never walked; we can only consider how many others are mad at God. We must forgive Our Lord, who loves us so much and knows the purpose and state of our being better than we ourselves know or understand.

As previously mentioned, to reiterate the following from *TrustfulSurrenderToDivineProvidence.pdf (archive.org)* in pdf form page 11:

> *"Let us never then attribute our losses, our disappointments, our afflictions, our humiliations to the devil or to men, but to God as their real source... So let us be careful not to say 'So-and-so is the cause of my misfortune.'* **Your misfortunes are the work not of this or that person but of God**. *And what should give you reassurance is that God, the sovereign good, is guided in all His actions by His most profound wisdom for holy and supernatural purposes."*

In the book of *Job* we can see that even He admits that it is the Lord who disciplines:

> *Blessed is the man whom God corrects; therefore, do not reject the chastisement of the Lord.* Job 5:17 CPDVTSB

> *For He wounds and He cures; He strikes and His hands will heal.* Job 5:18 CPDVTSB

> *And in the Book of Revelation, the following:*
> *Those whom I love, I rebuke and chastise.*
> *Therefore, be zealous and do penance* Rev 3:19 CPDVTSB

Mid-August 2022 – We know that the Lord disciplines and trains us through the experiences in our trials and tribulations. Our sufferings are for His Glory and help us to understand in a small way who He is and how much He loves us. His sacrificial passion demonstrates a love beyond our understanding. Reflecting on His life, and His Way, we learn to know and grow in His Love; the more we reflect and reciprocate, the more graces He bestows on us to help us be like Him. His Love, His Compassion, His Mercy, His Loving Kindness, and all that He is, demonstrate His Omnipotence and Grandeur in His Loving Sacrifice for our salvation.

In a very heartfelt and loving way, **every time we pray the Our Father, HE, OUR LORD Himself, ASKS US TO FORGIVE HIM.** He, like us, also asks forgiveness for the pains and sorrows inflicted upon us in our trials and tribulations, in our sufferings and all conflicts in this world. His plan is perfect and it has a divine purpose for the good of all those who love Him. It is imperative that we repent, forgive, and become merciful as He is merciful, and to love as He loves, unconditionally.

So the question may arise, **why do we have to suffer** if God can do anything. The truth is, that we live in the kingdom of Satan and to end that kingdom, we must unite with the Army of God, so that Satan can be divided and come to an end as noted in scripture.

> *And if Satan is at war with himself,*
> *and there is division in him,*
> *he will not keep his place but will come to an end.*
> Mark 3:26 BBE

Gather with
Jesus Christ
the Warrior!

THIS IS
A CALL
TO ARMS!

For I wrote you out of great distress and anguish of heart and with many tears, not to grieve you but to show you the depth of my love for you.
2 Cor 2:4 NIV

DO EARTHLY POSSESSIONS POSSESS YOU?

Today on the Queenship of Mary, (August 22, 2007) I was given the knowledge and insight so common in many families including the family of the Churches.

The Churches are just like a toddler fighting over things. They are like children fighting over a toy, an object of the earth, a created thing. Do they know love? Is the child possessed by the toy? Are they disobedient to the Lord's command? Is it a form of possession fighting for a toy and claiming it? Are they snared by it?

Like a toy, the churches dispute the issue about things created by man and fail to realize that Paul was teaching **"the Way."** What created thing will keep the Churches and each of us from the love of God? It does not matter who is wrong, they are both guilty; we are all sinners, and Loving unconditionally is key. What is worth the risk of separating ourselves from the love of God?

Who shall separate us from the love of Christ? shall tribulation, or distress, or persecution, or famine, or nakedness, or peril, or sword? Ro 8:35 KJV

Nor height, nor depth, nor any other creature, shall be Able to separate us from the love of God, which is in Christ Jesus our Lord. Ro 8:39 KJV

We know they are worthless and they are no gods at all. Who will bend? Jesus did! He came to earth and entered the sinners' home, taught them love and converted them to the faith of Our Heavenly Father, the faith of Jesus. He taught them to be humble and to forgive.

Apparently, knowing that it is a sin to create or even think of anything that is graven in an image of heaven, earth or under the earth, the Orthodox and others, acknowledge them in hate and condemn the sinner. Oh, but we are all sinners. So, the one who has the statute or is snared by it, is like the adulterer betraying God, and the one who accuses them is like the hater, a murderer. Both are guilty and without love. Who will bend? Stand with Christ!

Love unconditionally! We all wear blinders, if we do not have faith, we sin. The Lord says we must repent to know the truth.

Will we continue to allow "a created thing" to separate us from the love of God and the love of one another?

> *"Being then the children of God, we ought NOT TO THINK that the Divine Nature is like gold or silver or stone, an image formed by the art and thought of man. "Therefore, having overlooked the times of ignorance,* ***God is now declaring to men that all people everywhere should repent****, because He has fixed a day in which He will judge the world in righteousness through a Man whom He has appointed, having furnished proof to all men by raising Him from the dead."* Acts 17:29-31 NASB 1995

Statutes and things are a "great possession" of our homes, of the churches and even of our cities. What possesses us and keeps us from the love of God? Our trinkets? Our money? Our spouse? Our children? Our car? Our home? What is worth the risk of being separated from the love of God? Nothing! Can those who create them give up the big business as mentioned in the bible? We must make the Lord our Great WANT! Keep in mind the following scripture for end of times:

> *The rest of mankind, who were not killed by these plagues,* ***did not repent of the works of their hands****, so as not to worship demons, and the idols of gold and of silver and of brass and of stone and of wood, which can neither see nor hear nor walk;* Rev 9:20 NASB

There are many snares and the devil desires for us to continue in our disobedience to the Lord. Will we obey God or man? Can we love unconditionally? [2/2/2024 Well, let us reconsider that… If we decide to blame God for our difference, then perhaps it is simply to understand that undoubtedly, we are ALL sinners and our only option is the proof of our love 2 Cor 2:9-11. Perhaps this is so that we can realize who we are as sinners; and to know that as lovers of Jesus Christ, we truly are rebels in the kingdom of Satan. We are rebelling sinners against Satan, the father of sinners.] Now knowing that the Roman Catholic Church is the battleground and under attack, it is time for believers to gather as the Lord has asked. It is time to join the cause with Jesus, and divide the kingdom of Satan.

> *Do you not know that when you present yourselves to someone as slaves for obedience, you are slaves of the one whom you obey, either of sin resulting in death, or of obedience resulting in righteousness?* Ro 6:16 NASB

The devil deceives in many ways but his schemes are not very creative. He blinds us from the truth and we continue in disbelief. There are countless ways we become possessed by things and even other persons in this world.

Are we of a family that has quarreled over possessions at the death of a loved one or perhaps in a divorce dispute: a house, a car or even the little things, a ring, a hat, a picture and of course, money? What did we want that belonged to them and we did not get? Why do we grieve over things? These are attachments to the things of this world that drive Satan to keep us in his kingdom.

What did we not give to our neighbor in need desiring it only for ourself or our family? Or perhaps we have felt guilty because we have our stash of favorite food or things in our possession and do not want to share. Or, do we feel guilty when someone else is constantly sharing and we partake, not returning the favor? Or perhaps, we hide something because someone is coming? Is our selfishness and possessiveness aroused? Guilt reveals our sin! These are examples of forms of possession of the things of the earth that separate people from the love of God.

Do actions and reactions reveal our possessiveness?

Did our spouse give his parents cash from family funds, and for whatever reason objection and resistance is the response? Is money master here? Is it possessiveness? All our giving should be as to the Lord! We must stop our selfishness! We must stop our possessiveness, even toward one another, that is not love, it is demonic. We must trust the Lord!

We have been guilty of much. The Lord is pleased when we give with a joyful heart. We must ask the Lord to show us our sin and how to repent. We must desire to change our ways. The Lord says that corruption shall put on incorruption. We must desire it greatly and we must make every effort to become obedient to Our Lord. We must desire not to grieve the Spirit of God in us.

Perhaps, we think that someone who might be on food stamps having a huge modern TV or a new luxurious car or something very costly, is not deserving of it, because we work hard for our money and cannot afford it. Or perhaps someone who is a "squeaky wheel" boasting in themselves gets the bonus pay, are we jealous? Or perhaps the "whistle blower" saved the company from financial trauma or dissolution and gets fired, is it fair? Or still another example, perhaps we are not the one to get the promotion or raise that should have been given to us. These are examples of the sin of jealousy, envy, and resentment. They are also forms of being attached to things of this world. Our possessiveness revealed.

We must look at the events in our life and submit to God in every instance. In *1Cor 7:29-36* it says we must use the world as if it is not so important to us, it is not ours, and if we buy, as if the things we buy are not ours, again detaching ourselves from the world and the things in it. We must acknowledge and thank the Lord in all things. We must look for the lesson.

What attachment to the things of the earth are we allowing to keep us in bondage and away from the love of God, the love of one another, the unconditional love Jesus taught?

Would we give anything to someone we really, really love? Yes, that is how it should be with everyone and everything! Yes, that is a difficult quest.

These lessons are taught by Our Lord so that we may learn to live in His fullness. Learning who we are and accepting it is difficult, especially if you love Jesus. But now knowing who we are, we know and understand what we must do. Above all things we must remember to love unconditionally and to keep the truth in our hearts and on our tongues.

Know that these are all lessons to those who are humiliated and served unjustly on this earth. It is "the way" to become Christ like. Receiving these differences in the joy of the Lord and in the power of the cross is grace bearing. Contemplating the life of Christ we come to understand that the demons torment us in many ways. As the Lord said this is an evil and wicked generation and so it is. **We must learn to live in the cross of Christ where the victory is realized, and most importantly, where love is and our reward is found.**

For the person who thinks that their neighbor is unjust in having more than they have, it is a form of jealousy and a want for things of the earth. The Lord says

> *for where your treasure is, there your heart will be also.*
> Mat 6:21 KJV

> *"Sell your possessions and give to charity; make yourselves money belts which do not wear out, an unfailing treasure in heaven, where no thief comes near nor moth destroys.*
> Luke 12:33 NASB 1995

Jealousy and envy are demons that from the first began to destroy and devour our families. Jealousy was what made Cane kill Able. Jealousy and pride is what cast Satan out from heaven. Love is not found in a mind of envy and jealousy for things of the earth.

All things belong to the Lord and we should not be jealous of or for them and most importantly, we should not attach ourselves to anything of the earth.

Desires of the earth related to money are also temptations from the devil. The Lord said that simply by longing for money, you can separate yourself from the faith and pierce yourself with many grief's *(1Ti6:10).* (Read *Who is the servant of Money?*).

To employers the Lord says not to be unjust to the worker and to treat him equally. The man of greed and self-indulgence does not know love and his life is empty. Money possesses him.

In every event, although the Lord says that vengeance is His, we must make a sincere plea, that He will be merciful even to our brothers who have wronged us and more so wronged Our Lord in disobedience; mercy to those who are unjust and do not know Him, do not know love. We must repent. We must be merciful so that the Lord will also be merciful to all of us. We must desire to imitate Christ.

Surely, our preferences have taken over us! Are we possessed by them? In the same way, the churches are quarreling over things of the earth. The minds of men are scattered, there are many contentions and confusion among them.

Religion divides all believers in Christ. They are scattered. They are of little faith. All are guilty, participants in Satan's world. Is it worth the risk of being separated from our love for one another?

We must love God first above all things and each other unconditionally! What riches of the earth whether valuable or worthless do we attach ourselves to? Trust only in the Lord! What worth do we give to things or statues or money? All worth belongs only to the Lord, for He alone is Worthy!

> *Then Jesus beholding him loved him, and said unto him, One thing thou lackest: go thy way, sell whatsoever thou hast, and give to the poor, and thou shalt have treasure in heaven: and come, take up the cross, and follow me. And he was sad at that saying, and went away grieved: for he had great possessions. And Jesus looked round about, and saith unto his disciples, How hardly shall they that have riches enter into the kingdom of God! And the disciples were astonished at his words. But Jesus answereth again, and saith unto them, Children, how hard is it for them that trust in riches to enter into the kingdom of God! It is easier for a camel to go through the eye of a needle, than for a rich man to enter into the kingdom of God. And they were astonished out of measure, saying among themselves, Who then can be saved? And Jesus looking upon them saith, With men it is impossible, but not with God: **for with God all things are possible.*** Mark 10:21-27 KJV

> [6]*But Peter said, "I do not possess silver and gold, but what I do have I give to you: In the name of Jesus Christ the Nazarene—walk!"* Ac 3:6 NASB 1995

Is the earthly love we have for one another, a Godly love, or a possessive love? We love our spouses so much thinking that the love we know is the love the Lord desires of us. We are wrong. The Lord desires that we love Him first and each other even unto death as Jesus demonstrated. It is a greater love. In the following scripture we are told that we are concerned about the things of the world and how we please our spouses more than our Lord. Others may have it reversed desiring to please themselves more than their spouse. In any case, We do not know how to Love Our Lord. We must desire Him greatly and be truly devoted to Him in Spirit! In addition, as previously mentioned, we must all be chaste.

> *But this I say, brethren, the time has been shortened, so that from now on*
> *those who have wives should be as though they had none; and those who weep, as though they did not weep; and those who rejoice, as though they did not rejoice; and those who buy, as though they did not possess; and those who use the world, as though they did not make full use of it; for the form of this world is passing away.*
> *But I want you to be free from concern.*
> *One who is unmarried is concerned about the things of the Lord, how he may please the Lord;*
> *but one who is married is concerned about the things of the world, how he may please his wife, and his interests are divided. The woman who is unmarried, and the virgin, is concerned about the things of the Lord,*
> *that she may be holy both in body and spirit;*
> *but one who is married is concerned about the things of the world, how she may please her husband.*
> *This I say for your own benefit; not to put a restraint upon you, but to promote what is appropriate and to secure undistracted devotion to the Lord.* 1Cor 7:29-36 NASB

The Lord desires undistracted devotion. Will we be like the crowd that was confused and angry about giving up the work of their hands? Or will we do as the scripture in Acts has said:
> "Therefore having overlooked the times of ignorance,
> God is now declaring to men that
> **ALL PEOPLE EVERYWHERE should repent,**
> Acts 17:30 NASB 1995

Do we even care to please the Lord? Do we desire to obey Him? Do we desire to love Him greatly? Why do we insist in attaching ourselves to things of the earth?
> *Wrath is fierce and anger is a flood,*
> *But who can stand before jealousy?* Pr 27:4 NASB

> *"But who can endure the day of His coming?*
> *And who can stand when He appears? For He is*
> *like a refiner's fire and like fullers' soap* Mal 3:2 NASB 1995

For all things we must repent and confess with our mouth so that we might be liberated at the mercy of Our Lord. For all the things created of which we quarrel and are jealous or envious, and selfish, we must change our ways. If we think negatively of our brother, **we are guilty**.

Perhaps we think we have forgiven, but we have put stumbling blocks to keep us from true forgiveness. We want nothing to do with the person or church, we think we have forgiven. We will talk to them as little as possible, that is resentment, and true forgiveness has not been granted. Our eyes are full of splinters and being full of plank.
> *The light of the body is the eye:*
> *when your eye is true, all your body is full of light;*
> *but when it is evil, your body is dark.* Luke 11:34 BBE

> *No man, when the light is lighted, puts a cover over it,*
> *or puts it under a bed, but he puts it on its table,*
> *so that those who come in may see the light.* Luke 8:16 BBE

We must forgive to be forgiven by Our Lord. We must relent so that Our Lord will relent. Do not dwell in darkness - be a great light! We must open our mouth boldly and confess from the mountain tops. Be reconciled with our brothers, let our pride go.

*Confess your faults one to another, and pray one for another, **that ye may be healed**. The effectual fervent prayer of a righteous man availeth much.* James 5:16 KJB

Approach those with whom we must be reconciled and be reconciled. At least try, if they do not accept our apology pray for them and ask the Lord to bless them. Ask the Lord for the grace to know the Truth, He is the Truth. Can we love our enemy? We must! The Lord told Saint Faustina that as the Churches unite, His wounds will heal. When that happens, every believer on earth will be healed as well, when we unite.

ALL ARE GUILTY
FOR NOT LOVING UNCONDITIONALLY!

The offense is against Our Lord who gives us everything, to whom all things belong. He has taught us to share with an open hand with love and gratitude of all that He has given to us. We must acknowledge Him in all things and know that He truly is our provider. His desire to those who love Him and obey Him is to bless them.

The Lord says no eye has seen and no ear has heard what the Lord has in store for those who love Him.

Perhaps the road is rocky and cross bearing on earth for those who love Him, but the reward is great in our true home. We must greatly trust in the Lord. Rejoice over our humiliations in the Lord, that we may be like Him.

Let us then, embrace our brother in all they do, with all humility approach him and love him and let the Lord do the rest. Let us approach each other with a contrite heart. The battle began in the beginning, so let us put an end to it. Let us say to each other with all of our heart, mind, soul and strength:

"I am sorry, please forgive me, it is my fault."

Is there a difference between this sin and others? They all separate us from the love of God! We must stop pointing the finger. The importance here is to realize who we are. We are all guilty; we are all sinners. Satan is the father of sinners and we willingly partake in Satan's kingdom on earth. Therefore, this awareness, allows us to also realize that as believers of Jesus Christ, we must follow Jesus. We must **gather** as rebels in Satan's kingdom, join Jesus in His cause to divide, and let Jesus do the rest.

We must change our ways! Desire to love unconditionally and love the Lord greatly! Desire to stop doing our evil works! Know that nothing is ours, everything belongs to the Lord and give freely! Know that nothing on earth is worth separating us from the love of God!

This is a Call to Arms! Love, pray, fast, repent, and unite!

Prayer: TREASURES
Lord, You said that where my treasure lies, there my heart is.
Help me Lord, to remove myself from all treasures on earth
that only You will be the treasure I seek.
Fill me and make me Yours
I surrender to you: my heart, mind and soul,
my life and my being and everything I say and do.
You have given to me Your unconditional love
how can I offer anything less; I give to You my unconditional love with my free will, trusting You, Heavenly Father, more than anything in the world.
May Your Glory manifest sooner than later. I await Your coming with Joy and Love.
In the Name of Jesus. Amen.

WHAT ABOUT STATUES AND GRAVEN IMAGES?

American Heritage Dictionary:
Definition: ***graven image***
n. An idol or fetish carved in wood or stone…
1.   To sculpt or carve; engrave.
2.   To stamp or impress deeply; fix permanently.

In the original Ten Commandments the Lord specifically tells us **not to make** any graven image. Graven, cast or molten are three dimensional figures like statues. He is also specific in telling us **not to make** any that are **of any likeness** of anything that is in heaven above, or that is beneath the earth or in the water under the earth. He also commands that we do not bow down to them. The following is taken from the Ten Commandments, complete listing is in the back of the book:

> *³"You shall have no other gods before Me. ⁴**"You shall not make for yourself an idol, or any likeness of what is in heaven above or on the earth beneath, or in the water under the earth.** ⁵You shall not worship them nor serve them; for I, the LORD your God, am a jealous God, inflicting the punishment of the fathers on the children, on the third and the fourth generations of those who hate Me, ⁶ but showing favor to thousands, to those who love Me and keep My commandments. ⁷"You shall not take the name of the LORD your God in vain, for the LORD will not leave him unpunished who takes His name in vain.*   <u>Exodus 20:3-7 NASB</u>

Disobedience to this commandment is a sin, therefore when we sin, we are of the devil according to <u>*1 John 3:8*</u> noted below. This is given to us from the messenger of God. This is the Word of the Lord. It is a warning to the sinner. This is commanded by the Lord.

The person who makes or crafts them, sins.
Those who use or sell them, sin.

Those who bow or kneel in front of them, sin.

The people do not believe, because as always, they have preferred to disobey God, and **still reject His Word**. The devil has sinned from the beginning. **Jesus came for this purpose – to destroy the works of the devil!** In the book of Revelations it says that those who were not killed by plagues did not repent of the works of their hands, the making of idols made of gold, silver, brass, stone, or wood. They prefer to obey man rather than God. They prefer to keep to big business and savor their money.

> *Do you not know to whom you are offering yourselves as servants under obedience? You are the servants of whomever you obey: whether of sin, unto death, or of obedience, unto justice. (righteousness)* Ro 6:16 CPDVTSB

> *[8]the one who practices sin is of the devil; for the devil has sinned from the beginning. The Son of God appeared for this purpose, to destroy the works of the devil.*
> *[9]NO ONE WHO IS BORN OF GOD PRACTICES SIN, because His seed abides in him; and, he cannot sin, because he is born of God.* 1John 3:8 NASB 1995

WARNING IN THE BOOK OF REVELATIONS:
*[20] And the rest of the men which were not killed by these plagues **yet repented not** of the works of their hands, that they should not worship devils, and idols of gold, and silver, and brass, and stone, and of wood: which neither can see, nor hear, nor walk: [21] **Neither repented they** of their murders, nor of their sorceries, nor of their fornication, nor of their thefts.* Rev 9:20-21 KJV

Sometimes a statue merely tells a story, an angry or sad face, a pregnant woman or praying hands. Living by faith and not by sight the glory of the Lord may be seen through the conversions of those who did not believe at all and because of their trial or tribulation portrayed in a graven image, are converted to believe. Or perhaps a graven image sheds tears, could it be that as the Lord had said in the gospels, if you hold your peace, the stones will cry out? Perhaps it is a message of sorrow for the unrepentant sinner. Or perhaps, it is the devil making us to think that the graven image is of a divine nature, making us to sin. Is it the stones crying out or are we snared by them?

> *And he said in answer, I say to you, if these men keep quiet, the very stones will be crying out.* Luke 19:40 BBE

Some people do not believe that they are praying to idols believing that the image of that statue gives them an idea of what perhaps the heavenly being might look like. They do not realize that <u>Acts 17:20-31</u> says we should not even "think" that they are like an image of divine nature neither formed by the art or thought of men. Yes, people must stop praying to or at statues! **They must stop bowing down to them! The Lord commands it!** These are not good excuses to disobey God. Even in these cases, perhaps the Lord makes some things good to draw others near to Him. However, it is still a sin.

> *For they provoked him to anger with their high places, and moved him to jealousy with their graven images.* Ps 78:58 KJV

> *The graven images of their gods shall ye burn with fire: thou shalt not desire the silver or gold that is on them, nor take it unto thee, **lest thou be snared therein**: for it is an abomination to the LORD thy God.* De 7:25 KJV

We must pray that the Lord will help us to please Him, not provoke Him. In addition, **no statue is worth the risk!!!** The Lord says we can be snared by a graven image or even what it is made of? "Do not take it for yourselves or YOU WILL BE SNARED BY IT!"

The Lord will not give His praise to a graven image! In other words, He is jealous and wants us to praise Him, worship Him, adore Him, and love Him and only Him, not a statue nor any idol, not even your spouse or children. Our God is a jealous God and desires that we devote our love completely to Him above all else.

Why are there so many in the churches, in the cities, in the stores? Does it matter whether the statues be religious or not? No, they are graven images. Are those who approve them snared by them? Are they blind guides? Are they of the devil? Or perhaps they are snares in keeping Christ believers from being of the same mind, separated in love. They are obstacles that keep us from the love of God because the statues cause conflict and judgement between all believers of Jesus Christ.

> *"But woe to you, scribes and Pharisees, hypocrites, because you shut off the kingdom of heaven from people; for you do not enter in yourselves, nor do you allow those who are entering to go in.*   Matthew 23:13 NASB 1995

Do scribes and Pharisees live today? The truth is that they are here in great number! The dictionary describes them as people who think themselves of highest sanctity, most holy. The woes of St Matthew apply to them and many others. Blinded by their sin they refuse to repent. Can we all repent? Who do we desire to please?

> *Now while Paul was waiting for them at Athens, his spirit was troubled, for he saw all the town full of images of the gods.*   Ac 17:16 BBE

Jesus said "I am the Way." In the book of Acts in the New Testament Paul was teaching "**the Way**." Paul had persuaded and turned away a considerable number of people from graven images, the crafts of silversmiths and similar trades. In *Acts 19:23-29* The people who made them were angry because that was how they made their money to survive, it was "their work". It was and still is "Big Business." The disturbance caused by Paul's words was a "Big disturbance." The craftsmen also were concerned that if the people would believe that the graven images were worthless, they would be financially ruined and their goddess dethroned. They were in a rage and stirred confusion among the people.

They go on to say that the image "fell from heaven." If it fell from heaven then it was not made by men. But the argument here, is not about that, but rather that men do not want to stop making them as commanded by the Lord in the Commandments and disregarded the truth said by Paul, telling them the statues are basically worthless and junk. The worth put on a statue is that weighted by the mind of men and money is their god. A statute is truly an ugly thing compared to the beauty our eyes have not yet beheld of the heavens and our heavenly family.

People are driven by greed, murder, and deceptive practices simply to make people think something is valuable. This is a work of the devil that has not ceased, still practiced today as in the past. It is the work of the devil because it separates men from the love of God.

Jesus saith unto him, I am the way, the truth, and the life: no man cometh unto the Father, but by me. <u>John 14:6 KJV</u>

As Paul was teaching "**the WAY**" in the book of Acts he said that "gods made with hands are no gods at all". **He also says we are not to think of any image formed by the art or thought of man as of a Divine Nature.** They are worthless!!! The Word says that you can be snared by them. We must always acknowledge only the Lord. He is a jealous God! Yet, we know they are no gods at all.

Knowing therefore that they are no gods, fear them not,
For they can neither curse nor bless kings: Neither can they shew signs in the heavens among the heathen, nor shine as the sun, nor give light as the moon. The beasts are better than they: for they can get under a cover and help themselves. It is then by no means manifest unto us that they are gods:
***therefore fear them not**.* <u>Letter of Jeramiah 1:65-69 KJV</u>

This again, only confirms our sinfulness, and who we are. Perhaps, this imperfection will be perfected when the Kingdom of Jesus manifests. We must join Jesus in His cause to divide. We will be changed into incorruption and immortality and this earth will be purified. Perhaps, we are confronted with them so that our faith and love may be strengthened for we are in training, learning who we are.

Knowledge makes arrogant, but love edifies. 1Cor 8:1 NASB 1995

John 13:35 says that all men will know that we are disciples of Our Lord if we have love for one another. The devil is nothing but a stumbling block. There are many obstacles. A statue is an obstacle causing disruption; it is a created thing; it is a stumbling block among Christ believers.

Will the Catholic Church give up its statues for the love of his brother who does not like them? Or will his brother accept the Catholic Church as they are and not acknowledge statues for the Love of his brother in the Love of God? **Who will bend? Jesus did!** He went into the sinners' home and changed hearts.

We must realize that the Catholic Church is under attack. It is the rock in which the Lord promised victory. The Army of God must come to its defense and gather! In humility with a humble heart we must pray for one another, love one another, and let the Lord use us for His Glory, when we do become born again. We must wait on the Lord and meanwhile, be still, pray, fast, repent, and love, exalting the Lord!

Will we continue to allow "a created thing" to separate us from the love of God and the love of one another?

Is a statue worth the risk? We must love both God and one another! **We cannot have one and not the other!** How deep is our love? What measure holds us back?

We must **not** acknowledge statues. We must not kneel before them. If we insist on kneeling before anything, **kneel before the Real Presence of Our Lord, in the Blessed Sacrament. It is the Living Bread, the Living Bread of Life, the Presence of God**. He is not a symbol; He is truly alive in the Living Bread! Strive desperately to please the Lord!

The Lord says we must worship Him in Spirit and in Truth. He is Spirit. He is not a statue! He is not a graven image! God is Spirit and He specifically tells us to worship Him in Spirit.

Be careful! Be watchful! Repent!

We in the flesh must not judge those who appear to be sinning, we must trust in the Lord, pray for them, and ask Him

to bless them. We too are sinners. Let us then, embrace our brother in all they do, with all humility approach him and love him and let the Lord do the rest. We must concentrate on taking the speck out of our own eye. The Lord is merciful and makes all things good for those who love Him.

"Therefore having overlooked the times of ignorance, God is Now Declaring to Men that All People Everywhere Should Repent," <u>Acts 17:30 NASB 1995</u>

The Lord came to this earth to enlighten us and to show us the way. We know that there are many imperfections. We know that all believers in Christ are sinners. We know that He loves us and is merciful to us. Let us give all Praise and Glory to our Father in Heaven who through Jesus, Our Savior binds, beckons or chastises. Praise be and Glory be, to Our God and only to Him!

The bottom line is this, **Satan is in a united kingdom on earth. We live in a world that is in the power of the evil one, scripture confirms that**. It is difficult for us to escape the wiles of the devil without the grace of God. Does the severity of the sin as we perceive in the flesh, matter? Sin is sin, and according to scripture sinners are sons of the devil, period. Jesus did not differentiate; He was merciful to all. Satan tries to make us afraid of the antichrist? He is a devil just like us. The true question is:

Who wants to be true sons of God? Yes, that matters! Looking at the big picture there is only one remedy.

Love Unconditionally, Repent in Sackcloth and ashes, Forgive, and be Merciful! Gather!

The Lord wants to claim us as His own.

This is a Call to Arms! Love, pray, fast, repent, and unite!

WHAT ARE FALSE GODS?

Perhaps our distracted devotion and selfish love toward one another or the things of the earth make us to make Our Lord jealous because our minds are not focused on Him alone. In our ignorance we fail to give all our love, first to God. Instead, our lives become focused on our ambitions, our "things" or each other which then become the things we praise, instead of God.

Are false gods those things that distract us from a passionate urge and craving for the love of Our God? Do false gods exist at all? Perhaps we only need to redirect our devotion, attention, and desire toward Our God of Everlasting Love.

The Lord is a jealous God and wants us to love Him as He loves us. Our minds are easily distracted from true devotion and obedience to God. The following are three examples:

The year the SPURS won the basketball Championship the whole city was in an uproar. As soon as the winning game ended, the sound of cheering and praising could literally be heard all over the city even outside every home. It was incredible. They received so much recognition, praise, pride, and a form of worship. It would be amazing to even think that such an outroar could be heard for Jesus. Are they like false gods? We must direct our praise and adoration to the Lord, shouting in joy for the love of Him and in Him.

Another example: Blinded in earthly love, are our spouses our false god? Do we have them on a pedestal and strive to please them. Is our devotion to the Lord distracted and focused on our spouses as noted in *1Cor 7:29-36*. Do we think that the love we have for our spouse is sufficient? The love of God is much greater. We do not know how to love God. We love our spouses more than God, it is a small measure compared to His, we must change our ways.

Another example and question is: Are the people who eat meat like false gods to those who murder and kill creatures of the Lord? Or are people false gods to those who strangle animals to provide food to others (gods) concerned more about profits and fast production of meats? just like statues, are they more concerned with money, rather than obedience in not strangling an animal for food according to the ways of the Lord. How are our chickens killed in preparation to sell at meat markets? The Lord says that all He has created is good, so maybe it is strictly the intent of our hearts. Perhaps, we just need not to judge our food and be thankful always! Perhaps we need to sprinkle our food with ashes as mentioned in *Psalms*. May the Lord guide us to all truth and make us to obey Him so that we may stay in His Loving Light and Love. The following are scriptures related to eating meats and the sacrifice to idols:

> *that you abstain from things immolated to idols, and from blood, and from what has been suffocated, and from fornication. You will do well to keep yourselves from these things* Ac 15:29 CPDVTSB

> *¹ Now concerning those things that are sacrificed to idols: we know that we all have knowledge.* **Knowledge puffs up, but charity builds up**. *² But if anyone considers himself to know anything, he does not yet know in the way that he ought to know. ³ For if anyone loves God, he is known by him. ⁴ But as to the foods that are immolated to idols*, **WE KNOW THAT AN IDOL IN THE WORLD IS NOTHING, AND THAT NO ONE IS GOD**, *EXCEPT ONE. ⁵ For although there are things that are called gods, whether in heaven or on earth, (if one even considers there to be many gods and many lords) ⁶ **yet we know that there is only one God, the Father, from whom all things are, and in whom we are, and one Lord Jesus Christ, through whom all things are, and by whom we are.*** 1 Cor 8:1-6 CPDVTSB

> *⁷However not all men have this knowledge; but some, being accustomed to the idol until now, eat food as if it were sacrificed to an idol; and their conscience being weak is defiled. ⁸But food will not commend us to God; we are neither the worse if we do not eat, nor the better if we do eat. ⁹But take care that this liberty of yours does not somehow become a stumbling block to the weak. ¹⁰For if*

*someone sees you, who have knowledge, dining in an idol's temple, will not his conscience, if he is weak, be strengthened to eat things sacrificed to idols? [11]For through your knowledge he who is weak is ruined, the brother for whose sake Christ died. [12]And so, by sinning against the brethren and wounding their conscience when it is weak, you sin against Christ. [13]**Therefore, if food causes my brother to stumble, I will never eat meat again, so that I will not cause my brother to stumble**.*
1Cor 8:7-13 NASB 1995

Whatever is sold in the market, you may eat, without asking questions for the sake of conscience. 1Cor 10:25 CPDVTSB

But if anyone says, "This has been sacrificed to idols," do not eat it, for the sake of the one who told you, and for the sake of conscience. 1Cor 10:28 CPDVTSB

Other scriptures: Ro 14:21; Acts 15:20; Acts 21:25

According to the word there are many who have not repented "accustomed to the idol until now, eating food as if, it were sacrificed to an idol."

We must desire to give all our devotion to the Lord. Learning to live in Christ we stand firm in knowing that "there is no such thing as an idol in the world and that there is no God but one" for all glory, praise and honor belong to Him alone.

Thank God, we have hope, a great hope in His mercy, in His passionate Love and compassion towards us and our salvation. He is merciful and desires that we also be merciful. He is Love and desires for us to also Love as He loves. We must seek Him desperately to please Him desperately. We must desire him greatly! Our desire should be one with such passion and intensity as that of Our Father who sent His only son to die for us! Let us desire to love Him that much! Let us desire to die for the salvation of others.

__And so all Israel shall be saved__: as it is written, There shall come out of Sion the Deliverer, and shall turn away ungodliness from Jacob: For this is my covenant unto them,

when I shall take away their sins. As concerning the gospel, **they are enemies for your sakes**: *but as touching the election,* **they are beloved for the fathers' sakes**. *For the gifts and calling of God are without repentance. For as ye in times past have not believed God, yet have now obtained mercy through their unbelief: Even so have these also now not believed,* **THAT THROUGH YOUR MERCY they also may obtain mercy.** *For God hath concluded them all in unbelief,* **that he might have mercy upon all.**
O the depth of the riches both of the wisdom and knowledge of God! how unsearchable are his judgments, and his ways past finding out! For who hath known the mind of the Lord? or who hath been his counsellor? Or who hath first given to him, and it shall be recompensed unto him again? **For of him, and through him, and to him, are all things: to whom be glory forever. Amen**. <u>Ro 11:26-36 KJV</u>

Prayer: Lord, fill us with your grace that conquers all our enemies and make us obedient to You. Use us Lord to help our brothers, that they also may know Your unfathomable love! Make us Lord, to not lean on human understanding. Wonderful Creator of all, help us to remove ourselves from the custom of which we have been attached. Please do not let us remain accustomed to the idol. Make us to resist, rebuke and renounce all idols and all things that do not please you. Make yourself our only true want and desire, complete us Oh Lord, make us one with each other and with you. Help us Lord to give you the undistracted devotion that you desire. Help us to gather. Be our stronghold. In Jesus' Name I pray.

What about the queen of heaven in Scripture & Mary Mother of God?

When I saw the following scriptures in the Old Testament: *Jer 7:18, Jer 44:15-19 and Jer 44:24-29*, I was troubled, since they were worshiping the queen of heaven as an idol. This was on June 29, 2007 on the feast of St Paul and St Peter the apostles. I started to cry and then the Lord reminded me that I am not to be afraid of the devil for the Lord is all powerful and He is truth. Our Father chose His Beloved Mary to bear Jesus; He loves her with unfathomable love and so should we. I slept on the thought that troubled me. In the morning the Lord led me to write what is written in this question. It was Sunday June 30th (Birth of John the Baptist) and so I changed the calendar in my house to July and the calendar I saw had July pictured with the Queen of Heaven that stated what St. Bonaventure said as follows:

Men do not fear a powerful hostile army as the powers of hell fear the name and protection of Mary. (1221-1274)

"Fear the name and protection of Mary" is a holy fear of which St. Bonaventure speaks. It is a fear like fear of the Lord, fearing to be apart from Our Lord, loving Him so much, dreading the thought of offending Him. We must fear offending Mary, which would then offend Our Lord who loves her beyond our comprehension. We must also dread the thought of being apart from Her. He loves her so much she was chosen to bear the Man-God, Jesus, Our Savior. Her blood was commingled and was the first to mix and be created in union with Our Lord. It was a new blood in Jesus through Mary's flesh and blood. She can be looked at as the first connection between God and flesh. God united with the spirit of man in his vessel of clay, Mary's. It is a realization of what it means to be ONE with Our Lord, which we should also desire to be. **No matter how the Lord decides to make this happen to us, He has made it clear that He wants us to be ONE. It will happen through true love and submission to the King of Kings through**

Jesus Christ, Our Warrior of Love. Mary is a perfect example. We must take the first step in faith.

We must believe and know that God can do all things. It cannot be said enough "We must ask the Lord to forgive us for any and all things we have thought said or done to offend Him in regard to our ignorance about Mary." We must ask Him to teach us to love Her in a way pleasing to Him. The unconditional love of Our Lord and repentance are of utmost importance. We must imitate Jesus in His unconditional love and obey Him as He has proclaimed in the gospels regarding repentance. If you love me, He says obey His commandments. We must love our Christian brothers unconditionally; the battle is not ours. We must desire to obtain a mind of Christ. Remove the splinter from our own eye then we can help our brethren. We must desire to overcome every obstacle that keeps us from the love of God, the love for each other, even unto death.

Loving the Holy Family, Our Heavenly Father, Jesus, and Mary, gives us the opportunity to be filled with grace upon grace. We must desire it and believe it possible. When we do receive it, the devil will not be able to touch us anymore. We will sin no more.

Like in Jeremiah chapter 44, it cannot be ignored that there are voodoo dolls and statues that people use for witchery, black magic, idol worship and such which is most definitely an abomination in the sight of the Lord. This is not according to the doctrine and faith of the true Church. Even today the devil tries to take people away from the love of Mary and from the true church. The devil comes to devour our souls. If we do any of these, we must repent! Stop practicing these evil things! Stop speaking wickedness! The devil wants to possess us or use us. Desire mercy; desire to have a change of heart! We must ask the Lord and Blessed Mother Mary into our heart. Love one another in truth and sincerity with all humility.

> *"Then you will call, and the LORD will answer;*
> *You will cry, and He will say, `Here I am.*
> *' If you remove the yoke from your midst,*
> *The pointing of the finger and speaking wickedness,*
> <u>Isa 58:9 NASB 1995</u>

If we misunderstand the offering of cakes as the Holy Communion offered in the Catholic Church at the altar during mass, we do not know love. It is the devil lying to us because the devil does not want us to receive life in the Living Bread as the Lord has commanded us to eat. If we receive Holy Communion without contrition and love we bring judgment upon ourselves and we will be condemned as written in the Word, unless we repent.

The Holy Communion with which Our Lord has given is one that gives life everlasting. It is a transformation of Bread into Our Lord Jesus manifested. It is bread that is alive. It is a living creature; the Word of God became flesh in Jesus; now, Jesus says He is the Bread of Life. We must eat with unfathomable love and contrition so that we can become One with the Lord. This is a certainty! We must repent! Jesus is alive and He is here, He never left! He is here in a state of utmost humility because He loves us and wants us to live with Him as He originally intended since the beginning of time. The Bread of Life is our seed of life. When we go to the celebration of the Eucharist (our Holy Communion) we go to unite with Jesus at the mass. Our mouth is like a tomb and Our Lord will arise in our body in His time, if our intentions are right, we are of pure heart and speak no evil. This prayer, the mass, is one of Great Virtue. There is only one bread and only one body, let us then receive with great love unto the Lord.

The recognition given to the Mother of Our Lord is not one to be ignored! What is it about Mary? What is it about Jesus? that there is so much conflict? Reconsider their love and love them back!

> [22] *"Blessed are you when men hate you, and ostracize you, and insult you, and scorn your name as evil, for the sake of the Son of Man* Luke 6:22 NASB 1995

Mary is Blessed and all generations will call her blessed. She was hated, ostracized, scorned, and insulted by many. We must ask the Lord to help us with our understanding and love for her. Repent and be ready!

> [14] *For this cause I bow my knees unto the Father of our Lord Jesus Christ,* [15] **Of whom the whole family in heaven and**

> *earth is named, ¹⁶ That he would grant you, according to the riches of his glory, to be strengthened with might by his Spirit in the inner man; ¹⁷ That Christ may dwell in your hearts by faith; that ye, **being rooted and grounded in love,** ¹⁸ **May be able to comprehend with all saints what is the breadth, and length, and depth, and height;** ¹⁹ **And to know the love of Christ, which passeth knowledge, that ye might be filled with all the fulness of God.** <u>Eph 3:14-19 KJV</u>*

> *²⁰ Now unto him that is able to do exceeding abundantly above all that we ask or think, according to the power that worketh in us, ²¹ Unto him be glory in the church by Christ Jesus throughout all ages, world without end. Amen.*
> <u>Eph 3:20-21 KJV</u>

Preach unconditional love and repentance so that all truth may be made known. The devil has deceived the people of God
- keeping them from eating of the living bread,
- keeping them from loving each other,
- keeping them from loving the Holy Family
- keeping them from the true church
- keeping them from repenting as the Lord has desired
- keeping them from believing the Word of God and so much more.

Seek Love! May the love of Jesus and Mary fill our hearts.

> *In this way it is clear who are the children of God and who are the children of the Evil One;* ***anyone who does not do righteousness or who has no love for his brother, is NOT A CHILD OF GOD.*** <u>1John 3:10 BBE</u>

> *Now I beseech you, brethren, by the name of our Lord Jesus Christ, that **ye all speak the same thing**, and that there be **no divisions among you;** but that **ye be perfectly joined together in the same mind and in the same judgment.***
> <u>1 Cor 1:10-13 KJV</u>

> *For who hath known the mind of the Lord, that he may instruct him? But **we have the mind of Christ**.* <u>1 Cor 2:16 KJV</u>

Come back home to the Roman Catholic Church, where the Lion's Den will form, and the Army of God will be made whole. Let us love one another even unto death! There is no greater love! Eat of the bread of life, partake! Pray the Rosary it provides protection and pleases the Lord and Our Blessed Mother when we say it.

May Our Savior Reign and take His Throne on earth! Amen.

Prayer: Lord, give us a great love for Mother Mary. Teach us about her. Help us to obey her as you obeyed her. Help us to protect the name of Mary and allow us to be part of the Holy Family, Your Family. Make us pure, holy, and make our hearts like hers. Allow us to be fit for You, Our King. Give to us the zeal to proclaim the Holy Family as our own. Make us to do all that you desire. Make us worthy and loving servants. We desire to die in pure love for the sake of love, of which she was full. Take away any earthly fear that keeps us from you. Our hope is in You. We believe you will shower us with the graces that you have promised for Your Glory!

Father of Prestige and Highest Rank, Most Humble, Most Loving, Most Considerate, Most Kind, God of Goodness beyond understanding, Our Creator, We love you. We Exalt you. We adore You. We honor you. We believe. Teach us to Love Mary as you love her and fill us with your grace. In Jesus Name. Amen

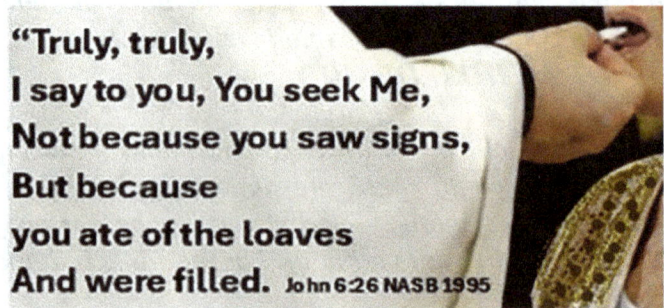

Why Was Jesus Silent in Front of The Courts?

*"In Humiliation His Judgment Was Taken Away;
Who will relate to His generation?* Ac 8:33 KJV

The great virtue of Humility comes through humiliation. We must be humble and willing to be humiliated so that we may be like Him. In our humiliation our judgment will be taken away obtaining the great virtue of humility.

Who has ever wondered why Jesus remained silent while everyone was mocking and condemning him?

Consider this as a small measure of the possibility for that reason. Example: The boss, the manager and the worker:

The worker after having discussed a situation with the manager, who was not willing to assume their responsibilities in authority, denied the truth of their conversation to the boss, who gave her that authority. She did not want to get herself in trouble.

Realizing that for those who are dishonest, "saving face" is more important. Their vain glory is everything to them, the devil is their master. Putting ourself "in Jesus" We can realize what the worker did: The worker caused the manager to lie and therefore sin.

As children of Our Lord, we must prefer to be meek and humble and let whatever comes our way to be for the Glory of God. We must not argue or make an unnecessary stand, remaining silent even if they are wrong, Jesus is our example.

We must ask the Lord for grace to remain in His Light and to lead us in response to every situation.

The worker caused the manager to sin in defense of themself.

Jesus remained silent in the courts to prevent us from getting deeper into our mischief and stop us from continuing to sin in that moment.

The following was taken from the book *Divine Mercy in My Soul* by Saint Maria Faustina Kowalska:

477 Silence is a sword in the spiritual struggle. A talkative soul will never attain sanctity. The sword of silence will cut off everything that would like to cling to the soul. We are sensitive to words and quickly want to answer back, without taking any regard as to whether it is God's will that we should speak. A silent soul is strong; no adversities will harm it if it perseveres in silence. The silent (198) soul is capable of attaining the closest union with God. It lives almost always under the inspiration of the Holy Spirit. God works in a silent soul without hindrance.

478 O my Jesus, You know, You alone know well that my heart knows no other love but You! All my virginal love is drowned eternally in You, O Jesus! I sense keenly how Your divine Blood is circulating in my heart; I have not the least doubt that Your most pure love has entered my heart with Your most sacred Blood. I am aware that You are dwelling in me, together with the Father and the Holy Spirit, or rather I am aware that it is I who I am living in You, O incomprehensible God! I am aware that I am dissolving in You like a drop in an ocean. I am aware that You are within me and all about me, that You are in all things that surround me, in all that happens to me. O my God, I have come to know You within my heart, and I have loved You above all things that exist on earth or in heaven. Our hearts have a mutual understanding, and no one of humankind will comprehend this.

Let us pray that we may also become blessed and crave, thirst, and desperately seek the love of God so that we also may learn to live where love is.

HOW GREAT IS THE MERCY OF OUR LORD?

For judgment will be merciless to one who has shown no mercy; MERCY TRIUMPHS OVER JUDGMENT.
Jas 2:13 NASB 1995

Blessed are the merciful: for they shall obtain mercy.
Mat 5:7 KJV

And so all Israel shall be saved: as it is written,
...they are enemies for your sakes: but,
... they are beloved for the fathers' sakes
.... Even so have these also now not believed, that
THROUGH YOUR MERCY *THEY ALSO MAY OBTAIN MERCY. For God hath concluded them all in unbelief, that he might have mercy upon all.* Ro 11:26-32 KJV

    The Lord is great in measure, so immeasurable we cannot begin to understand its capacity. His Love, His compassion, His Kindness, the Goodness of His very being, are all enormously and immeasurably grand!

    His Mercy is just as grand and enormously immeasurable as His love! We must also desire to be unconditionally merciful. In <u>Romans 11:26-32</u>, the Lord is saying **that if WE** are merciful to the unbelievers and to the merciless, they will be saved too! **There is Hope** for those we may have judged as hopeless including the living and the dead. We must pray and plead for them! Pray for the dead!

    These are the elect, those who are willing to die innocently for the love of the guilty. Be as He is, Sow and He sows, Love as He Loves!

    We are all sinners, one word spoken in condemnation towards another causes many others to sin. Therefore, we become the source of that sin multiplied. We must confess doubt. We must use sackcloth and ashes.

He is our teacher! His will, His way, His Light, His Truth... not ours!

    Stumbling blocks of darkness keep us from being the soul of fervent prayer.

The Lord's Mercy is so great. He is like a pregnant woman giving birth, waiting to burst out his mercy on everyone. If we would have even a little bit of understanding of His merciful kindness, goodness, and His great unconditional love we would want to urgently go and confess, to be full of light; sin brings darkness and darkness torments us. John 1:5-11 says that we would not receive Him, we did not comprehend. We are still rebels attached to Satan's kingdom and continue to refuse Him.

Praise the Lord, for His Mercy endures forever.
Exalted is Our Great Loving Bread of Life!

The following was taken from the book <u>Divine Mercy in My Soul</u> by Saint Maria Faustina Kowalska:

Today the Lord said to me, **Daughter, when you go to confession, to this fountain of My mercy, the Blood and Water which came forth from My Heart always flows down upon your soul and ennobles it. Every time you go to confession, immerse yourself in My mercy, with great trust, so that I may pour the bounty of My grace upon your soul. When you approach the confessional, know this, that I Myself am waiting there for you. I am only hidden by the priest, but I myself act in your soul. Here the misery of the soul meets the God of mercy. Tell souls that from this fount of mercy (7) souls draw graces solely with the vessel of trust. If their trust is great, there is no limit to My generosity. The torrents of grace inundate humble souls. The proud remain always in poverty and misery, because My grace turns away from them to humble souls.** (1602) **My daughter, just as you prepare in My presence, so also you make your confession before Me. The person of the priest is, for Me, only a screen. Never analyze what sort of a (89) priest it is that I am making use of; open your soul in confession as you would to Me, and I will fill it with My light.** (1725)

You will prepare the world for My final coming. (429)
Speak to the world about My mercy; ... It is a sign for the end times; after it will come (230) the day of justice. While there is still time, let them have recourse to the fountain of My mercy; (848) ...tell souls about this great mercy of Mine, because the awful day, the day of My justice, is near. (965). I am prolonging the time of mercy for the sake of [sinners]. But woe to them if they do not recognize this time of My visitation. (1160)
Before the Day of Justice, I am sending the Day of Mercy. (1588)

He who refuses to pass through the door of My mercy must pass through the door of My justice. (Diary 1146).

...you have to speak to the world about His great mercy and prepare the world for the Second (91) Coming of Him who will come, not as a merciful Savior, but as a just Judge. Oh how terrible is that day! Determined is the day of justice, the day of divine wrath. The angels tremble before it. Speak to souls about this great mercy while it is still the time for granting mercy. (Diary 635).

I beg you, my beloved reader, please repent. Be merciful and love unconditionally! I, a terrible sinner who continues to repent ask it of you, because I love you. You do not know the love of God unless you repent! Yet, I still do not know it in full, but I desire it.

Trust in Jesus! Pray with your whole heart, mind, soul, and strength. Meditate on His life and passion and that of the Holy Family where we find many answers. Trust Jesus even unto death!

WHO SHOULD WE TRUST?

Trust in Jesus! Trust in the Lord with all your heart, mind, and soul.

Trust in the LORD with all your heart and do not lean on your own understanding. Pr 3:5 NASB

The graces of My mercy are drawn by means of one vessel only, and that is — trust. The more a soul trusts, the more it will receive. 1578 (Jesus spoke this to Sr Faustina)

Our Lord said you are a slave to those whom you choose to obey as stated in *Romans 6:16*. We are not isolated to these occurrences and beliefs. The Lord also says to trust no man, **trust NO mortal man in whom there is no salvation.** To those who are running the race, loving unconditionally let us then submit to the Lord and bring Him down to earth, Our Lord, our stronghold in whom we trust, that He may deliver us from evil, even unto death! We must gather!

²Who will provide me, in the wilderness, with a lodging place along the road? And then I will forsake my people, and withdraw from them. For they are all adulterers, a union of transgressors. ³ And they have bent their tongue, like a bow, to send forth lies and not the truth. They have been strengthened upon the earth. ***And they have gone from one evil to another. But they have not known me, says the Lord.*** *⁴ Let each one guard himself against his neighbor, and let him* ***have no trust in any brother of his. For every brother will utterly overthrow, and every friend will advance deceitfully.*** *⁵And a man will deride his brother, and they will not speak the truth. For they have taught their tongue to speak lies; they have labored to commit iniquity. ⁶ Your habitation is in the midst of deceit.* ***In their deceitfulness, they have refused to know me, says the Lord.****" ⁷ Because of this, thus says the Lord of hosts: "Behold, I will refine them, and I will test them. For what else can I do before the face of the daughter of my people?*

⁸Their tongue is a wounding arrow; it has spoken deceit. **With his mouth, he speaks peace with his friend, and then he secretly lies in ambush for him.** *⁹ Shall I not visit upon them concerning these things, says the Lord? Or shall my soul not take vengeance on a nation of this kind?*
Jer 9:1-9 CPDVTSB

It is better to take refuge in the LORD **Than to trust in man.** Ps 118:8 NASB 1995

Do not trust *in princes,* **in mortal man,** *in whom there is no salvation.* Ps 146:3 NASB 1995

How blessed is the man who has made the LORD his trust, And has not turned to the proud, nor to those who lapse into falsehood. Ps 40:4 NASB 1995

"Blessed is the man who trusts in the LORD **And whose trust is the LORD.** Jer 17:7 NASB 1995

In God I will praise his word, **in God I have put my trust;** *I will not fear what flesh can do unto me.* Ps 56:4 KJV

But we had the sentence of death in ourselves, **that we should not trust in ourselves, but in God** *which raiseth the dead:* 2 Cor 1:9 KJV

And again, "I WILL PUT MY TRUST IN HIM." and again, "Behold, I and the children which God has given me."
Heb 2:13 KJV

A wise man scales the city of the mighty **And brings down the stronghold in which they trust.** Pr 21:22 NASB 1995

The image of the Divine Mercy has the words imprinted upon it "Jesus I Trust in You! It is those same words we must imprint in our minds, in our hearts and in our whole being without reserve. **Jesus, I Trust in you!**

WHY IS THE DIVINE MERCY CHAPLET SO IMPORTANT?

For judgment will be merciless to one who has shown no mercy; ***MERCY TRIUMPHS OVER JUDGMENT.***
Jas 2:13 NASB 1995

In 1933, God gave Sister Faustina a striking vision of His Mercy; Sister tells us:
…I saw a great radiance and, in the midst of it, God the Father. Between this radiance and the earth I saw Jesus, nailed to the Cross and in such a way that when God wanted to look at the earth, He had to look through the wounds of Jesus. And I understood that it was for the sake of Jesus that God blesses the earth." (Diary 60)

Of another vision on Sept. 13, 1935, she writes:
....I saw an Angel, the executor of divine wrath... about to strike the earth...I found myself pleading with (197) God for the world with words heard interiorly. As I was praying in this manner, I saw the Angel's helplessness; he could not carry out the just punishment.... (Diary 474)

Our Lord said to Saint Faustina:
…encourage souls to say the chaplet which I have given to you.1541 ... Whoever will recite it will receive great mercy at the hour of death. 687... When they say this chaplet in the presence of the dying, I will stand between my Father and the dying person, not as the Just Judge but as the Merciful Savior 1541... Priests will recommend it to sinners as their last hope of salvation. Even if there were a sinner most hardened, if he were to recite this Chaplet only once, he would receive grace from my infinite mercy…. I desire to grant unimaginable graces to those souls who trust in My mercy 687... Through the Chaplet you will obtain everything, if what you ask for is compatible with My will. 1731

THE CHAPLET OF DIVINE MERCY

Using ordinary rosary beads of five decades, pray as follows:
1. Begin with the Sign of the Cross,
2. Opening Prayers
    You expired, Jesus, but the source of life gushed forth for souls, and the ocean of mercy opened up for the whole world. O Fount of Life, unfathomable Divine Mercy, envelop the whole world and empty Yourself out upon us.
    Repeat three times:
    O Blood and Water, which gushed forth from the Heart of Jesus as a fountain of Mercy for us, I trust in You!
    1 Our Father, 1 Hail Mary and The Apostles Creed.

3. Then on the Our Father Beads say the following:
    Eternal Father, I offer You the Body and Blood, Soul and Divinity of Your dearly beloved Son, Our Lord Jesus Christ, in atonement for our sins and those of the whole world.

4. On the 10 Hail Mary Beads say the following:
    For the sake of His sorrowful Passion, have mercy on us and on the whole world.

    (Repeat step 3 and 4 for remaining four decades).

5. Conclude with (three times):
    Holy God, Holy Mighty One, Holy Immortal One, have mercy on us and on the whole world.

Optional Closing Prayer
Eternal God, in whom mercy is endless and the treasury of compassion -- inexhaustible, look kindly upon us and increase Your mercy in us, that in difficult moments we might not despair nor become despondent, but with great confidence submit ourselves to Your holy will, which is Love and Mercy itself.

End with the sign of the cross.

HOW CAN WE STOP WAR?

What is the source of quarrels and conflicts among you? Is not the source your pleasures that wage war in your members? <u>Jas 4:1 NASB 1995</u>

My loved ones, I make this request with all my heart, that, as those for whom this world is a strange country, you will keep yourselves from the desires of the flesh which make war against the soul; <u>1Peter 2:11 BBE</u>

For when we were in the flesh, the evil passions which came into being through the law were working in our bodies to give the fruit of death. <u>Ro 7:5 BBE</u>

And they that are Christ's have crucified the flesh with the affections and lusts. <u>Ga 5:24 KJV</u>

It is important to realize that every battle is not an earthly battle, it is not of human flesh; it is a spiritual battle. It is demons occupying the vessel of clay, flesh, in which people have chosen their master. The flesh is a prison, it must be confined. Every battle, every argument, is not initiated by the Lord! God is love and peace. He says to overcome evil with good.

Do not be overcome by evil, but overcome evil with good. Romans 12:21 NKJV

We must ask the Holy Spirit to take control of our lives so that we may empty ourselves of all evil. We must give our free will to the Lord. Padre Pio said the free will is the door in which Satan enters. We must submit ourselves to the Lord.

⁵⁵ But he turned, and rebuked them, and said, Ye know not what manner of spirit ye are of.
⁵⁶ For the Son of man is not come to destroy men's lives, but to save them. <u>Luke 9:55-56 KJV</u>

We must remember the life of Christ which we are to imitate and live to become like Him. They are **Each Unconditional: "love, mercy, forgiveness and repentance."**

The Lord said that those who live by the sword will die by the sword. The battle is not ours, and the Lord does not want us to fight in the way humans fight. He wants to fight the battle for us. Choose your Father, God vs Satan! Choose your sword, the Word of God!

> *the sword of the Spirit, which is the word of God.* _{Eph 6:17 KJV}

> **Repent;** *or else I will come unto thee quickly, and will fight against them with the sword of my mouth.* _{Rev 2:16 KJV}

> *He that leadeth into captivity shall go into captivity: he that killeth with the sword must be killed with the sword. Here is the patience and the faith of the saints.* _{Re 13:10 KJV}

Speak the Word of God in defense of His love and mercy. His Word is spirit and is life. Our God, Our Creator is the only authority of life and death, and these rights are His alone. Therefore, if we die we are the Lord's, and if we live, we are His still.

> *or whether we live, we live unto the Lord; and whether we die, we die unto the Lord: whether we live therefore, or die, we are the Lord's.* _{Ro 14:8 KJV}

It is better to die for the love of another than to die by the carnal weapon. The Lord tells us to love our enemies. The world in war with itself, does not listen. The world delighting and indulging in sin suffers much because it has not believed the word of God. It suffers because it continues to ignore the message of repentance, mercy, unconditional love, forgiveness, and unity.

Those who know Our Lord, Our Father and Our Heavenly Mother know that He is truly good. His ways are unfathomable in every characteristic of the fruits of the Holy Spirit in mercy, love, compassion, kindness, longsuffering, meekness and in all that He is. He is beyond measure all goodness beyond our understanding.

We must practice unconditional love and righteousness or at least desire it; He will help us though all things and hear our prayers. We must desire to obey by repenting and gathering.

Can we drop our weapons and say to our opponent, we will die so that their soul may be saved because we want to love them as Jesus loves them. He died for us and has saved us from our evil ways. All that we have, we have been given from above, we cannot take it with us when we die. We must not let anything on this earth keep us from the love of God.

He is our perfect example, Our Sheppard. His sheep know Him and hear his voice and follow Him.

LOVE and RIGHTEOUSNESS

27 But I say to you who are listening:
Love your enemies. Do good to those who hate you.
28 Bless those who curse you, and pray for those who slander you. 29 And to him who strikes you on the cheek, offer the other also. And from him who takes away your coat, do not withhold even your tunic. 30 But distribute to all who ask of you. And do not ask again of him who takes away what is yours. 31 And exactly as you would want people to treat you, treat them also the same.
32 And if you love those who love you, what credit is due to you? For even sinners love those who love them. 33 And if you will do good to those who do good to you, what credit is due to you? Indeed, even sinners behave this way. 34 And if you will loan to those from whom you hope to receive, what credit is due to you? For even sinners lend to sinners, in order to receive the same in return. 35 So truly, love your enemies. Do good, and lend, hoping for nothing in return. And then your reward will be great, and you will be sons of the Most High, for he himself is kind to the ungrateful and to the wicked. 36 Therefore, BE MERCIFUL, JUST AS YOUR FATHER IS ALSO MERCIFUL. Luke 6:27-36 CPDVTSB

We must desire to Love God first and allow Him to change us, transform us in His great love and mercy so that we also may be love and mercy and all that He is. We must desire to repent and clear ourselves of demons that persistently continue to try to steal, devour, and destroy our souls. We must be persistent and fervent in our desire to seek the Lord rebuking, resisting and renouncing Satan and all his works. We must pray more fervently and fast humbling ourselves before the Lord that He may possess us entirely so that we may do His will. We must repent to take the log out of our own eye!

> *You hypocrite, first take the log out of your own eye, and then you will see clearly to take the speck out of your brother's eye.* Mat 7:5 NASB 1995

> *Then you will call, and the LORD will answer;*
> *You will cry, and He will say, `Here I am.'*
> *If you remove the yoke from your midst, The pointing of the finger and speaking wickedness,* Isa 58:9 NASB 1995

VICTORY AT WAR
> *[17]But when they saw the army coming against them, they said to Judas: "How can we, few as we are, fight such a strong host as this? Besides, **we are weak since we have not eaten today.**" [18]But Judas said: "Many are easily hemmed in by a few; IN THE SIGHT OF HEAVEN THERE IS NO DIFFERENCE BETWEEN DELIVERANCE BY MANY OR BY FEW; [19]for victory in war does not depend upon the size of the army, BUT ON STRENGTH THAT COMES FROM HEAVEN.* 1 Maccabees 3:17-19 NAB

WOW!!! that is powerful!!!!! Today, there is such little faith. Let us change our hearts and simply BELIEVE!

Our Blessed Mother continues to tell us to pray the Rosary, it is a weapon against Satan. He hates it!!! It must be said with our whole heart, mind, soul, and strength to please the Lord. The Hail Mary is the call to heaven, sowing to reap, returning to Heaven those glorious living words of birth. The birth of our union with God. It is a remembrance of a moment of ONE. We must ask the Lord for the grace to pray fervently and righteously. We must repent, fast and pray so that we may obtain that strength that comes from heaven.

Let us stand firm, put down our weapons and say to them that choose the sword, "yes, we are willing to die so that their soul may be saved." Can we follow Jesus?

Who has that kind of faith? Who has that love? Who will trust in Jesus, our perfect example? Who will give everything up knowing that only Our God is above all gods, and He loves us? Who knows that He desires for all to be saved, the living and the dead? Who knows that Our Father in Heaven will be the one to determine whether we live or die and how? No man can change that! To whom do we submit? We must surrender to the way of Love in which Jesus came to teach us, to show us and to demonstrate for us. We must be willing to follow Him, so that we may be like Him.

> *[15] And the prayer of faith shall save the sick, and the Lord shall raise him up; and if he have committed sins, they shall be forgiven him. [16] Confess your faults one to another, and pray one for another, that ye may be healed. The effectual fervent prayer of a righteous man availeth much.*
> James 5:15-16 KJV

> *And we know that the Son of God is come, and hath given us an understanding, that we may know him that is true, and we are in him that is true, even in his Son Jesus Christ. This is the true God, and eternal life.* 1John 5:20 KJV

> *Greater love hath no man than this,*
> *that a man lay down his life for his friends.* John 15:13 KJV

In the Poem of a Man God Vol I page 156, the precept of the Lord is revealed in regard to war:
But Jesus takes the opportunity to speak to the children:
« **He is right. War is a punishment of God to chastise men, and it is a sign that man is no longer a true son of God.** *When the Most High created the world, He made all things: the sun, the sea, the stars, the rivers, the plants, the*

*animals, but He did not make arms. He created man and gave him eyes that he might cast loving glances, and a mouth to utter loving words, and ears to listen to such words, and hands to give help and to caress, and feet to run fast to assist our neighbors in need, and a heart capable of loving. He gave man intelligence, speech, affections and taste. But He did not give man hatred. Why? Because man**, a creature of God, was to be love as God is Love.** If man had remained a creature of God, he would have persevered in love, and the human family would have not known either war or death. »*

« But he does not want to make war, because he always loses. » (I had guessed right.)

Jesus smiles and says: « We must not reprove what is harmful to us simply because it is harmful to us. We must reprove a thing when it is harmful to everybody. If a person says: "I do not want that because I would lose", that person is selfish. Instead, the good child of God says: "Brothers, I know I would win, but I say to you: don't let us do that because you would suffer a loss". Oh! That fellow has understood the main precept! Who can tell Me which is the main precept? »

The eleven mouths say all together: « **"You shall love your God with all your strength, and your neighbor as yourself."** »

Who Will Listen to the Life Saving Commands of The Lord?

Life Saving Commands and Messages:
SMEAR YOUR DOOR WITH THE BLOOD OF THE LAMB!
Yes, this was the command of the Lord to save the lives of His people during the times of Pharaoh.

DO NOT LOOK BACK OR YOU WILL TURN INTO STONE!
This was the Lord's command at Sodom and Gomorrah.

BUILD AN ARK He said to Noah.
These messages were given by Our Father God in Heaven, the Great I AM, the Father of Abraham, lifesaving commands. No Bible, nothing written at the time, except in the heart of the believer, trusting the messenger of God.

UNLESS YOU REPENT, YOU SHALL LIKEWISE PERISH
Luke 13:3 NASB 1995

This message was given by Our Lord Jesus Christ while on earth, and His cousin John the Baptist and the apostles even after the death of Jesus Christ!
Repent or you will surely die. Every knee shall bow, every tongue shall confess! By confessing we are given the grace of increased light. We are given the grace to believe! Believing increases faith!

He is the Light of the world. We must desperately desire to be filled with His Light! It was divine inspiration, telling the believer what to say or do. "Who is it today that says "show me in the bible where it says that?" They have no faith and are full of doubt. They do not know Our Heavenly Father. They have not repented.

> *As I live, saith the Lord GOD, I have no pleasure in the death of the wicked; but that the wicked turn from his way*

*and live: turn ye, **turn ye from your evil ways**; for why will ye die, O house of Israel?* _{Eze 33:11 KJV}

*See that you **do not reject the one who speaks**. For if they did not escape when they refused the one who warned them on earth, how much more in our case if we turn away from **the one who warns from heaven**.*
_{Heb 12:25 NAB}

"I Have Come To Tell The World That God Exists. He Is The Fullness Of Life, And
TO ENJOY THIS FULLNESS AND PEACE, YOU MUST RETURN TO GOD."
_{Message from Our Lady of Medjugorje}

Today this is the message from the Mother of God, whom Jesus needed and so do we. Return To God! Pray! Love! Forgive! She encourages us to **obey Jesus and turn away from sin**. She speaks of the wickedness in this world and says that we bring catastrophe upon ourselves. It is a reflection of our sinfulness, it is darkness. Love and love will reflect; hate and hate will reflect. Jesus clearly said you reap what you sow. She comes crying and with much sorrow, to warn us, we must return to God, Love Him first above all things and even unto death. We must pray continuously. The following are three of her messages at Medjugorje (current messages can be viewed on their website)

Message of January 25, 2005
*"Dear children! In this time of grace again I call you to prayer. **Pray, little children, for unity of Christians, that all may be one heart**. Unity will really be among you inasmuch as you will pray and forgive. Do not forget: love will conquer only if you pray, and your heart will open. Thank you for having responded to my call."*

Message of February 25, 2005
"Dear children! Today I call you to be my extended hands in this world that puts God in the last place. You, little

*children, **put God in the first place in your life**. God will bless you and give you strength to bear witness to Him, the God of love and peace. I am with you and intercede for all of you. Little children, do not forget that I love you with a tender love. Thank you for having responded to my call."*

***Message of February 25, 2023**,*
Dear children!
*Keep converting and **clothe yourselves in penitential garments** and in personal, deep prayer; and in humility, seek peace from the Most High. In this time of grace, Satan wants to seduce you; but you, little children, keep looking at my Son and **follow Him** towards Calvary in **renunciation and fasting**. I am with you because the Most High permits me to love you and lead you towards the joy of the heart, in faith which grows for all those who love God above all.*
Thank you for having responded to my call.

Loving Mary

The Bible tells us that No One comes to the Father except through Jesus. However, knowing that the Lord commands and sends messages to the hearts of the men who believe and love Him, Jesus also said these words:

In <u>The Mystical City of God</u>, Vol. III p. 765 it states:
Just as I have told you, that he who sees Me sees my Father, and he who knows Me, knows also Him; **so, I now tell you, that He who knows my Mother, knows Me**; he who hears Her, hears Me; and who honors Her, honors Me. All of you shall have her as your Mother, as your Superior and Head, and so shall also your successors.

How can we even begin to think, that Loving Jesus alone is enough. If we want to live with our heavenly family, we must love them all. We must love her greatly! She is the vessel He used to unite Himself to this world. The WORD Became FLESH through her and in her. She is the vessel the world needs to unite itself to

Him. We need her, the one whom God Himself chose to need. Perhaps, Mary is the Bride in us. Blessed is she whose soul magnifies the Lord; may our soul be like hers. We must ask her into our hearts, into our life, so that Jesus will also receive us with as great a love as hers toward Him. The Word is God, the God of impossibilities. We must desire to be One with the Father, One with Jesus, One with the Holy Spirit, One with Mary Mother of God and one with each other. The Lord desires that we will all be one.

> *^{20}"I do not pray for these alone, but also for those who will believe in Me through their word; ^{21}that they all may be one, as You, Father are in Me, and I in You; **that they also may be one in Us**, that the world may believe that You sent me."*
> John 17:20-21

REGARDING PROPHECIES:
Three Days Of Darkness Prophecy

Only Beeswax Candles Blessed By Priests (Descendants Of Apostles) Will Give Light while the faithful pray, especially the Rosary of Life-Giving Grace. They will not light for the wicked during **the three days of darkness**, they must repent or they will perish. Wear your scapular!

> *^{39}But He answered and said to them, "An evil and adulterous generation craves a sign; and so no sign will be given to it except the sign of Jonah the prophet; ^{40}for just as Jonah was in the stomach of the sea monster for three days and three nights, **so will the Son of Man be in the heart of the earth for three days and THREE NIGHTS**. ^{41}The men of Nineveh will stand up with this generation at the judgement, and will condemn it because they repented at the preaching of Jonah; and behold, something greater than Jonah is here.* Mat 12:39-41

The Glorious Return

> *^{29}"But immediately after the tribulation of those days **The Sun Will Be Darkened, And The Moon Will Not Give Its Light, And The Stars Will Fall from the sky,** and the powers of the heavens will be shaken. ^{30}"And then the sign*

> *of the Son of Man will appear in the sky, and then all the tribes of the earth will mourn, and they will see the SON OF MAN COMING ON THE CLOUDS OF THE SKY with power and great glory.* Mat 24:24-30 NASB 1995

The three days of darkness as mentioned in the Bible and other remedies have been prophesied for end of times by many saints and prophets throughout the centuries. Whether the prophesies are true only God knows. They seem believable. However, looking at the above scripture Mat 12:39 it says three days and three nights, so it could mean three normal days, however, in the mouth of a whale would indicate darkness during the day too. Darkness is also mentioned in the book of Revelations and other parts of the bible. Not sure if it is specifically mentioned as three days of darkness. Mat 24:29-30 does mention total darkness but does not mention three days. In any case, realizing that men everywhere need to repent, because they are not sons of God, it gives more reason to question all prophesies. Even the Lord said that the elect need to be alert so as not to be fooled by the devil in disguise. We do know that if we prepare, repent, and follow Jesus, none of this should matter, therefore, repent and gather.

Garibaldi Warning Prophecy

Our Blessed Mother at Garibaldi in Spain told the visionaries that there will be a warning, a miracle, and the chastisement. The warning will be experienced by all, no matter what religion. People will wish they were dead but will not die, it will be an awakening. They will see their souls as God sees them. Perhaps the following scripture relates to the Garibaldi warning:

> *Therefore do not go on passing judgment before the time, but wait until the Lord comes who will both bring to light the things hidden in the darkness and disclose the motives of men's hearts; and then each man's praise will come to him from God.* 1Cor 4:5 NASB 1995

> *Do not let anyone deceive you in any way, for it will not come* [the coming of the Lord] *unless* **the rebellion takes**

***place first** and the man of sin, who is destined for destruction, is revealed.* 2Thessalonians 2:3 ISV

Hopefully the hearts of men will change if the Garibaldi warning does occur. Let's rephrase that: Hopefully the hearts of men will change because they desire to repent and Love the Holy Family, today and now. 2Thess 2:3 is proof that we must gather and rebel in the kingdom of Satan, as sinners, we are Rebels for Christ.

Food For End of Times Prophecy

This remedy was given by a woman who had the stigmata, Marie Julie Jahenny. The Miraculous Sustaining Grapes are grapes whose blessing has been transferred from the original to the new ones. One grape a day will sustain the people of Our Lord. It is said that the original grapes came from the mission fields of a little village from where St. Francis of Assisi lived. They must be prepared a certain way for the blessing to take effect.

Even today, people are concerned with what we are to do for food in the times of shortage or during the antichrist reign? Can we trust that the Lord will provide? How many people will believe? How many will have faith? How many will repent for Blaspheming the Mother of God? How many will believe her messages? How many will repent even at the last second - proclaiming sorrow with their whole heart, mind, and soul? How many will repent desiring to be reconciled one to another, desiring to remove barriers of division, fearing to be separated from Our Great Lord, who demonstrated such great forgiveness removing all barriers? How many will pray for wisdom, knowledge, and understanding out of desperation? We must trust that the Lord will lead us to do what is necessary. We must believe that the Lord will provide! We must gather!

In any case, we already know we must prepare for His coming. We must do as continuously mentioned in this book. Desire to be Perfect as Our Father is Perfect, Be Perfect as Mary Our Mother is Perfect. Desire an immaculate heart. Desire to rejoice in the Lord. Hope that our soul magnifies the Lord. The Lord said that corruption shall put on incorruption and mortality, immortality. He can do anything, we must believe it possible. Pray your rosaries, wear your scapular, repent in sackcloth, these are our defenses.

The following scripture is worth contemplating:

³⁰"Repent and turn away from all your transgressions, so that iniquity may not become a stumbling block to you. ³¹"Cast away from you all your transgressions which you have committed and make yourselves a new heart and a new spirit! For why will you die, O house of Israel?
Eze 18:30-31 NASB 1995

TODAY THIS IS THE MESSAGE:

We must divide the kingdom of Satan! Trust Jesus Christ Our Loving Warrior! Our Victor! **It is of utmost importance that all believers in Christ GATHER** and form the Army of God. As Satan rebelled in the heavens, we must rebel on earth, Satan's kingdom. We are Rebels for Christ and must start the rebellion.

³⁰The one who is not with Me is against Me; and the one who does not gather with Me scatters Mat 12:30 NASB

This is a Call to Arms! Love, pray, fast, repent, and unite!

WHAT IS THE SIGN OF JONAH?

THE STORY OF JONAH SUMMARIZED

Watching an animated movie, the story of Jonah was as follows: Jonah had a dream. The Lord wanted him to preach repentance in Nineveh, a wicked city. Jonah did not like what he saw in his dream and did not want to obey the Lord. He got on a boat going in the opposite direction from Nineveh. The captain of the boat and his crew laughed at him, believing he was running away from his wife. They began the journey, only to find themselves in a great storm. The captain and the crew were frightened fearing their death. They apparently were men of God, obedient and of great faith, ready to offer their first fruits to Our Lord. In fear of their life, the crew threw everything overboard as an offering to the Lord to appease his anger. The storm continued. The captain told the crew to get Jonah who was below deck. They wanted him to pray to his God for the safety of the crew. They brought Jonah and decided to cast lots to determine to whom the Lord was displaying his anger. The lot pointed at Jonah. Jonah told them to throw him overboard and that the storm would calm. The captain, a good man, did not want to do that. However, the storm continued and there was no other option. They asked the Lord to forgive them and threw him overboard. Jonah was then swallowed by a great fish in whose belly he remained for three days. Jonah repented and vowed to the Lord, that if he would save him, he would preach repentance as the Lord had asked. The fish spit him out on land. Jonah did as he promised.

Jonah went to the city of Nineveh, and was preaching repentance. Three men that heard Jonah went to the king and told the King that Jonah was preaching that all must repent or the Lord would destroy the whole city in a day. The king knowing that Jonah was a true prophet, **tore off his clothes and put on sackcloth and sat in ashes. He then made a decree that the whole city PEOPLE AND ANIMALS do the same**.

After having preached Jonah went out of the city to high ground where he could view the city. In the heat of the sun, he waited, became frustrated, and angry that there was no sign of destruction.

The Lord then allowed a huge tree to grow in a day. Jonah was happy because the Lord provided shade for him. That night the Lord allowed worms to eat the tree. The next day Jonah was angry that the tree was gone and he was once again in the hot burning sun. The Lord asked "Have you any right to be angry about the tree?" Jonah said he was angry to the point of death.

The Lord said it is only one tree for which Jonah did not toil. Yet he wanted the Lord to destroy a city that listened to his preaching that has repented.

The Lord told Jonah I AM A MERCIFUL GOD; MY PEOPLE HAVE REPENTED AND SO DO I REPENT." I love my people, hundreds of thousands who have listened to your message of repentance are saved because they have repented.

The Sign of Jonah is the resulting salvation of the people and the beasts (animals) through true bitter repentance with the use of sackcloth and ashes.

In Matthew 12:41 it clearly states that we will be condemned by the men of Nineveh, in THIS GENERATION at the JUDGEMENT because they repented at the preaching of Jonah implying that we did not repent properly.

Today's message is this: We must repent using sackcloth and ashes; if we do not repent the Lord will destroy the earth and everything in it as noted in the Book of Revelations; Repent, it is for the Lord and for the salvation of all.

> The men of Nineveh **will stand up with this generation at the judgment, and will condemn** it because they repented at the preaching of Jonah Mat 12:41 NASB

In _Matthew 11:21_ and _Luke 10:13_ we are reminded that if Tyre and Sidon would have done what we have done, **"they would have repented long ago, sitting in sackcloth and ashes."**

> Woe unto thee, Chorazin! woe unto thee, Bethsaida! for if the mighty works, which were done in you, had been done in

Tyre and Sidon, **they would have repented long ago in sackcloth and ashes**. <u>Matthew 11:21 KJV</u>

There is much to learn from the story of Jonah. The most important is, to repent using sackcloth and ashes both for people and animals. The Lord mentions in the New Testament that the only sign we will see is the sign of Jonah and the men of Nineveh will condemn us, at our judgement, because we did not repent. Apparently, the Lord acknowledges their actions of using sackcloth and ashes and so should we.

We can only wonder why we must use sackcloth in this age and time when very few use it. The revelation given, as best understood at this time, is that it provides a clearance to the heavens and direct communication to God. It is not a luxury item, it is not soft, comfy or lush. We must wail and morn and repent, releasing ourselves from the attachments we have had to Satan and his evil spirits. The sackcloth is like our telephone to heaven, but more than that. Since we cannot escape sin, we can escape this earth momentarily by using sackcloth, the devil hates it.

The story has several other lessons for us to reflect upon. The crew was willing to give their all and offer it to the Lord by throwing everything overboard. This is a demonstration of detachment to the things of this world and acknowledging the Lord in all our actions. They prayed, had faith, and trusted the Lord to calm the storm, because of their actions. This is also a demonstration of taking the first step in faith, when the captain threw Jonah overboard, calming the seas; and then again when the people repented, saving their city. Here we see that God Himself repented by not destroying the city.

This is also a demonstration of the timeline the Lord demonstrates throughout the Bible. This timeline is different from what preachers teach. It is a timeline of taking the first step in faith. The people repented and then the Lord responded. And the lesson here is that we, today, must take the first step in faith by repenting and gathering the army of God while in prayer, fasting and trusting God. The result of our actions is to allow Jesus Christ Our Warrior to fight our battle and not let the gates of hell prevail as He has promised.

(The measure you use is the measure you are measured with)

FIRST PEOPLE REPENTED **THEN GOD REPENTED!**

*But he answered and said unto them,
An evil and adulterous generation seeketh after a sign;
and there shall **no sign be given to it,**
but the sign of the prophet Jonas*: Matthew 12:39 KJV

*And I will give power unto my two witnesses,
and they shall prophesy a thousand two hundred and threescore days,* **clothed in sackcloth**. Revelation 11:3 KJV

WHAT IS AND HOW TO USE SACKCLOTH AND ASHES?

Definitions
Sackcloth: *A coarse cloth of camel's hair, goat hair, hemp or flax. ie: Burlap*
Ahes: *The remains of something burned; ie: paper, blessed palm; charcoal*

How To Use Sackcloth & What To Do!

Initially I felt odd using Sackcloth. I burned newspaper in an aluminum pan to make ashes. I obtained burlap cloth (5'x5') and used it according to Isaiah 58:5. I chose an area in my backyard big enough to lay the burlap. I spread ashes on the ground and put the burlap on top of the ashes. I laid face down on the burlap and my dog got next to me. I then began to pray, read scripture, and confess as the Lord led me to understand in *Neh 9:1*. After completing this act of obedience, I went inside and read the Word again. I opened the Bible and the Lord led me to read *Psalm 30:11*. The Lord turned my mourning into dancing and loosed my sackcloth requirement. I was stunned! After I did the above, I was drawn to used it as a quilt at night to sleep with, at which time I would also pray and continue in repentance. I stopped in 2011.

In 2022 I was drawn to use sackcloth again. I had not used it in years. I have been asking Our Lord, why do we have to use it? I have learned, only because I have been using it, that the Lord is teaching me again. He teaches in creative ways, not always while under the cloth, but the cloth is necessary.

There are many scriptures in the Bible about sackcloth. Here are a few that are highlighted to exemplify how sackcloth has been used in the New and Old Testament which we can imitate:

New Testament

*But he, answering, said to them, An evil and false generation is looking for a sign; and **no sign will be given to it but the sign of the prophet Jonah**:* Matthew 12:39 BBE

*Woe unto thee, Chorazin! Woe unto thee, Bethsaida! for if the mighty works had been done in Tyre and Sidon, which were done in you, **they would have repented long ago, sitting in sackcloth and ashes**.* Matthew 11:21 KJV

*And I will give unto my two witnesses, and they shall prophesy a thousand two hundred and threescore days, **clothed in sackcloth**.* Revelation 11:3 KJV

Old Testament

Using sackcloth and ashes as mentioned in the Old Testaments of the Bible:

*²In the first year of his reign I Daniel understood by books the number of the years, whereof the word of the LORD came to Jeremiah the prophet, that he would accomplish seventy years in the desolations of Jerusalem. ³ **And I set my face unto the Lord God, to seek by prayer and supplications, with fasting, and sackcloth, and ashes**:* Dan 9:2-3 KJV

***Put on sackcloth** and mourn, you priests;*
Wail, you ministers of the altar!
*Come, **spend the night in sackcloth**,*
You ministers of my God, For the grain offering

*and the drink offering Have been withheld from
the house of your God.* <u>Joel 1:13 NASB</u>

*Then his servants said to him, "Look now, we have heard that the kings of the house of Israel are merciful kings. Please, let us **put sackcloth around our waists and ropes around our heads,** and go out to the king of Israel; perhaps he will spare your life."* <u>1Kings 20:31 NKJV</u>

*"Wail, you shepherds, and cry; And **wallow in ashes**, you masters of the flock; For the days of your slaughter and your dispersions have come, And you will fall like a choice vessel.* <u>Jer 25:34 NASB</u>

*When I **clothed myself in sackcloth**; I became a byword for them.* <u>Ps 69:11 NAB</u>

*But as for me, when they were sick, my **clothing was sackcloth:** I humbled my soul with **fasting; and my prayer** returned into mine own bosom.* <u>Ps 35:13 KJV</u>

*Daughter of my people, **dress in sackcloth, roll in the ashes. Mourn** as for an only child with **bitter wailing**: "How suddenly the destroyer comes upon us!"* <u>Jer 6:26 NAB</u>

*I have **sewed sackcloth upon my skin**, and have laid my horn in the dust.* <u>Job 16:15 ASV</u>

*And in every province where the king's command and decree arrived, there was great **mourning** among the Jews, **with fasting, weeping, and wailing; and many lay in sackcloth and ashes.*** <u>Ester 4:3 NKJV</u>

*For I have **eaten ashes like bread, And mingled my drink with weeping,*** <u>Psalm 102:9 NKJV</u>

*Then David said to Joab and to all the people who were with him, "**Tear your clothes, gird yourselves with sackcloth, and mourn** for Abner."* <u>2 Sam 3:31 NKJV</u>

Other scriptures tell you to cover your loins, fall on your face and lay on it. Cast dust or dirt on your head. Spread ashes on a bed and lay on it. Eat ashes like bread, mingle weeping with drink. Other current applications might include filling a saltshaker with ashes and putting them on your food. Present yourself in a church, in home or outside in sackcloth and ashes and pray. Be humble so God can see us and hear us.

Do not be deceived to remove the sackcloth from you/ it is for the Lord, that He may hear our prayer of repentance/the destroyer will come suddenly, put on sackcloth (The two witnesses in the book of Revelations are perfect examples; In Esther 4:4, Mordechai refused to take off his sackcloth)

WHAT YOU MUST DO while Laying or Sitting on it:
According to <u>Nehemiah 9</u> they did the following:
1. Assembled with fasting in sackcloth with dirt/ashes on them.
2. Confessed their sins and those of their fathers and ancestors.
3. They read of the book of the law (Bible).
4. They worshipped the Lord.

<u>Nehemiah 9</u> and <u>Daniel 9</u> inspired this response:
Read Scripture, confess all sins yours and your fathers, the living and the dead, boldly and loudly while on or in sackcloth as taken from the Bible, also Worship the Lord.

*Now while I was speaking and **praying, and confessing my sin and the sin of my people Israel, and presenting my supplication** before the LORD my God for the holy mountain of my God,* <u>Dan 9:20 KJV</u>

*Now on the twenty-fourth day of this month the sons of Israel **assembled with fasting, in sackcloth and with dirt upon them.** The descendants of Israel separated themselves from* *all foreigners, and* **stood and confessed their sins and the iniquities of their fathers.** *While they stood in their place,* **they read from the book of the law of the LORD their God** *for a fourth of the day; and for another fourth* **they confessed and worshiped the LORD their God.** _{Neh 9:1-3 NASB 1995}

- Cry mightily unto God, Wail/Mourn/weep/cry out loud bitterly, as losing those you love most; including those least lovable, including the living and dead
- Beg the Lord desperately for His mercy on all, especially those most lost, as He was desperate for our Love,
- prostrate yourself before the Lord;
- We must desire to change our evil ways, remove violence, stop lying, stop sexual immorality, REPENT!
- PRAY that everyone will be saved and healed;
- FAST and Humble yourself before the Lord. We should also repent for the sins of our dead ancestors.
- DESIRE to love unconditionally and please the Lord.

The Lord told St Faustina that as the Churches unite, His wounds will heal. Perhaps, we also will be healed in all situations. Believe!

After prayer, confess your sins and those of your family and dead relatives, that perhaps the Lord will be merciful to them. If we are merciful, He will be merciful to them.

Sins to confess while using sackcloth & ashes:
While using Sackcloth and ashes or dirt, confess sins for yourself, your families, your ancestors and for others throughout the world. It is important to pray and confess for the dead and our ancestors. We must have hope for the salvation of all no matter how sinful they might have appeared to be. Many of them have been forgotten or neglected. The Dead will be first to rise, but we must help them. We must be merciful to them and ask the Lord to also be merciful, especially to the dead who have hurt us, physically or mentally. Some, suffer in purgatory. Confess with a contrite heart,

mind, and soul with a bitter appeal to the Lord. Doing this also liberates your soul and theirs, **do not hold grudges against the dead. Plead for their mercy.**

Read the book *Sackcloth & Ashes The Dead in Christ Shall Rise First* which includes a list of sins.

PRAY WITH YOUR OWN WORDS, Here Is A Start:
Break Every Yoke (inspired by Isaiah 58)
Lord, please teach us to bow down in an acceptable way and to be pleasing to You. Help us to trust you and to acknowledge you in all our ways. Give to us wisdom, knowledge and understanding. Teach us to be obedient. Lead us to those whom you want us to help. Make us and Mold us to be the repairer of the breach, the restorer of paths to dwell in, as you desire, that the yoke of many will be broken. Teach us to draw out our soul to the hungry, and to satisfy the afflicted soul. Guide us continually and like a spring of water, let not our waters fail. Please allow our health to spring forth speedily. Teach us to keep the Sabbath holy as a delightful day unto the Lord, that you may feed us with the heritage of Jacob our father. All Glory, Honor and Power are Yours Most Beloved Heavenly Father in the Name of Jesus. Amen.

Read the bible. Wool is sackcloth. This picture is of a scapular. It is worn around your neck. Buy only the **100% wool scapular,** shop around for best price. Do not substitute for medals or other material. One option: The Rose Scapular Company

WHY IS THE SCAPULAR A SIGN OF SALVATION?

The Sign of Jonah is the sign of salvation. It is the resulting salvation of the people and the beasts (animals) through true bitter repentance with the use of sackcloth and ashes.

*But he, answering, said to them, An evil and false generation is looking for a sign; and **no sign will be given to it but the sign of the prophet Jonah**: Matthew 12:39 BBE*

*Woe unto thee, Chorazin! Woe unto thee, Bethsaida! for if the mighty works had been done in Tyre and Sidon, which were done in you, **they would have repented long ago, sitting in sackcloth and ashes**. Matthew 11:21 KJV*

See that you give ear to his voice which comes to you.
For if those whose ears were shut to the voice which came to them on earth did not go free from punishment,
***what chance have we of going free if we give no attention to him whose voice comes from heaven**? Heb 12:25 BBE*

Mary presents a scapular to the world in more than one appearance. She said that anyone who dies wearing it will not suffer eternal fire. It is said to be "the sign of salvation."

A scapular made of wool is sackcloth therefore it also is the "sign of Jonah." It is the sign of salvation with repentance and love. It is sackcloth and must be worn in cloth made of wool (or animal hair like camel as John the Baptist wore) as presented by Mary, Mother of God, most Blessed. Whether the scapular satisfies Our Lord completely or not, we know there is a promise to be spared from eternal fire. In the right state of grace, in faith we know that the Lord keeps His promises. Our hope is for the salvation of all! Wear the scapular all the time.

SHOULD WE ALL WEAR SACKCLOTH?

Will the Lord know his sheep by the wool that they wear? We must repent and live a Christian life in love and mercy. We should wear sackcloth to please the Lord, and the scapular at Our Lady's request. We must honor them by wearing this garment (100% wool scapular) so that we may not suffer eternal fire. Since sackcloth is defined as animal hair, it seems that perhaps, wool is sackcloth and the sign of Jonah as mentioned in Mat 12:39. Our Lady promises that if we wear the scapular at the time of death, she will come for us on the first Saturday after our death, and take us to paradise or heaven, only the Lord knows.

The Lord asked Sister Faustina to wear a shirt of hair clothe, her superior denied her. She obeyed man rather than God.

The following was taken from this website:
http://www.truecatholic.org/scapular.htm
The Brown Scapular of Our Lady of Mt. Carmel
A magnificent assurance of salvation is Our Lady's Brown Scapular. One of the great mysteries of our time is that the great majority of Catholics either ignore or have forgotten the Blessed Virgin Mary's promise that **"whoever dies wearing this (Scapular) will not suffer eternal fire."** *She further says: "Wear it devoutly and perseveringly. It is my garment. To be clothed in it means you are continually thinking of me, and I in turn, am always thinking of you and helping you to secure eternal life."*
Many Catholics may not know that it is the wish of our Holy Father, the Pope, that the Scapular Medal should not be worn in place of the Cloth Scapular without sufficient reason. Mary cannot be pleased with anyone who substitutes the medal out of vanity, or fear to make open profession of religion. Such persons run the risk of not receiving the Promise. The medal has never been noted for any of the miraculous preservations attributed to the Brown Cloth Scapular.

During the Scapular Anniversary celebration in Rome, Pope Pius XII told a very large audience to wear the brown Scapular as a sign of consecration to the Immaculate Heart of Mary. Our Lady asked for this consecration in the last apparition at Fatima, when She appeared as Our Lady of Mount Carmel, holding the Brown Scapular out to the whole world. It was her last loving appeal to souls to wear her Scapular as a sign of Consecration to her Immaculate Heart. Blessed Claude de la Colombiere, the renowned Jesuit and spiritual director of St. Margaret Mary, gives a point which is enlightening. He said: "Because all the forms of our love for the Blessed Virgin, all its various modes of expression cannot be equally pleasing to Her, and therefore do not assist us in the same degree to Heaven, I say without a moment's hesitation the BROWN SCAPULAR is the most favored of all!" He also adds: "No devotion has been confirmed by more numerous authentic miracles than the Brown Scapular."

Why should we wear it?
According to http://www.carmelitedcj.org/saints/scapular.asp the scapular is not a magic charm or a free ticket into heaven. It is not an excuse to live an immoral life. The scapular is a visible sign that we are pledging to live a Christian life with Mary as our example. To wear the scapular is a sign of devotion to the Blessed Virgin Mary.

Our Lady told St. Simon Stock that she wished her children to wear the scapular, the garment she chose to signify her protection. Mary has promised that she will obtain the graces and protections necessary for those who show their devotion to her by wearing the scapular. She will not let her children fall into eternal fire, but rather protect them under her mantle, the brown scapular. By wearing the scapular, we visibly show that we desire to live a holy life, and we trust that God, through the intercession of Mary, will give us the graces we need to reach heaven. It is also a help to us in acknowledging the Lord in everything that happens around us.

March 2023 - The Catholic Church has not yet acknowledged the messages from Our Lady of Medjugorje. However, the following message seems to answer our questions about sackcloth. It would be so sad, if the church deflects us from any truth, yet we know they are under attack. Our Lady tells us to wear penitent clothing (sackcloth or perhaps the wool garment in scapular form as she previously presented in Mount Carmel.) Our Lord also asked Sister Faustina to wear sackcloth and she was denied. The question that arises, is if our religious leaders fall under the sins in the Woes in the Book of St Matthew, must we pray for them? Yes, always. We must repent even for them and all the times we have leaned on human understanding erroneously. This is not to say they are in error, but only that we must look for truth. We must be forgiving, and Trust the Lord and in His divine providence. We must ask Him to teach us all things and turn away from teachings we have hung on to in error. Pray without ceasing!

Today, February 25, 2023, Our Lady gave her message to the world through the visionary Marija. The following is the English translation of her message:

Dear children!
Keep converting and **clothe yourselves in penitential garments** *and in personal, deep prayer; and in humility, seek peace from the Most High.*

In this time of grace, Satan wants to seduce you; but you, little children, keep looking at my Son and **follow Him** *towards Calvary in* **renunciation and fasting***.*

I am with you because the Most High permits me to love you and lead you towards the joy of the heart, in faith which grows for all those who love God above all.

Thank you for having responded to my call.

AM I WITHOUT SIN?

If we do not obey any one of the Lord's commandments, then we are a sinner. Anything that is not of faith is sin. Doubt, malice, anger, hatred, envy, witchcraft, adultery, lies, sexual immorality, idol worship, not loving unconditionally and much more. Praying or longing for money is a sin, it is the master of this world. We must understand the mission Jesus came to accomplish: our salvation. He came not only to show us who we are, but what we must do to become His alone. It is difficult for us to escape sin without the grace of God.

We know that no one who is born of God sins;
1John 5:18 NASB 1995

We are all sinners, but we have this hope gifted to us that we may become true sons of God. We must desire it! We must believe!

*⁸**the one who practices sin is of the devil;***
for the devil has sinned from the beginning.
The Son of God appeared for this purpose,
to destroy the works of the devil.
*⁹**No one who is born of God practices sin**,*
1John 3:8-9 NASB 1995

We all fall short of the glory of God. Yes, we are born with sin. Are we then all devils? According to the Word of God, it seems very apparent that we are, yet, Our Lord loves us beyond our understanding! He came to show us the way to be like Him, to love like Him and to give us the great hope of our salvation. He came to convert us and to gather His Army. He came to divide the kingdom of Satan. We must respond and follow Jesus! We must help divide!

When perfection comes, we will be without sin as mentioned in *1 John*. We must run the race to attain perfection by desiring to love unconditionally, by repenting, and by gathering. We must run the race desiring to be born of God, that is, to be possessed by Our Lord! Let nothing on earth possess you! Belong to the Lord!

whosoever is born of God ...
that wicked one toucheth him not. *1John 5:18 KJV*

*We know that **No One Who Is Born of God Sins;** but He who was born of God keeps him, and **THE EVIL ONE DOES NOT TOUCH HIM.** We know that we are of God, and that **the whole world lies in the power of the evil one.** And we know that the Son of God has come, and has given us understanding so that we may know Him who is true; **and we are "in Him" who is true, in His Son Jesus Christ.** This is the true God and eternal life.* <u>1 John 5:18-20 NASB 1995</u>

*²²The light of the body is the eye; **if then your eye is true, all your body will be full of light.** ²³ But if your eye is evil, all your body will be dark. If then the light which is in you is dark, how dark it will be!* <u>Mat 6:22 BBE</u>

*And so, call to mind the place from which you have fallen, and **do penance**, and do the first works. Otherwise, **I will come to you and remove your lampstand from its place, unless you repent.*** <u>Re 2:5 CPDVTSB</u>

**PERFECT LOVE,
MAKE US TO LOVE YOU PERFECTLY!**

*Then Jesus saith to him:
**Begone, Satan: for it is written,
The Lord thy God shalt thou adore,
and him only shalt thou serve.*** <u>Matthew 4:10 DRB</u>

DOES HELL EXIST?

Hell is mentioned in the bible. We must believe! The Word of God is Spirit and it is Truth! We must desire not to go there! The Lord says people perish because of lack of knowledge. Surely the devil does not want us to believe because he wants us to go to hell. Another view, perhaps Satan does not feel worthy of forgiveness and so all he knows is suffering and disobedience; similarly, we love to sin, so we continue to suffer. We must change our ways and desire to love unconditionally.

Repent or Perish as warned repeatedly in the Word of God! Be merciful as Our Father is merciful so that we may obtain mercy.

*⁴**For if God did not spare angels when they sinned,** **but cast them into hell** and committed them to pits of darkness, held for judgment; ⁵and **did not spare the ancient world,** but protected Noah, a preacher of righteousness, with seven others, when **He brought a flood upon the world of the ungodly**; ⁶and if He **condemned the cities of Sodom and Gomorrah** to destruction by reducing them to ashes, having made them an example of what is coming for the ungodly; ⁷and if He rescued righteous Lot, who was oppressed by the perverted conduct of unscrupulous people ⁸(for by what he saw and heard that righteous man, while living among them, felt his righteous soul tormented day after day by their lawless deeds), ⁹then **the Lord knows how to rescue the godly from a trial, and to keep the unrighteous under punishment for the day of judgment,** ¹⁰**and especially those who indulge the flesh in its corrupt passion, and despise authority**.* 2Pe 2:4-10 NASB

*"Do not fear those who kill the body but are unable to kill the soul; but **rather fear Him who is able to destroy both soul and body in hell**.* Mat 10:28 NASB 1995

"But I will warn you whom to fear: fear the One who, after He has killed, has authority to cast into hell; yes, I tell you, fear Him! Luke 12:5 NASB 1995

And the tongue is a fire, the very world of iniquity; ***the tongue is set among our members as that which defiles the entire body, and sets on fire the course of our life****, and **is set on fire by hell**.* Jas 3:6 NASB 1995

"But I say to you that everyone who is angry with his brother shall be guilty before the court; and whoever says to his brother, `You good-for-nothing,' shall be guilty before the supreme court; and whoever says, `You fool,' shall be guilty enough to go into the fiery hell. Mat 5:22 NASB 1995

"You serpents, you brood of vipers, how will you escape the sentence of hell? Mat 23:33 NASB 1995

<u>Mat 5:29-30</u>, states that it is better to lose one part of our body than for our whole body to be thrown into hell. He mentions our "eye" and "our right hand", In <u>Mark 9:43</u> it mentions "our hand"; in <u>Mark 9:45</u> "our foot", <u>Mark 9:47</u> "our eye". It says that it is better to enter life lame than having two feet, or to enter life crippled than having two hands.

It is the Word of God that has left an imprint for our salvation and we must believe. Repent or perish!

"This is the judgment, that the Light has come into the world, and men loved the darkness rather than the Light, for their deeds were evil. Joh 3:19 NASB 1995

For judgment will be merciless to one who has shown no mercy; ***mercy triumphs over judgment****.* Jas 2:13 NASB 1995

The Lord is merciful to those who are merciful. We must be merciful to our brothers. We must love unconditionally and forgive unconditionally. We must desire not to sin. Jesus showed us the way to live, He is our perfect example.   Only the Lord can give us the grace to escape evil. We must repent as the Lord has warned, and desire to please the Lord. We must plead for mercy upon the unbeliever. We must desire to Love Him and each other, as He loves us. We must follow Jesus.

Act of Contrition – Orthodox
O God, we love thee with our whole hearts and above all things and are heartily sorry that we have offended thee. May we never offend thee any more. O, may we love thee without ceasing, and make it our delight to do in all things thy most holy will.
The Orthodox Book Of Common Prayer page 598

Eternal God, in whom mercy is endless and the treasury of compassion -- inexhaustible, look kindly upon us and increase Your mercy in us, that in difficult moments we might not despair nor become despondent, but with great confidence submit ourselves to Your holy will, which is Love and Mercy itself. (Sr Faustina)

The Mercy of Our Lord Is ours! Be Merciful As He Is!
We must amend our ways! **Imitate Jesus!**
We must RECIPROCATE the life He demonstrated!

We must join Jesus in His cause to divide Satan's kingdom!
Trust Jesus Christ the Warrior of Love! Our Victor!

**It is of utmost importance that
all believers in Christ GATHER and form the Army of God.**

> [30]*The one who is not with Me is against Me; and the one who does not gather with Me scatters* Mat 12:30 NASB

This is a Call to Arms! Love, pray, fast, repent, and unite!

WHERE IS THE KINGDOM OF SATAN?

Satan rebelled against God and with his devil followers they were cast out and down to earth.

And the great dragon was cast out, that old serpent, called the Devil, and Satan, which deceiveth the whole world: **he was cast out into the earth, and his angels were cast out with him.** Rev 12:9 KJV

Therefore rejoice, O heavens, and you who dwell in them! **Woe to the inhabitants of the earth and the sea! For the devil has come down to you**, *having great wrath, because he knows that he has a short time."* Rev 12:12 NKJV

It is therefore reasonable to believe that we live in the kingdom of Satan because it is written in The Living Word, our Holy Bibles. This earth is Satan's kingdom. Jesus even said it when He was on earth. He said *"My kingdom is not of this world."* Reflecting on what Jesus said on earth: The kingdom of God is not of this world and notably not here. *"***But now** *My kingdom is not from here"* so we agree that right now, it is not here, but it will be, we must obey and choose sides. We must join the rebellion and gather with the Army of Jesus Christ, Our Warrior!

"My kingdom is not of this world. **If My kingdom were** *of this world,* **My servants would** *fight, so that I should not be delivered to the Jews;* **but now** *My kingdom is not from here."* John 18:36 NKJV

Jesus came to gather His Army and unite believers who have faith in Him. Jesus is talking in code, "if it were, they would…" He said His servants would fight if His Kingdom was here. If we want to be His servants, our fight is to repent, stand firm in the faith of Jesus and unite. It is important that we gather with a repentant heart. Our fight begins by taking the first step in faith. We must gather as rebels against the kingdom of Satan in unconditional love.

> *"Whoever is not with me is against me, and whoever does not **gather with me** scatters.* _{Mat 12:30 NIV}

We know that Jesus is the hope of our salvation. We also know that the Lord wants to claim us and the earth as His own! His kingdom will come, but we must do our part. We must return to God! We must reciprocate! We must imitate Jesus! We must follow the lamb wherever He goes! He left us the living map to salvation!

We must reciprocate the event that started it all in Heaven. As Lucifer, a good angel at the time, rebelled against Heaven, we the sinners must gather as rebels, against Satan, the father of sinners, to end the kingdom of Satan. Jesus Christ the Warrior, will be without a doubt, Our Victor! Our Champion! And Our Lord's Kingdom will come! Satan himself is our example. He rebelled against heaven. It is our turn to rebel in the kingdom of Satan.

Satan is ruler of this world. The Lord refers to the evil one as ruler of this world. It is reasonable to believe that this is the kingdom of Satan and he is ruler of this world, it is his reign. These are just a few scriptures relating to the ruler of this world.

> *Now is the judgment of this world; now the **ruler of this world** will be cast out.* _{John 12:31 NKJV}

> *I will not speak with you much longer, for the **ruler of the world** (Satan) is coming. And he has no claim on Me [no power over Me nor anything that he can use against Me];* _{John 14:30 AMP}

> ***all the world is in the power of the Evil One***. _{1John 5:19 BBE}

Glory and Praise to Our Beloved Jesus who shows us the way! He desires for us to be perfect as Our Heavenly Father and He shows us how. Satan has been ruling this earth when he was cast out from heaven, and even when Jesus was here.

DO I DO AS OUR SHEPHERD HAS TAUGHT?

CONSIDER THIS: We need to pray for our obedience! Although with today's customs, using sackcloth and ashes might seem awkward, the Lord reminds us that the men of Nineveh will come to judge and condemn us because we have not repented. We have not acknowledged the sign of Jonah who told the people of Nineveh to repent and responded by doing so in sackcloth and ashes.

What have we failed to do and obey? It seems that everything we do is wrong, we are destined to be sinners unless we comply with the demands of Our Lord, Jesus Christ the Warrior. We must gather! He desires no divisions among us!

Throughout the Bible, the Lord says do this from generation to generation, but whispering down the lane changes things from generation to generation. We cannot escape this evil world and its sinfulness without Our Lord.

Are any of the following important for us to do and we have not, do not, and will not?

- Greeting those who enter your home and washing their feet as noted in *Luke 7:44 and John 13:14*

"If I then, the Lord and the Teacher, washed your feet, you also ought to wash one another's feet. Joh 13:14 NASB 1995

- Holy kissing of feet

"You gave Me no kiss; but she, since the time I came in, has not ceased to kiss My feet." Luke 7:45 NASB

- Anoint Head with Oil and/or Feet with Perfume

"You did not anoint My head with oil, but she anointed My feet with perfume." Luke 7:46 NASB

"But you, when you fast, anoint your head and wash your face" Mat 6:17 NASB

Let your clothes be white all the time, and let not oil be lacking on your head. Ec 9:8 NASB 1995

And they were casting out many demons and were anointing with oil many sick people and healing them.
<u>Mark 6:13 NASB</u>

Is anyone among you sick? Then he must call for the elders of the church and they are to pray over him, anointing him with oil in the name of the Lord; <u>Jas 5:14 NASB</u>

and the prayer of faith will restore the one who is sick, and the Lord will raise him up, and if he has committed sins, they will be forgiven him. <u>Jas 5:15 NASB</u>

Desire to have the bride, therefore, consecrate yourselves to Our Blessed Mother and Her Immaculate Heart, so that our heart may become like hers.

> **"He who has the bride** *is the bridegroom; but the friend of the bridegroom, who stands and hears him, rejoices greatly because of the bridegroom's voice. So this joy of mine has been made full.* <u>John 3:29 NASB 1995</u>

Be wise? do we need an oil lamp?

> ¹*Then shall the kingdom of heaven be likened unto* **ten virgins, which took their lamps, and went forth to meet the bridegroom.** ² *And five of them were wise, and five were foolish.* ³ *They that were foolish took their lamps, and took no oil with them:* ⁴ **But the wise took oil in their vessels with their lamps.** ⁵ *While the bridegroom tarried, they all slumbered and slept.* ⁶ *And at midnight there was a cry made,* **Behold, the bridegroom cometh; go ye out to meet him.** ⁷*Then all those virgins arose, and trimmed their lamps.* ⁸ *And the foolish said unto the wise, Give us of your oil; for our lamps are gone out.* ⁹ *But the wise answered, saying, not so; lest there be not enough for us and you: but go ye rather to them that sell, and buy for yourselves.* ¹⁰ *And while they went to buy, the bridegroom came; and* **they that were ready went in with him to the marriage: and the door**

> *was shut.* ¹¹ *Afterward came also the other virgins, saying, Lord, Lord, open to us.* ¹² *But he answered and said, Verily I say unto you, I know you not.* ¹³ **Watch therefore, for ye know neither the day nor the hour wherein the Son of man cometh.** _{Matthew 25:1-13 KJV}

> *Command the children of Israel, that they bring unto thee pure oil olive beaten for the light, to cause the lamps to burn continually.* _{Le 24:2 KJV}

We are lost, in a lost world dominated by evil and its' rules. We must remember that the weapons of our warfare are not carnal but mighty through God to the pulling down of strongholds.

We must do as the Lord has asked, divide the kingdom of Satan! Let there be no division among us! Come back home to the Roman Catholic Church, the battle ground. Pray the Rosary!

Trust Jesus Christ the Warrior! Our Victor!
It is of utmost importance that all believers in Christ GATHER and form the Army of God.

> ³⁰*The one who is not with Me is against Me; and the one who does not gather with Me scatters* _{Mat 12:30 NASB}

This is a Call to Arms! Love, pray, fast, repent, and unite!

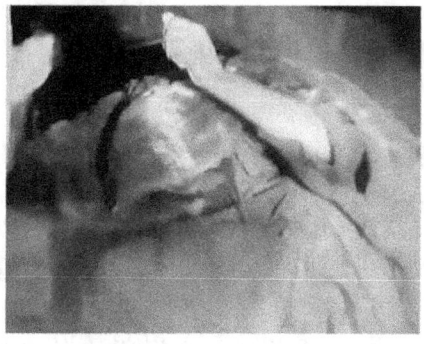

WHAT IS RELIGION?

Simply put, Religion equals Division. Division creates disunity among all believers of Jesus Christ. We are scattered. Christians help Satan by indulging in the ways of this world, partaking in Satan's kingdom. Christians thinking, they must have their way, because they think they know what is right. Pride, money, and glory are their sin. They do not love. The Lord said:

> *If anyone thinks that he knows anything,*
> *he has not yet known as he ought to know;* <u>1 Cor 8:2 NASB</u>

Jesus said that His kingdom is not in His world. The believers of Jesus Christ on earth are NOT united, if they were we would fight for Him as stated in scripture! It is evident that He came to proclaim war. He came to gather His army: God against Satan. He came to convert us, to be believers, and have faith in Jesus Christ as Our God and Savior. We must unite in unconditional love!

Is religion a discord among believers? Is religion a difference of the flesh, a separation of the minds? Yes, religion is a discord among believers and a separation of the minds. Is love being demonstrated here? No! Are they causing separation, controversy, and confusion among believers? Yes! Are they false Christ's being used for the glory of God? Yes! They are human beings that sin, they are not Christ Himself. They are each a false Christ, Satan disguised as angels of light. They are rebels in the kingdom of Satan. Are they too proud to lay down their crowns? Do they know who they are? They DO confess Jesus but are without love! We are either for Him or against Him. Who do we desire to follow? Let us reexamine ourselves and become selfless like Jesus.

> *Now I beseech you, brethren, by the name of our Lord Jesus Christ, that **ye all speak the same thing**, and that there be **no divisions among you**; but that ye be **perfectly joined together in the same mind and in the same judgment**. For it hath been declared unto me of you, my brethren, by them which are of the house of Chloe, that there are contentions*

> *among you. Now this I say, that every one of you saith, **I am of Paul; and I of Apollos; and I of Cephas; and I of Christ. Is Christ divided? was Paul crucified for you? or were ye baptized in the name of Paul*** _{1 Cor 1:10-13 NKJV}

In the above verse the Lord is clearly stating that because of religion, we are scattered. He is drawing a line on the ground. He wants us to choose our master. He is like Moses on the mountain, throwing down the ten commandments, telling the people to takes sides! So whose side are you on? God or Satan?

> *"He who is not with Me is against Me;
> and he who does not gather with Me scatters.*
> _{Mat 12:30 NASB 1995}
>
> *And if a house be divided against itself,
> that house cannot stand.* _{Mark 3:26 KJV}
>
> *Greater love hath no man than this,
> that a man lay down his life for his friends.* _{John 15:13 BBE}
>
> *Is it your opinion that I have come to give peace on earth? I say to you, No, but division:* _{Luke 12:51 BBE}

Let us look at scripture Mark 3:26. It says that if Satan is divided, he will come to an end. Well turn that around, in Satan's kingdom, Christians are divided and they are coming to an end. Satan is victorious because Christians are weak, lacking in faith with contradicting doctrines or beliefs. Christians are in discord complying with Satan's game. Christians think in the flesh, not in the spirit. They think their victory is their own. They suffer much and are persecuted out of disobedience. We must repent in sackcloth with use of ashes and allow the Lord to teach us and to be our Victor. He is Our Victor!

> [13]*For such are **false apostles**, deceitful workers, transforming themselves into the apostles of Christ.* [14]*And no marvel; for Satan himself is transformed into an angel of*

light. ¹⁵Therefore it is no great thing if his ministers also be transformed as the ministers of righteousness; whose end shall be according to their works. 2 Cor 11:13-15 KJV

We see in this world that discord is everywhere. **The kingdom of God is in discord** (scattered); **it indulges in Satan's kingdom**. Believers do not even know who they are. They are blind to their spiritual life. Many do not know that they are angels of light, ministers of righteousness, and false apostles, the devil in disguise. The devil keeps these vessels of clay captive and ignorant. Truth must be sought, the Lord reveals.

As believers in Christ we are still divided and sinful. The Lord wants to baptize us with the Holy Spirit; but it is not possible because we have not shown an interest in demonstrating unconditional love, as He has. We have not taken the first step of faith to unite in unconditional love. We must desire to be one with Him, one with the true Church, and with each other by gathering. Who will step down giving their throne to Jesus? Mercifully asking forgiveness and truly living the life of Christ.

These are the false Christs, false apostles: those who are not Jesus Himself, for there is only One Christ. Those who do not love unconditionally, are not merciful and do not know the way of the Shepherd nor do they live in the Truth.

> *By this the children of God and the children of the devil are obvious: anyone who does **not practice righteousness is not of God, nor the one who does not love his brother.***
> 1John 3:10 NASB 1995

> *For **who hath known the mind of the Lord**, that he may instruct him? But we have the mind of Christ.*
> 1Cor 2:16 NASB 1995

> **Let this mind be in you**, *which was also in Christ Jesus:*
> Php 2:5 DRB

For you have been called for this purpose, since Christ also suffered for you, **leaving you an example for you to follow in His steps***,* 1Pe 2:21NASB 1995

After you have suffered for a little while, the God of all grace, who called you to His eternal glory in Christ, will Himself perfect, confirm, strengthen, and establish you.
1Pe 5:10 NASB 1995

make my joy complete by being of the same mind, maintaining the same love, united in spirit, intent on one purpose. Php 2:2 NASB 1995

**We must sow as He sows, Be as He is,
Love as He Loves!**

Slaves, in all things obey those who are your masters on earth, not with external service, as those who merely please men, but **with sincerity of heart, fearing the Lord***.*
Col 3:22 NASB 1995

    Regarding the scripture that says we are servants of whom we obey, either to sin or to righteousness which is God, we must remember that in all things we must acknowledge God and do all that we do for Him. Therefore, in acknowledging God in all we say and do, then we are no longer serving our masters toward sin, but rather righteousness. We must do all that we do, and all that we say for the glory of God, always acknowledging Him! Even in our spending.

*Do not let kindness and truth leave you;
Bind them around your neck,
write them on the tablet of your heart.
So you will find favor and good repute
in the sight of God and man.*
**Trust in the LORD with all your heart and
do not lean on your own understanding.
In all your ways acknowledge Him,**

And He will make your paths straight.
Do not be wise in your own eyes;
Fear the LORD and turn away from evil.
It will be healing to your body and
refreshment to your bones. Proverbs 3:3-8 NASB 1995

Believers of Jesus Christ, Our Savior, and Redeemer of the world… be united in unconditional love. Stop speaking evil against one another. Stop your lies, deceit, and be reconciled. Choose your master!

This is a Call to Arms! Love, pray, fast, repent, and UNITE!

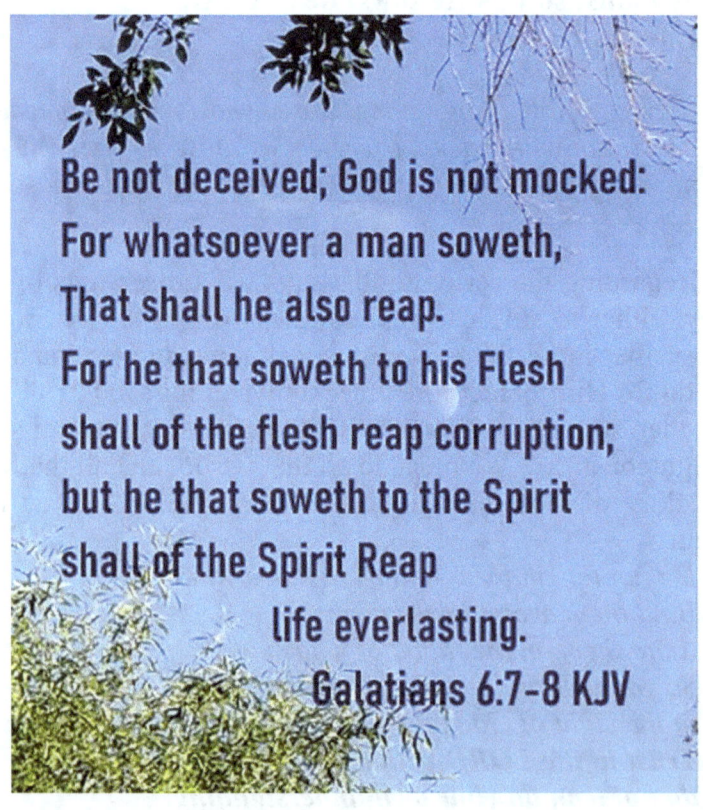

HOW CAN WE MAKE HIS JOY COMPLETE?

make my joy complete by being of the same mind,
maintaining the same love, united in spirit,
intent on one purpose. <u>Php 2:2 NASB 1995</u>

1. By being of the same mind...
*So that as Jesus was put to death in the flesh, do you yourselves be of the **same mind;** for the death of the flesh puts an end to sin;* <u>1Pe 4:1 BBE</u>

the god of this world (Satan) has blinded the minds of the unbelieving so that they might not see the light of the gospel of the glory of Christ, who is the image of God. <u>2Cor 4:4 NASB</u>

We must join Jesus in His cause to divide. We must unite to divide the kingdom of Satan for the salvation of all the living and the dead. Come back to the Roman Catholic Church. Rebuke Religion. Be of the same mind Be "FOR CHRIST!" Plead for mercy and salvation upon all, even the worst of sinners and unbelievers. Pray for them – repent using sackcloth and ashes

"Then you will call, and the LORD will answer;
You will cry, and He will say,
*'**Here I am.** ' **If you remove** the yoke from your midst,*
The pointing of the finger and speaking wickedness,
<u>Isa 58:9 NASB 1995</u>

2. Maintaining the same love...
UNCONDITIONAL LOVE, Desire to love even the worst of sinners. Can you love Satan, the father of sinners? Plead for the salvation of all!
With all lowliness and meekness, With longsuffering,
Forebearing one another in love <u>Eph Ch 4:2 KJV</u>

No one should seek his own advantage,
but that of his neighbor <u>1Cor 10:24 NASB</u>

> *Greater love hath no man than this,*
> *that a man lay down his life for his friends.* <u>John 15:13 KJV</u>

3. United in Spirit ...

We must desire to be Born of God, a new creation. Corruption shall put on incorruption, mortality, immortality. Only the Lord can do this, it is a new Pentecost. He is anxious to baptize us. We must unite in one house, one church. We must approach the Lord with a contrite heart, desperate love and equally desiring that love for our brothers, even unto death, for the salvation of all.

> *Endeavoring to keep the unity of the Spirit*
> *In the bond of peace* <u>Eph 4:3 KJV</u>

> *But Jesus answered, "You do not know what you are asking. Are you able to drink the cup that I am about to drink **and be baptized with the baptism that I am baptized with**?" They said to Him, "We are able."* <u>Mat 20:22 NKJV</u>

4. Intent on one purpose...

UNCONDITIONAL SALVATION FOR ALL the living and the dead and all those whom the Lord desires - Even Unto Death As the Lord has stated in His Word:

> *and he will speak words to you by which you will*
> *be saved, **you and all your household**.'*
> <u>Ac 11:14 NASB 1995</u>

We must imitate Him. Follow the Lamb wherever He goes as noted in the book of Revelations. We must be willing to do whatever He tells us, submitting and subjecting ourselves to all trials and tribulations as perfectly planned for the glory of God.

Act upon the ***Worldwide Agreement of Hope*** in this book

WHO ARE THE TRUE APOSTLES OF TODAY?

The Lord tells the church of Ephesus in the book of Revelations, that they have tested those who say they are apostles and have found them to be liars. This pertains to ALL churches of today.

He tells them their fault in *Rev 2:1-5*. He commands them to Repent because they do not love as they should! Scripture seems to point out that they are otherwise perfect. In truth, it seems that this applies to all churches. Most persons do not know how to love God and others as themselves, neither do the churches.

The Roman Catholic Church has a recorded history of the hierarchy of the descendants of the priesthood since Jesus, Apostle to Apostle. They can prove the lineage. Perhaps, it is they that consecrate the Holy Communion pleasing to the Lord. In addition, the Lord has promised victory in the rock, St Peter.

It seems reasonable to believe and evident that the Roman Catholic Church, is the Church, with the only apostolic history, that really matters for the coming of Jesus. It is the true church designated by the Lord in Our Living Word, the Holy Bible.

We are all flawed and imperfect. We are all sinners, including our church leaders, until born again. We must repent, we must unite! Without a doubt, Jesus told us that the gates of Hell will not prevail against the Church of St. Peter! We must have faith, knowing that as we gather, only the Lord can set things right.

> *And I say also unto thee, that thou art Peter, and upon this rock I will build my church; and the gates of hell shall not prevail against it.* Mat 16:18 KJV

According to the dictionary Pharisees are those who follow the law and think of themselves of highest sanctity. We know that the law made things imperfect, so the law is sinful. So, who today, are the blinded scribes, Pharisees, and hypocrites that do not know the love of God? Who are the angels of light and ministers of righteousness disguised as Satan? Certainly, it is everyone that is not Jesus Christ Himself.

So today's revelation, October 21, 2023 is the following scripture:

> *^{13}For such are **FALSE APOSTLES**, deceitful workers, transforming themselves into the apostles of Christ. ^{14}And no marvel; for Satan himself is transformed into an angel of light. ^{15}Therefore it is no great thing if his ministers also be transformed as the **ministers of righteousness;** whose end shall be according to their works.* <u>2 Cor 11:13-15 KJV</u>

The question remains, who are the true apostles? Are there any true apostles? Could it be that, the true apostles were apostles only after they were born again, and before that, they were known as "disciples?" I do not know. Do we have to wait until Pentecost to be born again? I think so, therefore that would make all disciples, false apostles, ministers of righteousness and angels of light, good devils until born again. Perhaps, the Lord has allowed us to believe, what we have believed, so that those who are converted as believers in Christ, could grow in number. And now, the number is here. It is time to help Jesus divide. Let us start the rebellion!

Repent and keep with the fruit of repentance. Receive Holy Communion; eat of the Bread of Life! Come back home to the Roman Catholic Church and receive the sacraments! Pray for unity! Jesus is Coming! Ask Him to teach you everything!

> ***We know the love of God in this way:*** *because he laid down his life for us. And so**, we must lay down our lives for our brothers*** <u>1 John 3:15 CPDVTSB</u>

Did Satan enter our churches when Peter denied Our Lord three times? Peter loved the Lord greatly and the Lord used him for His Glory! Just like Judas, this had to happen! Division has been necessary within the kingdom of Satan! The Lord has taught us who we are and that we must rebel. **We must unite if we want the Lord to return to us!** The Lord said that Peter is the Rock! It is the true Church! Prove your Love! Repent of this, so that you can believe! Use sackcloth and ashes! It is His Perfect Plan! The Gates of Hell will not prevail!

*"**Anyone who does not** take up his cross and **follow Me** cannot be My disciple."* Luke 14:27 NIV

…there is no way to heaven except the way of the cross. I followed it first. You must learn that it is the shortest and surest way. Diary of St Faustina 1487

Greater love hath no man than this, that a man lay down his life for his friends. John 15:13 KJV

Prayer: Make us Lord to gather and to make your Joy complete. Help us to agree among ourselves in unconditional love. Make us true followers of Jesus, in your love. Beloved Holy Ghost remove the dull of our hearing and let us hear. Remove the blinders, and open our eyes that we may see. Our hearts are waxed gross, melt away the wax so that the enemy may flee at the Your presence and make our hearts sound. Give our hearts understanding that we may be converted and made whole. Give to us a mind of Christ. Give to us the faith of Jesus, and strengthen us to take the first step of faith. Help us to be courageous and unafraid of the things to come. Help us to be still and keep our eyes on You. Unite us to Yourself. Fill us with your perfect love that we may love perfectly. Save all souls living and the dead in your omnipotent mercy. In Jesus Name Amen.

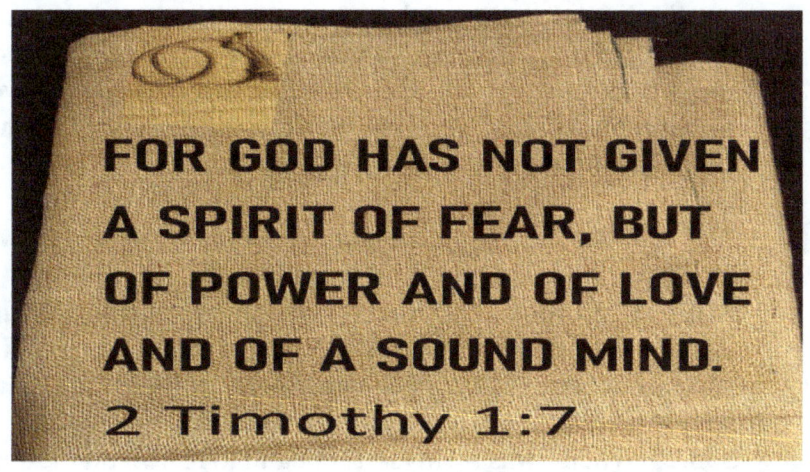

Who Do You Think Is The Person Most Prayed For?

Who do we think is the person most prayed for? Would that person on earth be the most filled with the Holy Spirit? I hope so! Millions of rosaries and masses are said every day in which the Pope is prayed for. Hoping that nondenominational churches and others are also praying for the Pope, may he find strength! Perhaps, he is the person most offered to the Lord. Keep praying for Him that He may obtain the guidance to do what is necessary for the Coming of Our Lord! Pray for Perfect Love, Perfect Faith, Perfect Charity!

The following was taken from the book <u>Divine Mercy in My Soul</u> by Saint Maria Faustina Kowalska:

531   November 24, 1935. Sunday, first day. I went at once before the Blessed Sacrament and offered myself with Jesus, present in the Most Holy Sacrament, to the Everlasting Father. Then I heard these words in my soul: **Your purpose and that of your companions is to unite yourselves with Me as closely as possible; through love You will reconcile earth with heaven, you will soften the just anger of God, and you will plead for mercy for the world. I place in your care two pearls very precious to My Heart: these are the souls of priests and religious. You will pray particularly for them; their power will come from your diminishment. You will join prayers, fasts, mortifications, labors and all sufferings to My prayer, fasting, mortification, labors and sufferings and then they will have power before My Father.**

532   After Holy Communion, I saw the Lord Jesus, who said these words to me: **Today, penetrate into the spirit of My poverty and arrange everything in such a way that the most destitute will have no reason to envy you. I find pleasure, not in large buildings and magnificent structures, but in a pure and humble heart.**

533   When I was by myself, I began to reflect on the spirit of poverty. I clearly saw that Jesus, although He is Lord of

all things, possessed nothing. From a borrowed manger He went through life doing good to all, but himself having no place to lay His head. And on the Cross, I see the summit of His poverty, for He does not even have a garment on himself. O Jesus, through a solemn vow of poverty I desire to become like You; poverty will be my mother. As exteriorly we should possess nothing and have nothing to dispose of as our own; so interiorly we should desire nothing. And in the Most Blessed Sacrament, how great is Your poverty! Has there ever been a soul as abandoned as You were on the Cross, Jesus?

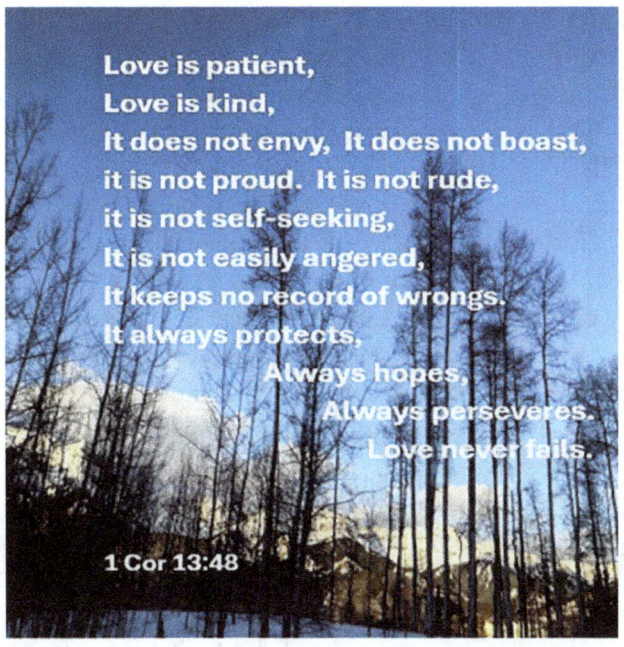

WHO IS GOD?

God is Alive and He is Spirit, pure love, infinitely perfect, Creator of all things in heaven and on earth and of all existence and in all of existence.

> *But as it is written, Eye hath not seen, nor ear heard, neither have entered into the heart of man, the things which God hath prepared for them that love him.* 1Cor 2:9 KJV

God is not a belief!!! God is certain!!! God is true and alive!!! Yet, who can truly define Him.
Jesus said He who knows me knows my Father; He who knows my Mother knows me.
God is in control and He knows our every thought and everything we say and do before we think it, say it or do it.
God is love beyond measure; words cannot even begin to edify His love, His greatness, His goodness, His kindness nor their bounty.
God is so Good! We must seek Him to know Him! He is too great to identify on a piece of paper and our minds are too small to truly comprehend. These notes are just a speck in knowing Him.
God is our creator, our maker. He gave to us His breath of life. He made us to love and to serve Him because He loves us and desires for us to love Him back.
You have heard many times that God is Love. Paul describes "love" as "a more excellent way" in *1Cor13:1*. In the book of *Matthew* Jesus tells us to love our enemies and to pray for those who persecute us. His love is a selfless unconditional love! He desires that we love as He loves.
He is the very essence of the fruits of the spirit magnified in unfathomable limits.

> *But the fruit of the Spirit is* **love, joy, peace, longsuffering, gentleness, goodness, faith, Meekness, temperance: against such there is no law**
> Gal 5:22-23 KJV

He is a merciful God who longs for us to return to Him, and to be like Him! He is the beginning and the end, the first and the last. He is the source and completion of our life and eternity. He is creative beyond creativity, the Creator of all. He is the same yesterday, today, and always. He was is and will always be. He is Light, Love and Life eternal. He is Lord of Lords and King of Kings. He is Holy, Righteous, Almighty, Immortal, Powerful and Immaculate, Pure in every way. He is our Redeemer and savior. His Word is eternal and all things will pass away, but His word will never pass away. His Word is eternally alive!

His Desire for us is Perfect Love and to be perfect as Our Heavenly Father is perfect. He desires for us to live in His loving embrace throughout eternity. He is gentle, kind and patient with us. We are slow to learn and He is our teacher, our leader, our guide, our lover, the very essence of our life.

He desires that we love our enemies and bless those who curse us. He desires for us to imitate Him so that perhaps our enemies may desire to change their ways and return to Him.

Our Father loved the world and all He created so much that He gave His only son to die for us so that we might live. He died for us to save us from our sinful and wicked ways. He came to teach us to repent, to be merciful and to love unconditionally. Jesus told Thomas "blessed are those who believe and have not seen".

Our Heavenly Father suffered with Jesus and in Jesus to help and teach us how to live in His great love, so that we may learn to follow Him. Jesus died for us, because in our sinfulness. we are dead already. But the promise of our redemption, in the death of Jesus and His resurrection is assurance of our eternal life in God's everlasting love. We must choose to live the life our Lord desires for us to inherit, eternal life. We must choose to be an advocate as He has been our advocate for salvation.

He came to teach us a more excellent way!

We must desire to be born of God submitting to Him, and by giving Him our free will; the door in which Satan enters. We must desire to inherit everlasting life by eating of the Bread of Life, the Bread of His Presence, God Himself. It is the living creature Jesus has become, so that we may become like Him. We must desire to obey Him, to love Him, to serve Him and to please Him in every way. We must believe in Him!

> *We know that **no one who is born of God sins;** but He who was born of God keeps him, and **the evil one does not touch him.*** 1 John 5:18 NASB 1995

> *For now we see in a mirror dimly, but then face to face; now I know in part, but then I will know fully just as I also have been fully known. But now faith, hope, love, abide these three; but the greatest of these is love.* 1Cor13:12-13 NASB 1995

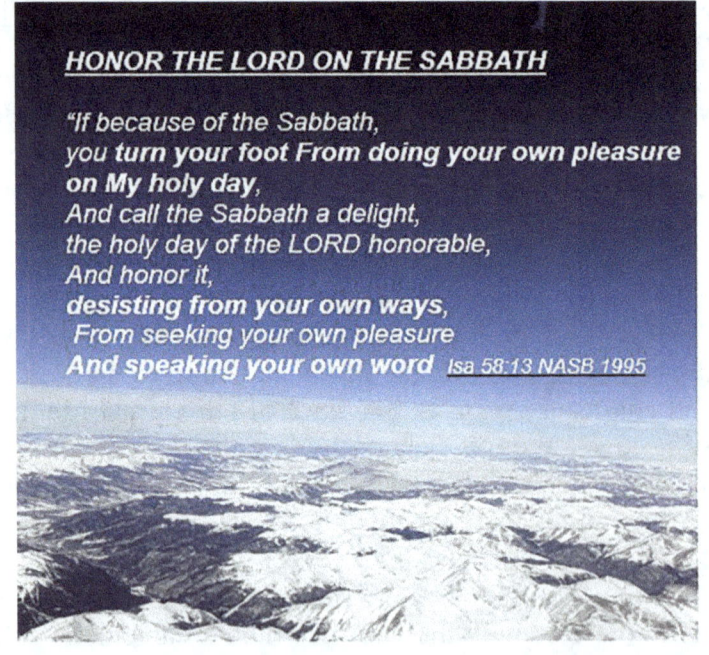

HONOR THE LORD ON THE SABBATH

"If because of the Sabbath,
you **turn your foot From doing your own pleasure on My holy day**,
And call the Sabbath a delight,
the holy day of the LORD honorable,
And honor it,
desisting from your own ways,
 From seeking your own pleasure
And speaking your own word Isa 58:13 NASB 1995

WHAT ABOUT THE SABBATH?

So there remains a Sabbath rest for the people of God.
Heb 4:9 NASB 1977

'So the sons of Israel shall observe the Sabbath, to celebrate the Sabbath throughout their generations as a perpetual covenant.' Ex 31:16 NASB 1995

[8] *"Remember the sabbath day, to keep it holy.* Ex 20:8 NASB 1995

    The Sabbath is to be kept holy according to the Fourth of the Ten Commandments of Our Lord. It is a commandment throughout all time, perpetual, from generation to generation. It is most definitely a day we are to rest and sanctify our souls. It is a day designated by the Lord, for the Lord.
    On the Sabbath Jesus healed and helped others. He read scripture and taught. When His disciples were with Him they picked the heads of grain rubbing them and ate them. In *Col 2:16* it says that no one is to judge acts regarding food or drink in respect to the Sabbath. In *Heb 4:9* it reaffirms that the Sabbath is a day of rest for the people of God.
    In the days before Christ you could not do anything on the Sabbath. The story in the New Testament about the man picking up his mat because Jesus healed him, was considered sin, one, because he picked up his mat and two, because he was healed. Jesus very clearly states that **it is lawful to do good and to help one in need on the Sabbath.** We are not to buy and sell on the Sabbath, nor are we to work, it is a day of rest, a day of sanctification.
    We must pray that the Lord will make us to keep the Sabbath a holy day to the Lord, pleasing to Him so that we may avoid sinning. Again, it is difficult for us as sinners to escape sinning.
    We must attempt to obey all the commandments of Our Lord! We must desire it and ask the Holy Spirit to help us! For those of us who find it difficult to have a day of rest, we must pray for it and ask the Lord to grant it. Perhaps we have worked on the

Sabbath and we should not have, and so now we suffer. Obey the Commands of Our Lord! Repent!

The following scriptures pertain to the Sabbath:

New Testament

Or have ye not read in the law, ***that on the Sabbath day the priests in the temple profane the Sabbath, and are guiltless?*** *Mat 12:5 NASB 1995*

But the Lord answered him and said, "You hypocrites, does not each of you on the Sabbath untie his ox or his donkey from the stall and lead him away to water him? Luke 13:15 NASB 1995

And He said to them, "What man is there among you who has a sheep, and if it falls into a pit on the Sabbath, will he not take hold of it and lift it out? "How much more valuable then is a man than a sheep! So then, ***it is lawful to do good on the Sabbath.****" Mat 12:11-12 NASB 1995*

Old Testament:

And He has violently treated His tabernacle like a garden booth; He has destroyed His appointed meeting place. The ***LORD HAS CAUSED TO BE FORGOTTEN** **The appointed feast and Sabbath*** *in Zion, And He has despised king and priest In the indignation of His anger. La 2:6 NASB 1995*

Therefore no one is to act as your judge in regard to food or drink or in respect to a festival or a new moon or a Sabbath day— Col 2:16 NASB 1995

"It is to be a Sabbath of ***solemn rest for you, that you may humble your souls; it is a permanent statute****. Le 16:31 NASB 1995*

'For six days work may be done, but on the seventh day there is a Sabbath of ***complete rest, holy to the LORD; whoever does any work on the Sabbath day shall surely be put to death.*** *Ex 31:15 NASB 1995*

*"If because of the Sabbath, you **turn your foot From doing your own pleasure on My holy day**, And call the Sabbath a delight, the holy day of the LORD honorable, And honor it, **desisting from your own ways**, From seeking your own pleasure **And speaking your own word**** Isa 58:13 NASB 1995*

"How blessed is the man who does this, And the son of man who takes hold of it; Who keeps from profaning the Sabbath, And keeps his hand from doing any evil." Isa 56:2 NASB 1995

*"It is to be a Sabbath of **complete rest** to you, and you shall **humble your souls**;" Le 23:32 NASB 1995*

*but the seventh day is a Sabbath of the LORD your God; in it **you shall not do any work**, Ex 20:10 NASB 1995*

*but during the **seventh year the land shall have a Sabbath rest**, a Sabbath to the LORD; you shall not sow your field nor prune your vineyard. Le 25:4 NASB 1995*

*Thus says the LORD, "Take heed for yourselves, and **do not carry any load on the Sabbath day** or bring anything in through the gates of Jerusalem. Jer 17:21 NASB 1995*

*In those days I saw in Judah some who were treading wine presses on the Sabbath, and bringing in sacks of grain and **loading them** on donkeys, as well as wine, grapes, figs and all kinds of loads, and they brought them into Jerusalem on the Sabbath day. So **I admonished them on the day they sold food**. Also men of Tyre were living there who imported fish and all kinds of merchandise, and sold them to the sons of Judah on the Sabbath, even in Jerusalem. Then I reprimanded the nobles of Judah and said to them, "What is this evil thing you are doing, by **profaning the Sabbath day**? "Did not your fathers do the same, so that our God brought*

> *on us and on this city all this trouble? Yet you are adding to the wrath on Israel by profaning the Sabbath." It came about that just as it grew dark at the gates of Jerusalem before the Sabbath, I commanded that the doors should be shut and that they should not open them until after the Sabbath. Then I stationed some of my servants at the gates so that no load would enter on the Sabbath day.*
> <u>Ne 13:15-19 NASB 1995</u>

> *'Observe the Sabbath day to keep it holy, as the LORD your God commanded you.'* <u>De 5:12 NASB 1995</u>

> *As for the peoples of the land who bring wares or any grain on the Sabbath day to sell,* **we will not buy from them on the Sabbath or a holy day;** *and we will* **forego the crops the seventh year and the exaction of every debt.**
> <u>Ne 10:31 NASB 1995</u>

> *"And from Sabbath to Sabbath, All mankind will come to bow down before Me," says the LORD.* <u>Isa 66:23 NASB 1995</u>

According to scripture, the Sabbath is a day of complete rest. A day of not doing our own pleasures nor doing whatever we want, nor speaking our own words, but rather, resting, keeping to the Lord, doing good deeds and speaking the Word of God.

In the first scripture shown above in the Old Testament section, the Lord has caused the Sabbath to be forgotten, he was angry at our disobedience. However, the Lord makes all things good for those who love Him. So, looking at the good side, we become truly aware that we are all sinners. **As in game playing, plots and codes are devised, likewise, the Lord has been making WAY for us to understand**. At the cross He said "We know not what we do." In the things the Lord did or said while on earth, we become aware, that it is necessary to unite the army of God and know that the battle is not ours. Jesus came to let us know who we are and what we must do. We are sinners, and must separate ourselves from Satan, the father of sinners! Join Jesus in the cause to divide the kingdom of Satan.

WHY MUST I GIVE MY FREE WILL TO THE LORD?

We should desire to give our free will to the Lord so that we can be born of the will of God like Jesus. It is said that free will is one of the doors in which Satan enters. Our Lord gives us the right to be children of God if we are born of the will of God.

Consider this, you have heard, and probably want to believe, that in Him we live, move, and have our being. But, how can that be, if you do not believe in Divine Providence? How can that be if you do not trust that everything that happens in your life is for the glory of God? How can that be if you do not believe that everything in your life and those around you, are part of His Perfect Plan? In acknowledging the Lord in all we do and all we say, we give Him credit in all things. We have to believe in Divine Providence and Our Lord's perfect plan.

The Deity of Jesus Christ
*"In the beginning was the Word, and the Word was with God, and the **Word was God**. He was in the beginning with God. All things came into being through Him, and **apart from Him nothing came into being that has come into being. In Him was life, and the life was the Light of men.** The Light shines in the darkness, and the darkness did not comprehend it.*

The Witness John
*There came a man sent from God, whose name was John. He came as a witness, to testify about the Light, so that all might believe through him. He was not the Light, but he came to testify about the Light. There was the true Light which, coming into the world, enlightens every man. He was in the world, and the world was made through Him, and the world did not know Him. He came to His own, and those who were His own did not receive Him. But as many as received Him, to them **He gave the right to become children of God,** even to those who believe in His name, **who were born**, not*

*of blood nor of the will of the flesh nor of the will of man, but **of (the will)** God.*

The Word Made Flesh

And the Word became flesh, and dwelt among us and we saw His glory, glory as of the only begotten from the Father, full of grace and truth. John testified about Him and cried out, saying,
"This was He of whom I said, `He who comes after me has a higher rank than I, for He existed before me.' "For of His fullness we have all received, and grace upon grace. For the Law was given through Moses; grace and truth were realized through Jesus Christ. No one has seen God at any time; the only begotten God who is in the bosom of the Father, He has explained Him."
<u>John 1:1-18 NASB 1995</u>

If you think you are making your own choices, then think again of who is your master. We must acknowledge the Lord in our lives and in His perfect plan. We must submit to His Holy Will.

In this book read, *Why do I Suffer?*

WHO WILL FOLLOW JESUS?

The hope of our salvation comes through perfection and there is only one way to be perfect. The Lord left instructions, **He is our living instruction sheet**; and before He comes, we must follow Jesus. It is attainable. The truth is that the answer is in "THE WAY." We must not lean on human understanding.

We need to demonstrate the life Jesus taught, reciprocate everything, return to God. We must divide the kingdom of Satan by uniting in the faith of Jesus Christ the Warrior of Love.

When Jesus came to this earth, metaphorically speaking, He was like the sun inhabiting the dark abyss. In our dark world, light made itself present; and love touched this earth. Love beyond love illuminated like a seed of a blooming flower. And when Mary was overshadowed by the Holy Spirit, the love she experienced is one we have not seen in movies, it was like a supernova. She was one with God himself. His love was of a magnitude beyond our understanding and she was filled with it. The joy she felt was also one we cannot even begin to understand. The Lord desires to give each one of us that same love. He wants our soul to magnify Him, and our Spirits to rejoice in Him. Our life, in such a submittal, would be one we wished we would have responded to even at birth.

We must unite and follow His example. It is important that we take the first step of faith.

Unconditional forgiveness – as Jesus forgave on the cross, we must forgive the worst of sinners, who have hurt us. Even our ancestors who left this earth in discord, the dead like Judas who was used for the glory of God. Hitler to the Jews, who was like the Romans to Jesus, yet Jesus loved and forgave. Perhaps even Satan, he also is the Lord's creation, maybe the Lord used him first to teach us to be His humble and loving children. These are difficult lessons to contemplate to learn of the love of God. Pray for them, the living and the dead. Plead for mercy. Bless them and desire to love them.

Unconditional repentance – repent in sackcloth (burlap) using ashes or dirt, and confess the sins of our ancestors and our own so that the dead in Christ can rise first. Pray for the religious, especially those who think of themselves as being of highest sanctity (holiness) like pharisees.

Unconditional mercy – instead of demonstrating anger be compassionate, instead of vengeance demonstrate forgiveness. Be Merciful as Jesus is, Trust Him! Desire to love everyone. Plead to the Lord for mercy for those who have made others to suffer most. Pray for all haters and ask the Lord to be merciful to them. Pray that the dead will not reject their rising and their second chance at salvation. Believe! If there is hope for us, there is hope for them! We must plead for the living and the dead.

Unconditional love – undoubtedly, we must divide the kingdom of Satan, all Christians must unite no matter what the stumbling block. Let us pray that believers in Christ will repent and desire to love unconditionally. Come back to the Roman Catholic Church where the Lord has promised victory! It is the battleground.

May we be blessed! May the Lord strengthen us and fill us with His unfathomable love!

> *These things I have spoken to you, so that in Me you may have peace. In the world you have tribulation, but take courage; I have overcome the world."* John 16:33 NASB

> **We know the love of God in this way:**
> **because he laid down his life for us. And so,**
> **we must lay down our lives for our brothers.**
> 1 John 3:15 CPDVTSB

> **So may they all be one.** *Just as you, Father, are in me, and I am in you,* **so also may they be one in us: so that the world may believe** *that you have sent me.* John 17:21 CPDVTSB

> *By this, all shall recognize that you are my disciples:*
> *if you will have love for one another."* John 13:35 CPDVTSB

> *Greater love hath no man than this,*
> *that a man lay down his life for his friends.* John 15:13 KJV

The victory is in the cross, learn to love it and live in it!
GATHER – Join the Army of Jesus Christ the Warrior!

What Should My Greatest Passionate Desire Be?

Our greatest and most passionate desire must be to love Our Lord perfectly and to be perfect as Our Heavenly Father is perfect.

Our desire should be one of great passion and urgency, intensely craving the love of God. We must desire to reciprocate, and to love Him **and each other** as He loves us. We must desire to follow Jesus!

We must be willing to be all that He has asked of us and that is to "BE PERFECT AS MY HEAVENLY FATHER IS PERFECT!" We must also make our desire known to Him passionately with a contrite and loving heart.

7/31/2022. I was enlightened to believe that we must also desire and be willing to "Be A Virgin As My Heavenly Blessed Mother Is A Virgin!" My first thought was that the Lord is funny, however, we must know that **for God all things are possible** and it is very likely that it can only be attained with the greatest love finding His favor, hoping for salvation for all mankind. The elect will be chaste. We must also desire to be chaste. One of the requirements of the 144,000 in the book of Revelations is to be chaste.

8/4/2022 The Lord had me take note of the following scripture I believe to be confirmation of what is mentioned above, that is, that He wants all of us, men and women alike to ask Him to make us to be a Virgin as Our Heavenly Blessed Mother is a Virgin, so that He can present us to Christ as His bride.

Scripture:

*For I am jealous for you with a divine jealousy; for I betrothed you to one spouse (one husband), **that I might present you as a chaste virgin to Christ**. 2 Corinthians 11:2*

There is neither Jew nor Greek, there is neither slave nor free man, there is neither male nor female; for you are all one in Christ Jesus. Galatians 3:28 NKJV

Perhaps, the Lord will find favor in us if we take the first step in faith, by uniting in unconditional love, willing to die for the salvation of all, as Jesus did. Or perhaps, the Lord will look kindly upon us and yes, make us a virgin, transforming us from corruption to incorruption, mortality to immortality, perfect as our Heavenly Father is Perfect if we simply believe. Yes, we can be a virgin, because He is a God of the impossible.

PRAYER: Dearest and Most Beloved Lord and King of All Creation, Omnipotent God of the impossible, throughout this book we have been requesting that you make us Perfect as Our Heavenly Father is Perfect as You have requested and desired. However, you have enlightened us to believe that you also desire for us to Be as Your Beloved Bride, Mother of God, Our Blessed Mother, a Virgin as She is a Virgin. And so Lord we request that you make us, all that She is, Holy, Immaculate, Loving, Perfect and a Virgin, and more than we can conceive as You desire, so that You may also find favor in us. Free us from this prison of clay, and make us a choice vessel. We thank you Lord for the Perfect Plans you have for us. We will continue to hope in the fulfillment of your Promise and Deliverance. In the Name of Jesus.

BE PERFECT, THEREFORE, AS YOUR HEAVENLY FATHER IS PERFECT.

MATTHEW 5:48

Who Are The 144,000 In The Book Of Revelation? Can We Be Part of That Number?

These are the 144,000 as mentioned in the Book of Revelations:

*These are the ones who have not been defiled with women, for **they have kept themselves CHASTE**. These are the ones **WHO FOLLOW THE LAMB** wherever He goes. These have been purchased from among men as first fruits to God and to the Lamb. And **NO LIE was found in their mouth; they ARE BLAMELESS**.* Rev 14:4-5 NASB 1995

So can we be part of that number? The Lord says all things are possible for God! We know that His ways are higher than ours! Truly, we do not understand much! Our minds are so small! We are like dumb sheep! But can we be part of that number? Let us consider each of the requisites:

NOT BEEN DEFILED, THEY ARE CHASTE

Can we become a virgin, after we have been so guilty in the flesh? Changing our ways and deciding to be chaste for the Lord from now on, is a good act of repentance and an act of faith. Would this please the Lord and is it enough? Perhaps, it is virginity of mind, pure, non-judgmental, striving to be holy and **having a mind of Christ**. Having no doubt that the God of the impossible can do anything, as previously discussed, we know that he can make us Chaste, as He said **Be a Virgin as My Heavenly Blessed Mother is a Virgin!** The elect will be chaste. We must live in Hope, believing He can make us to qualify under His requisites! We must desire to reap what we sow. Take the first step in faith, **Be Chaste!**

FOLLOW THE LAMB WHEREVER HE GOES

We must desire to **follow Jesus!** Imitate Him! On July 29, 2022 the following scripture left an impression of great mercy. It states that the **unbeliever will obtain mercy through the mercy of**

the believer, that is through OUR mercy the Lord will be merciful. To the Lord they are beloved and God has concluded that He will have mercy on all, if we are merciful. We must demonstrate the greatest love by uniting and forming the Army of God, by being merciful to the worst of sinners living and dead, even Satan. We must desire to reap what we sow. Be an advocate, **Love unto death!**

> *And so all Israel shall be saved: as it is written, ... they are enemies for your sakes: but ..., they are beloved for the fathers' sakes. For the gifts and calling of God are without repentance. For as ye in times past have not believed God, yet have now obtained mercy through their unbelief:*
> *Even so have these also now not believed, THAT*
> ***THROUGH YOUR MERCY***
> ***THEY ALSO MAY OBTAIN MERCY.***
> *For God hath concluded them all in unbelief,*
> ***that he might have mercy upon all.***
> *O the depth of the riches both of the wisdom and knowledge of God! how unsearchable are his judgments, and his ways past finding out! For who hath known the mind of the Lord? or who hath been his counsellor? Or who hath first given to him, and it shall be recompensed unto him again?* ***For of him, and through him, and to him, are all things: to whom be glory forever. Amen.***
> Ro11:26-36 KJV

Do we follow the Lamb wherever He goes? As our Blessed Mother said in the wedding of Cana: *Do whatever He says*! Reciprocate! Return to God! **We Can Follow Jesus!**

NO LIE WAS FOUND IN THEIR MOUTH

We know that **we must not lie**, it is one of the Commandments, so stop the lies. Jesus said that He is the Truth. If we desire to be in Him, we must not be deceitful, manipulative or tell lies. We must desire to reap what we sow. **We Can Be Truthful!**

THEY ARE BLAMELESS

We can be blameless as previously discussed in this book. We must know that God is in control. We must believe in Divine Providence and Trust in Jesus. **We Can Be Blameless!**

Again, all things are possible for God! We do not understand His ways. We must not lean on human understanding. His definition of words is not as we perceive it. Heavenly interpretation verses earthly interpretations of words such as "fear," "jealously," and "blameless" are not as we understand it . What is the heavenly interpretation of "virgin"? We know that Blessed Mary is a virgin. If that is the case, We know the Lord can make us like her…. Just like He can make us Perfect as Our Heavenly Father….

Read your Bibles! Strive to Obey God, Love and unite!

Are The Keys to The Kingdom of Heaven Used as The Lord Intended?

> [19] *And I will give unto thee the keys of the kingdom of heaven: and whatsoever thou shalt bind on earth shall be bound in heaven: and whatsoever thou shalt loose on earth shall be loosed in heaven.* _{Mat 16:19 KJV}

January 28, 2023

What about the keys to the kingdom of heaven? They have been given to Peter, the rock, The Roman Catholic Church. So, what is the key and has it been used as the Lord intended? How do we open that door?

IS THIS THE KEY? Thinking first of the dead and not ourselves, **for they shall rise first** as noted in 1Thess 4:16?
The Lord desires that everyone be saved, even the dead, living in spirit, including the wicked.

> and ***I have the same hope in God***
> *as these men themselves have,* ***that***
> ***there will be a resurrection***
> *of both the righteous and* ***the wicked***. _{Acts 24:15 NIV}

What are we to do to help this happen? We must pray for them, love, and forgive even the worst of sinners. We must pray to liberate them. We must follow Jesus and be the advocate for the remaining unbelievers and the dead, willing to die for our brethren demonstrating unconditional love. Plead to the Lord for mercy for those who have made others to suffer most. Pray for all haters and ask the Lord to be merciful to them, also praying that the dead will not reject their rising and accept their second chance at salvation. Believe! If there is hope for us, there is hope for them! We must plead for the living and the dead.

> ⁵ *Jesus answered, "Very truly I tell you,* **no one can enter the kingdom of God unless they are born of** *water and the* **Spirit**. *⁶ Flesh gives birth to flesh, but the* **Spirit gives birth to spirit.** *⁷ You should not be surprised at my saying, 'You must be born again.'* John 3:5-7 NIV

Sadly, because the second Pentecost has not occurred, and I think no one is born again in this generation, based on John 3:5-7, I can only wonder, if anyone has ever made it to heaven after Jesus resurrected. We must pray for mercy upon everyone both living and all the deceased.

Satan, Pharaoh, Judas, Hitler are perfect examples of sinners difficult to forgive, yet, Jesus shows mercy to all. Can we be merciful to Putin, Zelenskyy, Hamas and to others who cause grief in this world? Wars are the result of our own sinfulness and reluctant heart. We refuse to repent. We fail to acknowledge the Lord in all our ways.

Now is time to make amends! It is time to forgive unconditionally and love unconditionally. No one wins in war. We must repent as in the old days in sackcloth and ashes. We must request forgiveness and mercy for everyone especially all ancestors. We must pray for them! Plead for their salvation!

IS THIS THE KEY? That we take the first step of faith detaching ourselves from the kingdom of this world, Satan's kingdom! Will the key to open the door of heaven turn, when the churches combine and unite the Kingdom of God on earth. As noted in Daniel Chapter 2, **even though they do not adhere, they will combine.**

> **As they return to unity with the Church**
> **My wounds heal, and** 13 **in this way they**
> **alleviate My Passion.** Diary of St. Faustina ¶1218

Our faith must be executed, we must act by taking the first step in faith. Know that the Lord has used all churches for the glory of God, as He used Judas, for whom we should also pray. Satan is on guard, lurking everywhere, keeping the minds of people away from the true Bread of Life and the true Church. This world is Satan's kingdom, and we partake and party in it all the time.

We must become like gladiators and enter the lion's den, by combining. I am not saying that the Catholic Church is the Lion's Den, I am saying that as we combine, a Lion's Den will form, and the Lord will be our Victor. Jesus did not come to bring peace as noted in scripture. He came to declare war against Satan. The Battle against Satan will manifest. Right now, we are all in Satan's court, sinning and not loving as we should. He who is without sin, let him cast the first stone! It is time to combine and to make amends and love unconditionally. Join Jesus in His cause to divide, join the Army of God! Let the rebellion begin!

> *Do not let anyone deceive you in any way, for it will not come* [the coming of the Lord] *unless **the rebellion takes place first** and the man of sin, who is destined for destruction, is revealed.* 2Thessalonians 2:3 ISV

> *^{38} For I am convinced that neither death, nor life, nor angels, nor principalities, nor things present, nor things to come, nor powers, ^{39} nor height, nor depth nor any other created thing will be able to separate us from the love of God that is in Christ Jesus Our Lord.* Ro 8:38-39 NASB

IS THIS THE KEY? That the Church use its authority to bind everyone and all Christ believers to heaven, and loosen from heaven and earth the wounds inflicted upon Our Lord Jesus Christ!

The Lord gives the church the power to bind and loosen. Who has the authority to give the executive command to end all evil? The Pope? Or those who combine in the Army of God and take this authority? Or perhaps, after we combine, Jesus Himself! For the Lord said that a divided kingdom cannot stand.

Sadly, Christians presently cannot stand because they are divided joined to the kingdom of Satan. We are participants in Satan's kingdom on earth. Combine and allow the Lord to demonstrate His glory! Join the war Jesus started! Unite to combine the Army of Our Lord Jesus Christ, Our Warrior! We must love, pray, fast and repent! We must take the first step in faith!

> ^{16}*And Simon Peter answered and said, Thou art the Christ, the Son of the living God.* ^{17}*And Jesus answered and said unto him, Blessed art thou, Simon Barjona: for flesh and blood hath not revealed it unto thee, but my Father which is in heaven.* ^{18}*And I say also unto thee, That thou art* **Peter, and upon this rock** *I will build my church; and* **the gates of hell shall not prevail against it.** ^{19}*And* **I will give unto thee** *the keys of the kingdom of heaven: and* **whatsoever thou shalt bind on earth shall be bound in heaven**: *and whatsoever thou shalt loose on earth shall be loosed in heaven.* Mat 16:16-19 KJV

The rock, which crushes the kingdoms in the statue, in the book of Daniel, promises victory. It is apparent that the Lord identifies Peter as the rock in *Mat 16:18.* Jesus told us that Peter is the rock and that the gates of hell will not prevail against it. Jesus made Peter the chief Apostle and head of the Church on earth. The Roman Catholic Church is the true Church. It has recorded the history and lineage of priests since Peter, the apostle. The Roman Catholic Church is the appointed rock upon which the Lord Himself built His Church. Although many use their wicked tongue to speak against them, we must know that it is not by the Word of God that those words are spoken. So then, enter the Lion's Den! We must combine!

This earth is Satan's kingdom, the Lord even said it while on earth. He wants to claim us and the earth as His own! We must gather!

> *Jesus answered, "My kingdom is not of this world. If my kingdom were of this world, my servants would have been fighting, that I might not be delivered over to the Jews. But my kingdom is not from the world.* John 18:36 ESV

Will You Be Part of Today's Finale?

so the dream is true and its interpretation is trustworthy
<u>Dan 2:45 NASB 1995</u>

DANIEL'S INTERPRETATION IS TRUE AND TRUSTWORTHY!

In the book of Daniel chapter 2, King Nebuchadnezzar is troubled by a dream. He refuses to tell anyone of his dream and demands a revelation and an interpretation from his advisors. He threatens to kill them all if they do not respond. Daniel, being included in that threat, goes to the King. He is granted permission to withdraw and pray with his three companions. Daniel returns to tell the King **that God has shown the King what will happen in the future. Daniel gives God the glory and acknowledges that only the Lord can reveal such things.** Daniel says that he is no different from any other living person. He tells the King what he dreamt and its interpretation.

Today, part of the dream has not yet occurred. Now, is the time to make it happen, we must take the first step of faith.

The King's Dream was of a large, single, awesome, and extraordinary statue. The statue represents different kingdoms, in different eras. The statue had a head of gold, which Daniel said represented King Nebuchadnezzar. The chest and arms were of silver, the belly and thighs of bronze, legs of iron, and its feet were partly of iron and partly of clay. Daniel goes on to explain that a rock was cut out, not by human hands, and it struck the feet of the statue causing the whole statue to be shattered.

The toes of the statue represent division. In Daniel 2:43 he says **that we do not adhere to one another, but we will combine.** The great mountain referred to in Daniel 2:35 is the Divine Kingdom of God. So, although, we as believers in Christ find it difficult to adhere to one another, that is, agree with one another, our willingness to love unconditionally and gather will bring victory. We must put aside all doctrines that have caused imperfection. If we are willing to demonstrate love as Jesus did, as noted in *1 John 3:16,* willing to lay down our lives for our brethren, the Lord will be our reward.

We are Christians arguing with one another, and preach the thoughts of men. The Lord wants His joy to be complete by obeying Him and being like-minded, loving unconditionally, being one in spirit with one purpose. What is that purpose? The purpose is to join Jesus in his cause to divide the kingdom of Satan and by uniting the Kingdom of God on earth. It is for the salvation of all mankind, the living, and the dead.

> *^{28}And we know that God causes all things to work together for good to those who love God, to those who are called according to His purpose.* Ro 8:28 NASB

The great mountain is referring to all believers in Christ and the unity of the churches which includes the living and the dead living in spirit. We will be united in one cord that cannot be broken. The Kingdom of God will no longer be scattered, we will be united to the Kingdom of God. The kingdom of Satan will be divided into two. God against Satan. The Kingdom of God will reign.

> *^{49}"I have come to cast fire upon the earth; and how I wish it were already kindled! ^{50}***"But I have a baptism to undergo, and how distressed I am until it is accomplished!*** Luke 12:49-51 NASB 1995

We must kindle the fire and set it ablaze to tumble the kingdom. He is waiting for us to be unconditionally merciful and to love unconditionally as He loves. We must become ONE! We must allow activation of the key to heaven. **We must take the first step in faith**. The Lord has already given us the answer…

We must repent in sackcloth and ashes and join forces. Uniting to the Roman Catholic Church is the battleground where the Lord promises that the gates of hell will not prevail. Peter is the Rock, maybe he is the rock in Daniel's interpretation that was not made by human hands. We may not understand it, nevertheless, Jesus said that Peter is the rock.

The fourth kingdom, is the united church! **The divided nations are but two: God vs Satan.** Jesus came to divide the kingdom of Satan. It is not this place or that, it is in the hearts of men loving unconditionally, today, and now. Today the importance of this dream is what follows in Daniel's revelation: we will not adhere to one another, but we will combine.

We must take the first step in faith and join the cause Jesus began by dividing the kingdom of Satan, to form THE DIVINE KINGDOM! Unite against all odds! Love unconditionally!

Like Noah, Like Moses, Like Joshua, Like Mary! Like Jesus! and many others. No matter what it looks like, give up your platform and your churches, tell your congregation to go to the Roman Catholic Church and to worship and exalt the Lord there, the Christians, all Christ believers, must unite! Pray the Rosary! Do not worry about money, trust in Jesus! Perhaps, we as a congregation can help each other in need. **Eat of the UNLEAVENED bread (*Ex 34:25*), His body, and drink of the wine, His blood.** We must be changed! We will be transformed! the Bread of Life gives life. It is time to combine and to make amends. It is time to forgive unconditionally and love unconditionally. Take the first step in faith! Do it!

[35]Then the iron, the clay, the bronze, the silver, and the gold were crushed to pieces all at the same time, and like chaff from the summer threshing floors; and the wind carried them away so

that not a trace of them was found. **But the stone that struck the statue became a great mountain and filled the entire earth.** <u>Dan 2:35 NASB</u>

Rome

⁴⁰Then there will be a fourth kingdom as strong as iron; just as iron smashes and crushes everything, so, like iron that crushes, it will smash and crush all these things. ⁴¹And in that you saw the feet and toes, partly of potter's clay and partly of iron, ***it will be a divided kingdom****; but it will have within it some of the toughness of iron, since you saw the iron mixed with common clay. ⁴²And just as the toes of the feet were partly of iron and partly of pottery; so some of the kingdom will be strong, and part of it will be fragile. ⁴³In that you saw the iron mixed with common clay,* ***they will combine with one another in their descendants; but they will not adhere to one another,*** *just as iron does not combine with pottery.*

The Divine Kingdom

⁴⁴And in the days of those kings the God of heaven will set up a kingdom which will never be destroyed, and that kingdom will not be left for another people; it will crush and put an end to all these kingdoms, but it will itself endure forever. ⁴⁵Just as you saw that a stone was broken off from the mountain without hands, and that it crushed the iron, the bronze, the clay and the silver, and the gold, the great God has made known to the king what will take place in the future; so, the dream is certain and its interpretation is trustworthy." <u>Dan 2:40-45 NASB</u>

Bless the Lord for He is Good. His Mercy is Everlasting! His Love is beyond understanding! May we truly become perfect as Our Heavenly Father, Heavenly Mother, and as Jesus is perfect! Almighty Loving God, please give to us the grace of unconditional love; remove our fear of loving unto death! Unite us and make us ONE body, ONE of great faith, ONE in unconditional love, ONE pleasing to you! Help us to take the first step in faith in gathering the Army of God. Blessed is He who comes in the Name of the Lord! Blessed is Our Creator and Loving God that makes all things possible! Jesus, We Trust in You!

UNITE IN UNCONDITIONAL LOVE EVEN UNTO DEATH!

This is a Call to Arms! Love, pray, fast, repent, and UNITE!

A DIFFERENT KIND OF WAR

TAKE ACTION ON THIS: = ACTS 19:19
*And many of those who practiced magic
brought their books together and*
began burning them *in the sight of everyone;*
<u>Acts 19:19 NASB 1995</u>

LET US DESIRE TO OBEY AND FOLLOW JESUS
IN ALL THINGS, IN THE NAME OF JESUS.

May we each do our part to put an end to even this war starting in our homes. Pray, fast, be merciful and may the WORD OF GOD Prosper and infiltrate this land which has been given to us by Our Creator, Eternal Love and mercy itself.

[5]"Arise, bless the LORD your God forever and ever!
O may Your glorious name be blessed
And exalted above all blessing and praise!
[6]"You alone are the LORD. You have made the heavens,
The heaven of heavens with all their host,
The earth and all that is on it,
The seas and all that is in them.
You give life to all of them
and the heavenly host bows down before You.
[7]"You are the LORD God, ... <u>Neh 9:5-7 NASB95</u>

BLESSED ARE YOU WHO COMES IN THE NAME OF THE LORD!

GATHER!

**This is The End of Section PART II
Who Is Who and What Is What?**

PART III

PRAISE
PRAYERS
MESSAGES
MISCELLANEOUS
&
COMMANDS
OF THE LORD

Part III is taken in-part
from the original book entitled:
<u>THE GREAT DELIVERANCE</u>
<u>Stop a Grieving World</u>
(Green book cover with white split leave)

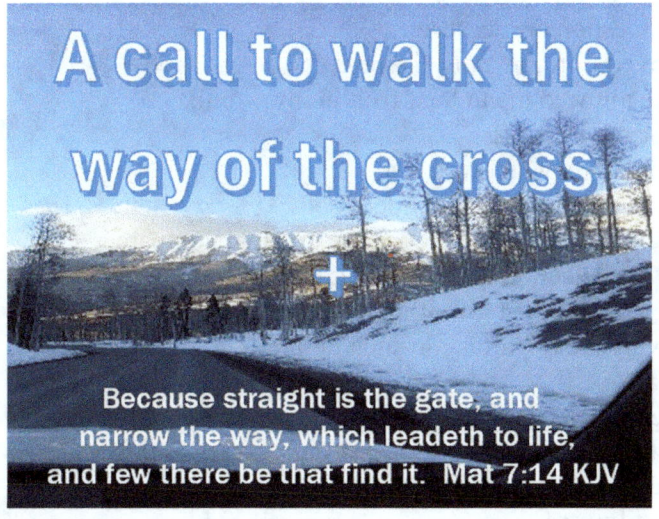

The following is the remaining message from the 5th Mystery of the Rosary meditations. The Lord wants us to love and exalt THE BREAD OF LIFE, in the form of Bread itself.

THE EUCHARISTIC HOST LIKE MY BABY

My Baby
Oh, My precious baby
Holding you in my arms
Defenseless and so lovingly, I embrace you.
Just born you are helpless
Your head, I have to hold
And near my heart,
loves sweet beat comforts both
Revealing Unconditional love,
total dependence
Engaged in new sight of responsibility
Love has shown itself without restraint
Innocent Love,
infant love
weak yet strong
Free and without reservations untold
Willingly our love deepens
without question or measure.
My Beloved Lord, in Your likeness
You have allowed me to bear fruit in my womb
in Your same likeness,
Blessed are You who gives life,
and whose greatness is not understood
except for the small measure we are given to compare.
Thank You Father, Son, and Holy Ghost
for the gift of life, the gift of love and
for allowing me to partake in such delight.

The Eucharistic Host
Oh, my Exalted Eucharistic Host
My Seed of Life unseen
My Infant Inward
Appearing defenseless,

yet defending

What Seed enters my mouth
What King enters this tomb
Accepting You in my mouth
Make me holy and true, loving. and pure
The embrace of my tongue You receive
With sweet alms and reverence
Eucharistic love returns to me
Such sweet high, mystical ecstasy,
so loving a communion
Love beyond love ignites
Life beyond Life recognized

Oh what Heavenly Bread is this
What food has nourished me
What Glorious King arises within
Oh my beloved, My soul is Yours
My flesh and body too

What greatness is this within me
Oh, beloved consumed by Your presence
Nothing else matters
There is no other want

Oh, Love Everlasting
Do not leave me
Be my strength, Be my all
Gracious, Immortal Beautiful Savior
My Want of You Is Without Ceasing

My Love, My Light
Let Us Be One Throughout Eternity.
Arise and remain within me;
Let us be whole. In the Name of Jesus.

THE GREATEST ANGUISH VS LOVE
His heart has become so hardened
that even a speck of light cannot be seen

Lost in hope. lost in time
hopeless in a helpless earth

the road broadens
He reaps what He sows
in sorrow and anguish to an extreme
there is no end to self-punishment

Oh My Lord, shine your light upon him
soften his heart and show him your mercy
Heal him Dear Lord

Forgive us, forgive him
Deliver us Oh Lord, from all hatred, jealousy, envy, and pride
In the Name of Jesus

ST. MICHAEL THE ARCHANGEL
St. Michael the Archangel, defend us in battle. Be our protection against the wickedness and snares of the devil. May God rebuke him, we humbly pray, and do thou, O Prince of the Heavenly Hosts, by the power of God, cast into Hell Satan and all evil spirits who prowl through the world seeking the ruin of souls. Amen.

THE CHAPLET OF ST MICHAEL
O God, come to my assistance.
O Lord, make haste to help me.
Glory be to the Father, and to the Son, and to the Holy Spirit, as it was in the beginning is now and ever shall be world without end. Amen.

Say one **Our Father and three Hail Mary's** *after each of the following nine salutations in honor of the nine Choirs of Angels*

By the intercession of St. Michael and the celestial Choir of **(1)**

*... may the Lord **(a)** ...*

1) Seraphim — a) make us worthy to burn with the fire of perfect charity.

2) Cherubim — b) grant us the grace to leave the ways of sin and run in the paths of Christian perfection.

3) Thrones — c) may the Lord infuse into our hearts a true and sincere spirit of humility.

4) Dominions — d) give us grace to govern our senses and overcome any unruly passions. Amen.

5) Powers — e) protect our souls against the snares and temptations of the devil.

6) Virtues — f) preserve us from evil and falling into temptation.

7) Principalities — g) may God fill our souls with a true spirit of obedience.

8) Archangels — h) give us perseverance in faith and in all good works in order that we may attain the glory of Heaven

9) Angels — i) grant us to be protected by them in this mortal life and conducted in the life to come to Heaven. Amen.

*Say **one Our Father in honor of each of the following** leading Angels: St. Michael, St. Gabriel, St. Raphael, and our Guardian Angel. (Added: all other archangels and angel's unknown to us)*

Concluding prayers: *O glorious prince St. Michael, chief and commander of the heavenly hosts, guardian of souls, vanquisher of rebel spirits, servant in the house of the Divine King and our admirable conductor, you who shine with excellence and superhuman virtue deliver us from all evil, who turn to you with confidence and enable us by your gracious protection to serve God more and more faithfully every day.*

Pray for us, O glorious St. Michael, Prince of the Church of Jesus Christ, that we may be made worthy of His promises. Almighty and Everlasting God, Who, by a prodigy of goodness and a merciful desire for the salvation of all men, has appointed the most glorious Archangel St. Michael Prince of Your Church, make us worthy, we ask You, to be delivered from all our enemies, that none of them may harass us at the hour of death, but that we may be conducted by him into Your Presence. This we ask through the merits of Jesus Christ Our Lord. Amen.

A NEW CHAPLET OF MERCY
(as inspired in the prayer life of Fr. Einer R. Ochoa (1997)

Simple version:

Contemplate the Cross

Start with the Apostle **Creed** on the first bead

Pray the **Our Father**

Three **Hail Mary's** on the next three beads

On the next bead say,

> *"Sacred hearts of Jesus and Mary, I Offer you my mind, my body, my heart, and my soul that the will of God be done in me"*

Ten times *"Jesus I trust in You"*

Glory be…
Pray the mysteries of the rosary

Finish with the *"Salve Regina"* (Hail Holy Queen)

OBEDIENT MIND TO CHRIST

For though we walk in the flesh, we do not war after the flesh: (For the weapons of our warfare are not carnal, But mighty through God to the pulling down of strong holds;) Casting down imaginations, and every high thing that exalts itself against the knowledge of God, and bringing into captivity every thought to the obedience of Christ; And having in a readiness to revenge all disobedience, when my obedience is fulfilled. 2Cor 10:3-6 KJV

Lord make me, and my mind obedient to You; bless me, protect me and keep me from all harm. Remain with me and in me always. I also ask

Your protection upon the minds and bodies of all beloved on earth. In the Name of Jesus. I pray.

THE ARMOR OF GOD

Finally, I am strong in the Lord, and in the power of his might. I put on the whole armour of God, that I may be able to stand against the wiles of the devil. I wrestle not against flesh and blood, but against principalities, against powers, against the rulers of the darkness of this world, against spiritual wickedness in high places. Wherefore I put on the whole armour of God, that I may be able to withstand in the evil day, and having done all, to stand. I Stand therefore, having my loins girt about with truth, and having on the breastplate of righteousness; And my feet shod with the preparation of the gospel of peace; Above all, taking the shield of faith, wherewith I shall be able to quench all the fiery darts of the wicked. And I take the helmet of salvation, and the sword of the Spirit, which is the word of God: Praying always with all prayer and supplication in the Spirit, and watching thereunto with all perseverance and supplication for all saints; Ephesians 6:10-18 KJV personalized as a prayer

I believe I wear the Armor of God for all eternity, and I also ask Your protection Dear Lord, upon all beloved on earth. In the Name of Jesus. Amen.

Worldwide Agreement of Hope-Pray Without Ceasing

We know that not one person can pray without ceasing, we must sleep. Yet, in *1Thes 5:17* we are told to "Pray without ceasing". My Hope is that in unison we can accomplish this! **Let us all agree to make the call to Heaven** and **act by Praying the Rosary all the time**, anywhere, everywhere, or in His Humble Presence at the Church! (Individually or in forming groups organized to cover time 24/7):

Everyone, Everywhere And Anywhere Around The World, help cover every moment on the clock: start a group Every Hour, another group Every Half Hour, another Every Quarter Hour, On the Hour and/or EVERY DAY and if you cannot do this then pray **AT ANY MOMENT**, while Rosaries are being prayed above, just pray, even if just one prayer, one Hail Mary and more! Be sure to…

1. **UNITE YOURSELF to the following intentions and purpose:**

    Beloved Lord Jesus Christ increase in us and give to us Your perfect love that we may love you perfectly, prepare us and give to us the grace to make Your joy complete *by being of the same mind, maintaining the same love, united in spirit, intent on one purpose,* fulfill your desire that all will be saved, deliver us from evil and as a Father to His Children, Answer us! In the Name of Jesus *(Scripture taken from Php 2:2)*

2. **REFLECT** on the same intentions with All Your Heart Mind and Soul. **After each Rosary, or before we Sleep/ Work/ Or Become Distracted   Pray this:**

    Beloved Holy and Loving Lord, I surrender this vessel of clay to you and ask you to allow my Holy Spirit to continue in prayer in the Worldwide agreement of Hope that my Mind and every member of my body, my soul and spirit may continue in prayer in perfect undistracted devotion for you, I unite myself to those praying in the same mind, maintaining the same love, united in spirit, intent on one purpose. With You Lord, all things are possible, unite us to yourself and deliver us from evil. In Jesus Name Amen

I believe we can do this, resulting in constant unceasing prayer worldwide. Even if some of us sleep or are momentarily distracted and we are not all praying at the same time, if our desire, and want, are the same, with all our hearts, mind, and souls **We Will Be There in Spirit**. The prayer of sleep/distraction in this agreement will unite us as well - **Simply Believe!**

All things are possible through Christ our Great Omnipotent Loving God! Desire to Love Him Greatly! Desire to Love Mary Mother of God as He Loves Her!

Pray Without Ceasing! We can do this together! Desire to be ONE! One Love, One Hope, One with Our One God! One with Jesus, the Finisher of Our Faith! (YOUTUBE has Live Rosaries being said, join them.)

Pray the Rosary! The Hail Mary is the call to Heaven asking for the Lord to return. It is reciprocating the annunciation from Angel Gabriel to Mary. Now we are asking for our new birth, to be born true children of God.

This is a call to Arms, Let us join the cause Jesus began in dividing the kingdom of Satan. We must gather!

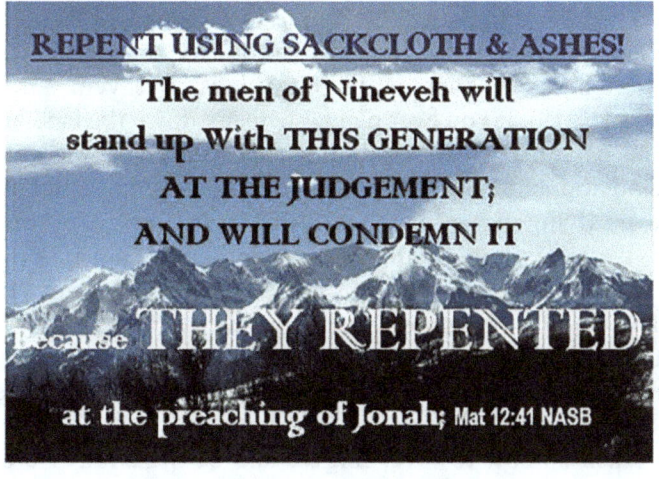

STEPS TO THE NARROW ROAD

4/30/2023
*"Enter by the narrow gate; for wide is the gate
and broad is the way that leads to destruction,
and there are many who go in by it.* Mat 7:13 NKJV

In the book The Great Deliverance Stop a Grieving World, there is a long list of escalating steps, which is excluded here. A brief discussion is written in its place.

According to the Bible, there are so many commands, statutes, and precepts. It may seem impossible to remember them all. Without a doubt, trying to obey them, could be worrisome. While writing the book Sackcloth and Ashes; The Dead in Christ Shall Rise First, I remember getting somewhat angry at the Lord. I was jotting down sins to confess while using sackcloth and ashes (which I believe we must all do! I believe it is required.). It became apparent to me that the things He says to do from generation to generation is impossible for us to do. Our minds are so little and we are irresponsible regarding the things of heaven. Afterall, we are only human. Also, if you ever played whisper down the lane, the story changes from person to person. Although we continue to sin, we must confess and attempt to be reconciled one to another as the Lord has asked.

We are living in the kingdom of Satan on earth. His kingdom is not divided, we are in union with him, sinning and living in our lustful, and selfish ways. Consequently, Jesus came not to bring peace, but rather division. The God of the impossible has shown us The Way to find the narrow road. On the cross He said "Father, forgive them for they know not what they do." He has made us aware that as sinners, Satan is the father of sinners. So are we children of Satan, therefore, devils? He came to convert us, teach us how to love, forgive and be merciful. He came to divide and to gather His army. We must gather as mentioned throughout this book.

If you want to be part of the elect, we must HOPE and know all things are possible through our Almighty God. We must desire to comply with the requirements mentioned for the 144,000. The ultimate questions are these…

Who is Willing to be Merciful Like Jesus?
Who Will Become Chaste, for God's Sake?
Who Will Not Lie, Living Only in Truth?

Who Will Be Blameless, living in Divine Providence, and giving God the Glory and credit for All that Happens in Our Lives?

Who is willing to love unto death for the worst of us, both the living and dead?

We must take the first step in faith, repent in sackcloth with use of ashes as Jonah preached and unite to form the Kingdom of God.

OUR CROSS ☩ is to UNITE even though we do not adhere, we must combine to the Roman Catholic Church (Peter is the key) and give up our platforms REGARDLESS of whatever stumbling block we may encounter. We cannot serve God and money. Acknowledge the Lord when you do use it or anything of this world! Do not be afraid. The Lord wants His Army to unite into the kingdom of God! This is a spiritual war and Jesus Christ the Warrior will fight for us! We must stand still knowing that He is with us! He will fight the battle, not us, we are only vessels of clay submitting to the power of an Almighty and Glorious God who loves us. **We must Love, Pray, and Exalt Him!**

Allow your vessels of clay, to be set free by Jesus Christ the Warrior. Be free indeed! We are held captive in these prisons of clay. Awake all you sleepers! In the Name of Jesus!

Rebels against the kingdom of Satan… Rebels for Jesus Christ the Warrior of Love, Army Rise up! Let the rebellion begin! Repent in sackcloth using ashes and Gather! **THIS IS A CALL TO ARMS! Love, pray, fast, repent, and unite!**

> *"**If Satan has risen up against himself** and
> is divided, he cannot stand,
> **but he is finished!*** Mark 3:26 NASB95

CONCLUSION: So, who will partake? As noted in *Will You Be Part of Today's Finale?* Afterall, Daniel's interpretation is true and trustworthy!

> ***they will combine with one another*** *in their descendants;*
> ***but they will not adhere to one another*** Daniel 2:43 NASB

Praise worship and exalt the Lord. Repent and Receive Holy Communion, the Bread of Life with a contrite and loving heart. Your mouth is a tomb, allow the Lord to arise. Believers wake up!

THY KINGDOM COME, ON EARTH AS IT IS IN HEAVEN!

[14] Blessed are those who wash their robes, so that they will have the right to the tree of life, and may enter the city by the gates. [15] Outside are the dogs, the sorcerers, the sexually immoral persons, the murderers, the idolaters, and everyone who loves and practices lying. Rev 22:14 NASB

Let us pray for *"the dogs, the sorcerers, the sexually immoral persons, the murderers, the idolaters, and everyone who loves and practices lying."* Let us pray for all sinners, and all guilty even unto death for the salvation of all, both living and dead. Plead for mercy!

**IF WE ARE MERCIFUL TO THE UNBELIEVER THEN THE LORD WILL ALSO BE MERCIFUL TO THEM
WE MUST LIVE IN LOVE AND MERCY
WE MUST DESIRE TO AMEND OUR WAYS
DESIRE HIS LOVE AND LOVE EVERYONE BACK**

Here is hoping that everyone will be led to repent using sackcloth and ashes and be led to become Christ like. Here is hoping that the Lord will prepare us all and we will be ready for His Coming. Here is hoping that we will not be afraid to love unconditionally and be willing to unite the Kingdom of God, and divide the kingdom of Satan.

Desire to please him and love him first above everyone and everything. When he says "remember me" reciprocate to him "Lord remember me, receive me as your own." Trust in Jesus no matter what!

Do these things because it is written in His Word, the Word of God. If you have any doubt about what is written in this book, then diligently seek with all your heart, mind, and soul; ask the Lord. **Use sackcloth it is like a clearing for the Lord to hear and teach each one of us. But first we must repent in sackcloth with ashes or dirt upon us.** So, before judging, Repent, as noted. Submit to Him and He will guide and teach as He has promised in His covenant. May we all become of one mind in Christ! Please discern and pray! There is only ONE TEACHER! Jesus!

LET THE LOVING REBELLION BEGIN! In the Name of Jesus!

STEPS TO THE REBELLION OF LOVE

Do not let anyone deceive you in any way, for it will not come [the coming of the Lord] *unless **the rebellion takes place first** and the man of sin, who is destined for destruction, is revealed.*
<u>2Thessalonians 2:3 ISV</u>

- **A. WHO does this apply to:**
  1. All believers and lovers of Jesus Christ!
  2. We are rebels in the kingdom of Satan, as sinners we will rebel against the father of sinners.
- **B. WHAT is the purpose?**
  To join Jesus in the cause to divide the Kingdom of Satan for the salvation of all.
- **C. WHERE is this accomplished?**
  The battleground is the Roman Catholic Church. Jesus promises that the gates of hell will not prevail in the church of the apostle Peter. We must gather everywhere, throughout the world.
- **D. WHEN will this be accomplished?**
  As exemplified throughout the Bible, we must take the first step in faith and then the Lord will respond. We must gather in faith trusting Jesus Christ, Our Warrior of Love and Our Victor! He will fight the battle. Our vessels of clay will Trust and Be Still, keeping in prayer, exalting the Lord. The Lord knows when the flock has gathered in full.
- **E. WHY should we do this?**
  To follow Jesus as He has asked us to do. Be as He is in unconditional love, unconditional mercy, unconditional forgiveness, and repent unconditionally for the living and the dead for the salvation of all.
- **F. HOW will this be accomplished?**
  1. Repent
  a. Go to the confessional and confess your sins, be reconciled one to another.
  b. Confess your sins and those of your ancestors.
     Plead for mercy for them, hoping that the Lord will save all living and all the dead.

    c. Repent in sackcloth using ashes. The Lord repeatedly tells men everywhere to repent as the people of Nineveh. Sleep in it, for learning.
2. **Love Unconditionally.** Be kind, love, and accept all humiliation for the glory of God, follow the example of Jesus
3. **Pray and exalt the Lord** without ceasing
    a. Pray the Rosary! The Hail Mary is the call to Heaven. It is reciprocating the annunciation from Angel Gabriel to Mary. Now we are asking for our new birth, to be born true children of God. We are asking for Jesus to return to us!
4. **Gather and Unite.** We as believers and lovers of Jesus Christ, must form the rebellion by uniting and praying without ceasing, exalting the Lord. **Stand firm, be still** and Let the Lord be Our Victor! Submit your vessels of clay to God Almighty through Jesus. The battle is the Lords'!
5. **And of course, follow the requisites of the 144,000: Be chaste, blameless, truthful, follow Jesus, be love and mercy itself.**
6. **Believe the impossible is possible** through Jesus and desire to be Perfect as Our Heavenly Father is, Perfect as Our Blessed Mother is.

BLESSED IS HE WHO COMES IN THE NAME OF THE LORD!

And at the sounding of the seventh angel there were great voices in heaven, saying, The kingdom of the world has become the kingdom of our Lord, and of his Christ, and he will have rule forever and ever Rev 11:15 BBE

And they overcame him by the blood of the Lamb and by the word of his testimony. ***And they loved not their own lives, even unto death*** *Rev 12:11 CPDVTSB*

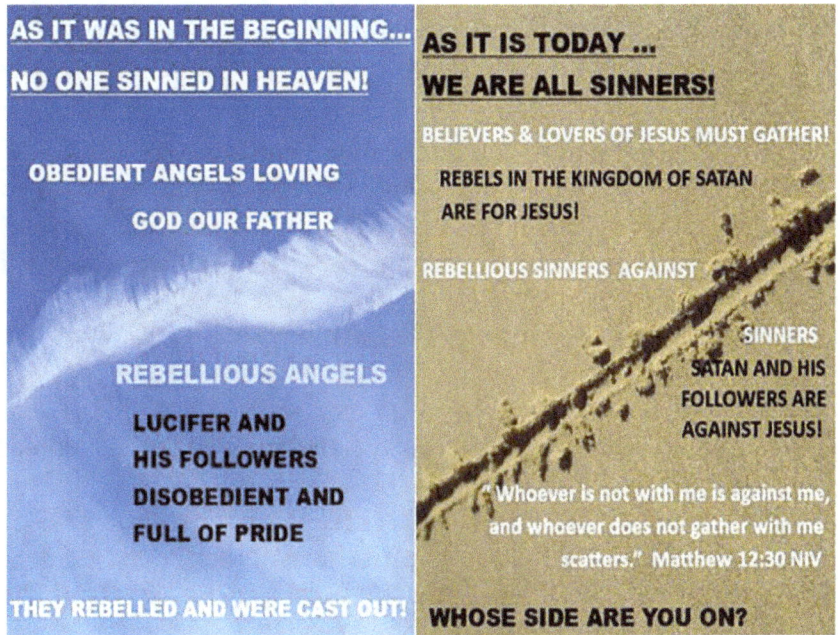

*And so all Israel shall be saved: as it is written,
... they are enemies for your sakes: but
..., they are beloved for the fathers' sakes.
... Even so have these also now not believed,
that THROUGH **YOUR MERCY**
THEY ALSO MAY OBTAIN MERCY.
For God hath concluded them all in unbelief,
that he might have mercy upon all. <u>Ro11:26-32 KJV</u>*

It is important for us to know who we are. It is important to realize that we are rebels in the kingdom of Satan and must gather as Jesus has taught. We must join Jesus in His mission to divide.

IMITATING THE BIBLE EVENTS

1. Baptism of Water by John the Baptist
   People on earth are baptized with water

2. Confessing one to another or in the confessional
   Confessing to God by repenting in Sackcloth asking mercy for our ancestors so that they will be with the dead first to rise, pray that they will not reject their second chance at salvation

3. Breaking of the Bread at the Last Supper
   Receiving Holy Communion, The Bread of Life

4. Apostles gathered and received the Holy Spirit at Pentecost after Christ resurrected
   REBELS FOR CHRIST **GATHER and unite** and receive the Baptism of the Holy Spirit through the second Pentecost before Jesus comes again administered by Jesus Himself. Spirit to Spirit. Men are born again, Born of God.

5. Good angels' rebel in Heaven the Kingdom of God. It was a rebellion of hate.
   Sinners rebel on earth against Satan's kingdom.
   It is a Rebellion of Love!

6. Jesus came to earth born of man, lowest of men.
   Jesus comes to earth out of Heaven, the Highest of Kings. He is our Victor and claims His kingdom on earth

"The time is fulfilled, and the kingdom of God is at hand; repent, and believe in the gospel" (Mk 1:15).

THOSE WHO ARE WITH ME GATHER

Believers In Jesus Christ Wanting to be Born of God
These are Rebels in the Kingdom of Satan

SINNER / GOOD DEVIL - LOVES JESUS

**THEY CANNOT ESCAPE SIN UNLESS
ALL REBELS JOIN JESUS IN THE CAUSE
TO DIVIDE THE KINGDOM OF SATAN**

vs

THOSE WHO ARE AGAINST ME SCATTER

These do not believe,
do not love, and
Do not follow Jesus;
their father is the devil (John 8:44)

THIS SINNER / DEVIL LOVES TO SIN

We know that no one who has been born of God sins; but He who was born of God keeps him, and the evil one does not touch him 1John 5:18 NASB

What does it mean when scripture says "on these two commandments hang all the law and the prophets"? It means that with obedience to the greatest commandment all others are obeyed automatically!

THE NEW TESTAMENT
THE GREATEST COMMANDMENT

Master, which is the great commandment in the law?
Jesus said unto him,
Thou shalt love the Lord thy God with all thy heart,
and with all thy soul, and with all thy mind.
This is the first and great commandment.

And the second is like unto it,
Thou shalt love thy neighbour as thyself.
On these two commandments **hang all the law** *and the prophets.*
Mathew 22:36-40 KJV

THE OLD TESTAMENT
THE TEN COMMANDMENTS

¹Then God spoke all these words, saying,
² "I am the LORD your God, who brought you out of the land of Egypt, out of the house of slavery.
³ "You shall have no other gods before Me.
⁴ "You shall not make for yourself an idol, or any likeness of what is in heaven above or on the earth beneath or in the water under the earth. ⁵ "You shall not worship them or serve them; for I, the LORD your God, am a jealous God, visiting the iniquity of the fathers on the children, on the third and the fourth generations of those who hate Me, ⁶but showing lovingkindness to thousands, to those who love Me and keep My commandments.
⁷ "You shall not take the name of the LORD your God in vain, for the LORD will not leave him unpunished who takes His name in vain.
⁸ "Remember the sabbath day, to keep it holy. ⁹ "Six days you shall labor and do all your work, ¹⁰but the seventh day is a sabbath of the LORD your God; in it you shall not do any work, you or your son or your daughter, your male or your female servant or your cattle or your sojourner who stays with you. ¹¹ "For in six days the LORD made the heavens and the earth, the sea and all that is in them, and rested on the seventh day; therefore the LORD blessed the sabbath day and made it holy.
¹² "Honor your father and your mother, that your days may be prolonged in the land which the LORD your God gives you.
¹³ "You shall not murder.
¹⁴ "You shall not commit adultery.
¹⁵ "You shall not steal.
¹⁶ "You shall not bear false witness against your neighbor.
¹⁷ "You shall not covet your neighbor's house; you shall not covet your neighbor's wife or his male servant or his female servant or his ox or his donkey or anything that belongs to your neighbor."
¹⁸ All the people perceived the thunder and the lightning flashes and the sound of the trumpet and the mountain smoking; and when the people saw it, they trembled and stood at a distance. ¹⁹Then they said to Moses, "Speak to us yourself and we will listen; but let not God speak to us, or we will die." ²⁰ Moses said to the

people, *"Do not be afraid; for God has come in order to test you, and in order that the fear of Him may remain with you, so that you may not sin."* ^{21} *So the people stood at a distance, while Moses approached the thick cloud where God was.*

^{22} *Then the LORD said to Moses, "Thus you shall say to the sons of Israel, 'You yourselves have seen that I have spoken to you from heaven.* ^{23} *'You shall not make other gods besides Me; gods of silver or gods of gold, you shall not make for yourselves.* ^{24} *'You shall make an altar of earth for Me, and you shall sacrifice on it your burnt offerings and your peace offerings, your sheep and your oxen; in every place where I cause My name to be remembered, I will come to you and bless you.* ^{25} *'If you make an altar of stone for Me, you shall not build it of cut stones, for if you wield your tool on it, you will profane it.* ^{26} *'And you shall not go up by steps to My altar, so that your nakedness will not be exposed on it.'*

<u>Exodus Ch. 20:1-26 NASB 1995</u>
NASB 1995 Copyright © 1960, 1962, 1963, 1968, 1971, 1972, 1973, 1975, 1977, 1995 by The Lockman Foundation, La Habra, Calif. All rights reserved. For Permission to Quote Information visit http://www.lockman.org

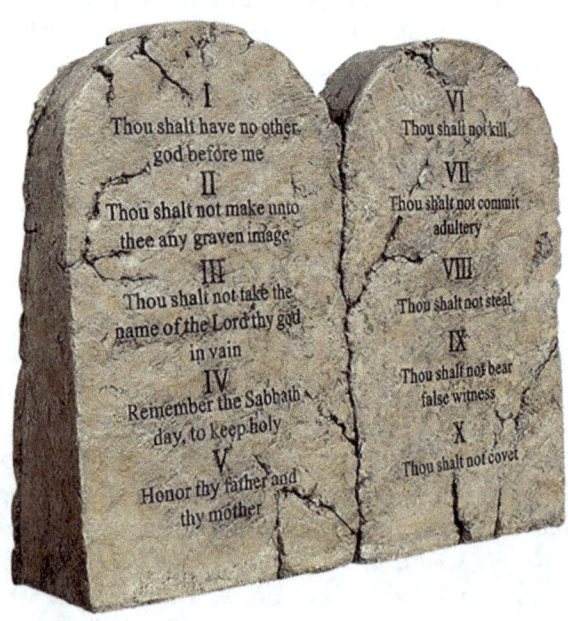

You will find additional important commands from Our Lord in the Renewal of the Ten Commandments. These are the commands on the new stones, after Moses threw the original ones at the wicked people. Have they been ignored? They are as follows:

RENEWAL OF THE TEN COMMANDMENTS
The Two Tables Replaced

[1] Now the LORD said to Moses, **"Cut out for yourself two stone tablets like the former ones, and I will write on the tablets the words that were on the former tablets which you shattered.** *[2] " So be ready by morning, and come up in the morning to Mount Sinai, and present yourself there to Me on the top of the mountain.* *[3] "No man is to come up with you, nor let any man be seen anywhere on the mountain; even the flocks and the herds may not graze in front of that mountain."*
[5] The LORD descended in the cloud and stood there with him as **he called upon the name of the LORD.** *[6] Then the LORD passed by in front of him and proclaimed, "The LORD, the LORD God, compassionate and gracious, slow to anger, and abounding in lovingkindness and truth; [7] who keeps lovingkindness for thousands, who forgives iniquity, transgression and sin; yet He will by no means leave the guilty unpunished, visiting the iniquity of fathers on the children and on the grandchildren to the third and fourth generations."*
[8] Moses made haste to bow low toward the earth and worship. [9] He said,

> *"If now I have found favor in Your sight, O Lord, I pray, let the Lord go along in our midst, even though the people are so obstinate, and pardon our iniquity and our sin, and take us as Your own possession."*

The Covenant Renewed
[10] Then God said, "Behold, I am going to make a covenant Before all your people I will perform miracles which have not been produced in all the earth nor among any of the nations; and all the people among whom you live will see the working of the LORD, for it is a fearful thing that I am going to perform with you. *[11]* **"Be sure to observe what I am commanding** *you*

this day: behold, I am going to drive out the Amorite before you, and the Canaanite, the Hittite, the Perizzite, the Hivite and the Jebusite. [12] **"Watch yourself that you make no covenant with the inhabitants of the land** into which you are going, **or it will become a snare in your midst.** [13] "But rather, you are to tear down their altars and smash their sacred pillars and cut down their Asherim

[14] —for **you shall not worship any other god, for the LORD, whose name is Jealous, is a jealous God--**
[15] otherwise you might make a covenant with the inhabitants of the land and they would play the harlot with their gods and sacrifice to their gods, and someone might invite you to eat of his sacrifice, 16 and you might take some of his daughters for your sons, and his daughters might play the harlot with their gods and cause your sons also to play the harlot with their gods.

[17] **"You shall make for yourself no molten gods.**

[18] **"You shall observe the Feast of Unleavened Bread** For seven days you are to eat unleavened bread, as I commanded you, at the appointed time in the month of Abib, for in the month of Abib you came out of Egypt.

[19] "**The first offspring from every womb belongs to Me**, and all your male livestock, the first offspring from cattle and sheep. [20] "You shall redeem with a lamb the first offspring from a donkey; and if you do not redeem it, then you shall break its neck

You shall redeem all the firstborn of your sons None shall appear before Me empty-handed.

[21] "**You shall work six days, but on the seventh day you shall rest**; even during plowing time and harvest you shall rest.

[22] "**You shall celebrate the Feast of Weeks, that is,** the first fruits of the wheat harvest, **and the Feast of Ingathering** at the turn of the year.

[23] **"Three times a year all your males are to appear before the Lord GOD, the God of Israel.** [24] "For I will drive out nations before you and enlarge your borders, and no man shall covet

your land when you go up three times a year to appear before the LORD your God.

^{25} "You shall not offer the blood of My sacrifice with leavened bread, nor is the sacrifice of the Feast of the Passover to be left over until morning.

^{26} "You shall bring the very best of the first fruits of your soil into the house of the LORD your God.

"You shall not boil a young goat in its mother's milk."

^{27} Then the LORD said to Moses, **"Write down these words, for in accordance with these words I have made a covenant with you and with Israel."** *^{28} So he was there with the LORD forty days and forty nights; he did not eat bread or drink water And he wrote on the tablets the words of the covenant, the Ten Commandments.*

Moses' Face Shines

^{29}It came about when Moses was coming down from Mount Sinai (and the two tablets of the testimony were in Moses' hand as he was coming down from the mountain), that Moses did not know that the skin of his face shone because of his speaking with Him. ^{30}So when Aaron and all the sons of Israel saw Moses, behold, the skin of his face shone, and they were afraid to come near him. ^{31}Then Moses called to them, and Aaron and all the rulers in the congregation returned to him; and Moses spoke to them. ^{32}Afterward all the sons of Israel came near, and he commanded them to do everything that the LORD had spoken to him on Mount Sinai. ^{33}When Moses had finished speaking with them, he put a veil over his face.

^{34}But whenever Moses went in before the LORD to speak with Him, he would take off the veil until he came out; and whenever he came out and spoke to the sons of Israel what he had been commanded, ^{35} the sons of Israel would see the face of Moses, that the skin of Moses' face shone. So Moses would replace the veil over his face until he went in to speak with Him.

Exodus 34 NASB 1995
Copyright © 1960, 1962, 1963, 1968, 1971, 1972, 1973, 1975, 1977, 1995 by The Lockman Foundation

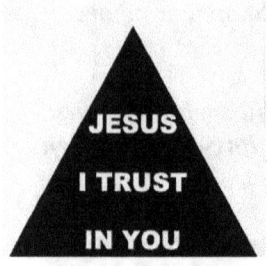 The copyright of this book is dedicated to Our Glorious God through Jesus Christ. No enemy (devil) will come against this book, or internet, or sell or copy this book **with intent to profit, change or destroy.**

Upon sense, sight, or nearness of this book, or audiobook, or copies thereof, the devil will be bound and banished; his tongue shall be shut up forever and he will be made immobile. The devil will not keep any believer in Christ from holding, reading this book nor believing all truth according to will of God. He will not move anyone or anything ever again. The devil will not tamper with anyone or thing, used for the spread of the good news and these heartfelt prayers. Thank You Father for hearing my prayer, In the Name of Jesus.

This book is issued solely to glorify God and increase our one-on-one connection with Him and each other.

Praise be to Our Loving Father to whom I bow and kneel in love and adoration. May we all be His alone through Jesus Christ. I pray that this message and these prayers reach the world.

Spirits of double mindedness, division, separation be bound, cast out and banished forever. Readers be unveiled; Get behind me Satan, you are nothing but a stumbling block in the eyes of the Lord! Thank you, Heavenly Father, for hearing my prayer, all Glory, Honor and Power is Yours, In the Name of Jesus.

May we become a new creation in Christ!
Yea!!! Arise Holy Spirit arise within us!
May He Bless us indeed! In the name of Jesus!
Please share this book for the unity of all believers in Christ.
UNITE! The Army of God is waiting… Let the rebellion begin!

THE END

REFERENCES

PUBLIC DOMAIN BIBLES QUOTED

ASV - The American Standard Version
From Wikipedia: **The American Standard Version** (ASV) is rooted in the work that was done with the Revised Version (RV) (a late 19th-century British revision of the King James Version of 1611). In 1870, an invitation was extended to American religious leaders for scholars to work on the RV project. A year later, Protestant theologian Philip Schaff chose 30 scholars representing the denominations of Baptist, Congregationalist, Dutch Reformed, Friends, Methodist, Episcopal, Presbyterian, Protestant Episcopal, and Unitarian. These scholars began work in 1872. The RV New Testament was released In 1881; the Old Testament was published in 1885.
The ASV was published in 1901 by Thomas Nelson & Sons. In 1928, the International Council of Religious Education (the body that later merged with the Federal Council of Churches to form the National Council of Churches) acquired the copyright from Nelson and renewed it the following year.
The divine name of the Almighty (the Tetragrammaton) is consistently rendered Jehovah in the ASV Old Testament, rather than LORD as it appears in the King James Bible.
The **ASV** was the basis of four revisions. They were the Revised Standard Version, 1971, the Amplified Bible, 1965, the New American Standard Bible, 1995, and the Recovery Version, 1999. A fifth revision, known as the World English Bible, was published in 2000 and was placed **in the public domain**. The ASV was also the basis for Kenneth N. Taylor's Bible paraphrase, The Living Bible, 1971. This Bible is in the public domain in the United States. We are making it available in the same format in which we acquired it as a public service.

BBE - The Bible In Basic English was printed in 1965 by Cambridge Press in England. Published without any copyright notice and distributed in America, this work fell immediately and irretrievably into the **Public Domain** in the United States according to the UCC convention of that time.

CPDVTSB - The Sacred Bible - Catholic Public Domain Version (Catholic Public Domain Version of the Sacred Bible)

DRA – Douay-Rheims 1899 American Edition
The Douay-Rheims Bible is in the **public domain**. The Douay–Rheims Bible is a translation of the Bible from the Latin Vulgate into English made by members of the Catholic seminary English College, Douai, France. It is the foundation on which nearly all English Catholic versions are still based.
It was translated principally by Gregory Martin, an Oxford-trained scholar, working in the circle of English Catholic exiles on the Continent, under the sponsorship of William (later Cardinal) Allen. The New Testament appeared at Rheims in 1582; the Old Testament at Douai in 1609. The translation, although competent, exhibited a taste for Latinisms that was not uncommon in English writing of the time but seemed excessive in the eyes of later generations. The New Testament influenced the Authorized Version.
Between 1749 and 1752, English bishop Richard Challoner substantially revised the translation with an aim to improve readability and comprehensibility. It was first

published in America in 1790 by Mathew Carey of Philadelphia. Several American editions followed in the 19th and early 20th centuries; prominent among them the Douay-Rheims 1899 American Edition Version.

KJV - King James Version.
Scripture quotations from The Authorized (King James) Version. Rights in the Authorized Version in the United Kingdom are vested in the Crown. Reproduced by permission of the Crown's patentee, Cambridge University Press
In 1604, King James I of England authorized that a new translation of the Bible into English be started. It was finished in 1611, just 85 years after the first translation of the New Testament into English appeared (Tyndale, 1526). The Authorized Version, or **King James Version**, quickly became the standard for English-speaking Protestants. Its flowing language and prose rhythm has had a profound influence on the literature of the past 400 years. The King James Version present on the Bible Gateway matches the 1987 printing. **The KJV is public domain** in the United States.

WEB - The World English Bible
The World English Bible is a 1997 revision of the American Standard Version of the Holy Bible, first published in 1901. It is in the **Public Domain**. Please feel free to copy and distribute it freely. Thank you to Michael Paul Johnson for making this work available.

OTHER BIBLES QUOTED

DRB – Douay Rheims Version - Bishop Challoner Revision
Section Headings Courtesy BereanBible.com © 2013, 2014 Used by Permission

GNT - Good News Translation® (Today's English Version, Second Edition) © 1992 American Bible Society. All rights reserved. Used by permission.
Bible text from the Good News Translation (GNT) is not to be reproduced in copies or otherwise by any means except as permitted in writing by American Bible Society, 101 North Independence Mall East, Floor 8, Philadelphia, PA 19106-2155 (www.americanbible.org). Learn more at www.gnt.bible . Discover. BIBLE resources for your ministry at www.get.bible/gnt

NAB - New American Bible, Books of the Bible | USCCB
New American Bible, revised edition © 2010, 1991, 1986, 1970 Confraternity of Christian Doctrine, Washington, D.C. and are used by permission of the copyright owner. All Rights Reserved. No part of the New American Bible may be reproduced in any form without permission in writing from the copyright owner.

NABRE- New American Bible Revised Edition
The *New American Bible, revised edition* © 2010, 1991, 1986, 1970 Confraternity of Christian Doctrine, Inc., Washington, DC and are used by permission of the copyright owner. All Rights Reserved. No part of this work may be reproduced or transmitted in any form or by any means, electronic or mechanical, including photocopying, recording,

or by any information storage and retrieval system, without permission in writing from the copyright owner.

NIV - New International Version
Holy Bible, New International Version®, NIV® Copyright © 1973, 1978, 1984, 2011 by Biblica, Inc.® Used by permission. of Zondervan. All rights reserved worldwide. www.zondervan.com The "NIV" and "New International Version" are trademarks registered in the United States Patent and Trademark Office by Biblica, Inc.™

NKJV – New King James Version
The Holy Bible, **New King James Version**, Copyright © 1982 Thomas Nelson. Used by permission. All rights reserved.

NRSV - New Revised Standard Version Catholic Edition
The **New Revised Standard Version** Bible: Catholic Edition, copyright © 1989, 1993 National Council of the Churches of Christ in the United States of America. Used by permission. All rights reserved worldwide.

NASB – New American Standard Bible
New American Standard Bible Copyright © 1960, 1971, 1977, 1995, 2020 by The Lockman Foundation, La Habra, Calif. Used by permission. All rights reserved. For Permission to Quote Information visit www.lockman.org

NASB 1995 – New American Standard Bible 1995
NASB 1995 Copyright © 1960, 1962, 1963, 1968, 1971, 1972, 1973, 1975, 1977, 1995 by The Lockman Foundation, La Habra, Calif. Used by permission. All rights reserved. For Permission to Quote Information visit http://www.lockman.org

OTHER BOOKS AND QUOTES REFERENCED

Marian Fathers of the Immaculate Conception of the R.V.M. (2007). *Diary of Saint Maria Faustina Kowalska.* Marian Press, Stockbridge, MA 01263.
All Divine Mercy images and content of any kind in this book have been "Used with the permission of the Marian Fathers of the Immaculate Conception of the B.V.M."

De Sales, St. Francis. (1994). *Philothea, or An Introduction to the Devout Life.* Tan Books and Publishers, Inc. PO Box 424, Rockford, Illinois, 61105.

Sister Mary of Jesus also known as Mary of Agreda. Translated from the Original Authorized Spanish Edition by Fiscar Marison. (2006). *The Mystical City of God Vol. 1.* Tan Books and Publishers, Inc. PO Box 424, Rockford, Illinois, 61105.

Sister Mary of Jesus also known as Mary of Agreda. Translated from the Original Authorized Spanish Edition by Fiscar Marison. (2006). *The Mystical City of God Vol. III.* Tan Books and Publishers, Inc. PO Box 424, Rockford, Illinois, 61105.

Alpha House Inc. (1927). ***The Lost Books of the Bible and the Forgotten Books of Eden.*** World Bible Publishers Inc.

The Holy Orthodox Catholic Church in Canada and the Americas. (2003). ***An Orthodox Book of Common Prayer*** First Edition. The Holy Orthodox Catholic Church in Canada and the Americas, Diocese of the Southwest, Printed in Canada.

Valtorta, Maria. (1992). ***The Poem of a Man-God Vol I.*** Grafiche Dipro, 31056 Roncade TV, Italy for Centro Editoriale Valortiano srl

General Secretariat of the Franciscan Missions Inc. ***The Prayer of St. Francis.*** P O Box 130; Waterford, WI 53185

WEBSITES USED AS REFERENCE

Father Jean Baptiste Saint-Jure. ***Trustful Surrender to Divine Providence.*** The following is a beautiful paragraph from page 139 of the booklet: (September 2022 – I cannot find the booklet, but the following is also an internet source of same book in pdf form page 11): ***TrustfulSurrenderToDivineProvidence.pdf (archive.org)***

St Bonaventure. Quote. Web: ***It Is Impossible to Love Mary More Than Jesus Did| National Catholic Register (ncregister.com)***

Messages from Medjugorje Website: ***Medjugorje Visionaries - Medjugorje WebSite***

St. Teresa of Calcutta Quotes "The fruit of silence is prayer, the fruit (catholic-link.org)**:**

http://www.carmelitedcj.org/saints/scapular.asp

http://www.truecatholic.org/scapular.htm

http://www.ewtn.com/expert/answers/rosary_scripture.htm

THE GREAT DELIVERANCE
STOP A GRIEVING WORLD

The Great Deliverance Stop a Grieving World is a book that was republished in 2023 by Ewing Publishing, the cover is green with a white leaf and its' reflection. The 2023 version is the same as its original version of 2010 however it is properly documented in regard to references and sources used throughout the book.

The original book published in 2010 is no longer in circulation. The original cover is of black birds and clouds.

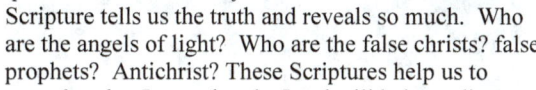

The Great Deliverance Stop a Grieving World has many quotes from the *Word of God*. Scripture tells us the truth and reveals so much. Who are the angels of light? Who are the false christs? false prophets? Antichrist? These Scriptures help us to realize who we are and what we need to do. I pray that the Lord will help us discern and lead us to all truth. He is our Teacher! We must ask Him for wisdom, knowledge and understanding! Helping us to not lean on human understanding and help us to believe what is true if we have been misled by out preachers, teachers, and such. This is His promise to us:

> *10" For this is the Covenant that I will make with the house of Israel after those days, says the Lord:* **I Will** *Put My Laws into Their Minds, And* **I Will** *Write Them on Their Hearts, and* **I Will** *Be Their God, And They Shall Be My People.11" And* **They SHALL NOT TEACH EVERYONE** *his fellow citizen, and everyone his brother, saying, 'Know the Lord,'* **FOR ALL WILL KNOW ME**, *from the least to the greatest of them. 12" For I Will Be Merciful to their iniquities, AND I WILL REMEMBER THEIR SINS NO MORE." Heb 8:10-12 NASB 1995.*

The Lord led me to repent using sackcloth & ashes and then I started sleeping in it. I have included a long list of sins to confess for ourselves, the world and even the deceased. I believe the sackcloth has provided a clearance for the Lord to teach me. I am no different than you. All this is explained in the book.

One thing I am sure of, is that Our God is very real and alive! He is a certainty and speaks to us. He knows your every thought, and is closer to you than your next breath. Jesus, Son of God teaches us unconditional love, unconditional mercy, and unconditional forgiveness. Reflect on His glorious passion, reflect on the life of the Holy Family where we find Victory. He is the Way! Reciprocate!

Jesus Christ the Warrior has new topics and some that have been modified and updated. After returning to sackcloth in June of 2022, The Lord began to teach me again in a distinct way. This book deals with His coming and the importance of Uniting to form the Army of God today and now. Be part of it!

> *I pray that the eyes of your heart may be enlightened in order that you may know the hope to which He has called you, the riches of His glorious inheritance in his holy people,* Eph 1:18 NIV

This book has a list of many sins to confess, tells you how to use sackcloth and ashes supported by scripture

The objectives in the book are meant to Glorify God and increase our one-on-one connection with Him and each other. Salvation and Restoration for All! In Jesus' Name. All things are possible if you choose to believe! Doubt is the greatest insult to Our Divine Lord. Ignorance is the devil's strength.

The devil loves tormenting you. An Orthodox priest told me that the devil cannot touch the people of God. I have found that to be true. If you think you love God first and greater beyond compare and are willing to die for a stranger because you want to die more than anything in the world **simply to be with Our Great and Magnificent Father of Everlasting Love**, who is greater beyond compare, who is so loving, so kind, so gentle, so compassionate and so merciful as you have never known or understood; if you long to be with Him, if you crave the passion of His love and return it to Him passionately, then you probably do love Him.

If you do not know how to love God first, if you do not hope in Him, do not adore Him, do not believe, are not willing to lay down your life for a friend, then buy the book entitled **ONE**, it is a deep beginning. It is imperative that we love God first. He is very real – the devil hopes you do not believe me – I Trust in Jesus and have increased faith, I believe you do believe! Glory to Jesus who deserves more than we can ever offer to Him. I love Him so much; I now understand the expression of John of the Cross:
"I die because I do not die".

ONE, One Love, One Hope, One God ISBN: 9781418434250

WE LAY DOWN OUR CROWN
Sealed By The Spirit Of God
by Gloria

This book includes prayers from **ONE**, Confessions, more prayers, and talks about being a Prisoner of the Lord, being Born Again and The Real Born Again. In this book the Lord typed: SEALED BY THE SPIRIT OF GOD on a copyright page dedicated to Our Glorious God through Jesus Christ. And He tore off the first page with the worldly copyright. He Changed IN GOD WE TRUST to JESUS I TRUST IN YOU! There is also a miracle prayer, the Lord combined three prayers, the new is entitled BE EXALTED BREAD OF LIFE I LOVE YOU LORD! The Sign of Jonah is repentance is sackcloth and ashes. This book tells you how and what to do according to scripture. It includes the following taken from this book: *Why the Hail Mary?* And **part** of *Who is the King?* And much more!

***

I give to you my love for Jesus with the heart of Mary and the love of Mary with the heart of Jesus now and eternally -- Gloria

Books by Gloria:
WE LAY DOWN OUR CROWN Sealed By The Spirit Of God
ISBN: 9781420875904

MULTIMEDIA MUSIC CD

The following CD's ** are available at Amazon or spotify. These CD's are prayers or narrations by Gloria in the books by Gloria. Please note these CD's are homemade and have no musical instruments in them. Songs sung without musical instruments are in italics. Come to the Wedding was put together in ten minutes, sung. Finding Mary was going to be spoken and the Lord led me to sing, so this is it. May the Lord Bless you indeed!

*** **Come to the Wedding - the Invitation**
*** **Be Exalted Bread of Life – I Love You Lord**
*** **Loves True Desire** - 1. Sincere Desire 2. Be Perfect as My Father is 3. The Joy 4. The Desire of Love 5. Prayer for Everlasting Unity 6. What Great Love Does My Soul Acknowledge? 7. What More Can I
Say? 8. Be Exalted Bread of Life I Love You Lord 9. Psalm 19:7-14
10. A New Chaplet of Mercy 11. Critical Moment 12. Altar of Grace
13. The Chaplet of St Michael 14. 3x The Sign of the Cross in Thanksgiving 15. Offering of self
*** **Why the Hail Mary? The Call to Heaven!** (approx 70 min)
1. The Hail Mary 2. Why the Hail Mary? 3. Be Not Hid from Me 4. *Ven Maria* 5. Psalm 116:15 6. *Finding Mary* 7. Circle to the
Most Greatest Hope 8. *The Call to Heaven* 9. I Love You Lord 10. Honor thy Father and thy Mother 11. From Darkness into Light 12. Important Notice say "Yes" 13. Concluding Prayer from Who is the King?
*** **Re-Pentecost in Honor of the Holy Ghost**
*** **Prayers Novena for Departed Souls**

www.ingramcontent.com/pod-product-compliance
Lightning Source LLC
LaVergne TN
LVHW020409070526
838199LV00054B/3571